HUMAN RESOURCE PRACTICE
in the
HOSPITALITY
INDUSTRY

JOHN ROBERTS

Hodder & Stoughton
A MEMBER OF THE HODDER HEADLINE GROUP

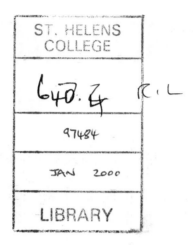
British Library Cataloguing in Publication Data

Roberts, John
  Human Resources in the Hospitality and Catering Industry
  I. Title
  647.940681

ISBN 0 340 607564

First published 1995
Impression number   10 9 8 7 6 5 4 3 2 1
Year   1999 1998 1997 1996 1995

Typeset by Wearset, Boldon, Tyne and Wear.
Printed in Great Britain for Hodder & Stoughton Educational, a division of Hodder Headline Plc, 338 Euston Road, London NW1 3BH by Bath Press Ltd, Avon.

DEDICATION

—

This book is dedicated to my wife, Maggie, and sons, Steven and Mark, who provided positive support, encouragement and critical analysis; additionally to the following individuals who assisted me in my early years within the hospitality industry: Raymond Zarb, ex-chef patron of the Marquis de Montcalm Restaurant, who provided me with my first real catering job and so much else, and Vincent Kitchener, ex-catering lecturer, Westminster Technical College, who worked throughout his life to help others.

This book also provides tribute to Steve Long, past leader of Bedminster Down Boys Club, Bristol. He knew nothing of the hospitality industry, but did devote his life to the training and development of young people and adults, inspiring myself and many others. He believed in involving others in the decision-making process and continually strove to empower individuals long before certain theorists stumbled onto the method. His argument was simple: involve individuals, provide them with the mechanisms and skills and facilitate their development. Through this approach he saw many an individual, youngster and adult improve their skills and abilities – the side of human resource management that sometimes gets lost in the more functional approaches.

CONTENTS

——

CHAPTER 3
Personnel policies, procedures and practices

CHAPTER 4
Recruitment and selection

CHAPTER 5
Training and development

CHAPTER 6
The future of human resource management in the hospitality industry

ACKNOWLEDGEMENTS

—

A significant amount of research was conducted in preparation for this text. Certain individuals and organisations allowed me to spend time in their companies, and provided significant amounts of information and assistance. They include: Victor Arciniega, Senior Human Resource Director, McDonald's; Nick Armitage, Human Resource Manager, Whitbread Restaurants & Leisure; Chris Ashcroft, Personnel Director, Compass; Jane Biss, Personnel & Recruitment Manager, J. D. Weatherspoon; Janet Gray, Head of Human Resources, Jarvis Hotels; David Haworth, Training Manager, Village Leisure Hotels; Chris Jeffries, Training Manager, Thresher; Margaret Lang, Human Resource Manager, Catering Direct; Trevor Norgett, Personnel & Training Manager, Haven Leisure; Bob Russell, Director, Payne & Gunters; Andrew Sample, People Development Manager, Harvester Restaurants; Bob Tapp, Brand Personnel Manager, Quicksnacks & Buffets, Travellers Fare Ltd; Roddy Watt, Chief Executive, Berkeley Scott Personnel Consultants.

I wish to acknowledge the positive contribution of the following individuals and organisations, who provided information and material, not all of which I have been able to include directly within the text: C. Amor, General Manager, Craigellachie Hotel of Speyside; P. M. Balfe, Personnel Manager, Le Manoir aux Quat' Saisons; E. Bird, Manager, Nidd Hall Country House Hotel; O. Blades, Sales & Marketing Manager, Avon Data Systems Ltd; M. Boella, Principal Lecturer, University of Brighton; D. S. Bohanna, Human Resources Controller, Quadrant Services; T. Bovey, Personnel & Training Officer, Torquay Leisure Hotels; V. Browen, Personnel & Training Manager, Bromwich Catering; J. Burley, Personnel Assistant, Runnymede Hotel; N. Cartwright, Human Resources Manager, Travellers Fare Ltd; G. Crawford, Personnel Manager, Cross Channel Catering Co.; C. Cromble-Holme, Personnel & Training Executive, Richoux Restaurants; L. Cullen, Staff Recruitment Coordinator, HF Holidays Ltd; C. Dixon, Director of Human Resources, Letherby & Christopher; F. Dowswell, Company Training Officer, Marston Hotels; K. Doyle, Human Resources Manager, National Leisure Catering; J. Endersby, Personnel Manager, Center Parcs Ltd; D. Fieldhouse, Personnel & Training Manager, Shaw Catering Company Ltd; P. Fry, Personnel Administrator, Quadrant Catering; S. P. Gade, Consultant, Touche Ross (GBS); J. Gibbs, Resourcing & Training Director, Bass Taverns; M. Hales, Regional Personnel & Training Manager, Compass Services; J. Herring, Personnel Manager, Mercury

Taverns plc; R. Hubbs, Consultant, Key Note Market Information; Human Resource Dept, TGI Friday's; J. Hyam, Consultant; J. Kearsey, Personnel Manager, Unicorn Hotel, Bristol; I. R. King, Personnel Manager, Toby Restaurants; C. Lark, Personnel & Development Manager, Pizzaland; J. Laycock, Personnel Director, Campanile UK Ltd; A. Lee, Personnel & Training Manager, Regent's Park Marriott; C. Lindsay, Personnel & Training Manager, Instore; B. Lunde, Human Resource Manager, Portman Hotel, London; G. Lyle, Training & Development Manager, Stakis Hotel, Glasgow; A. Makinson, Group Personnel Manager, De Vere Hotels; A. Martin, Personnel & Training, Lightwater Valley Ltd; C. Marzano, Training Manager, Massarella Catering Group Ltd; R. D. Mascio, Personnel Manager, Caledonian Hotel; M. McDonald, Group Personnel & Training Manager, Cala Hotels; A. Meldrum, Personnel & Training Manager, Park Lane Hotel, London; D. Mitchell, Group Personnel Manager, Savoy Group; S. Mullings, Bourne Leisure Group; D. Myers, Group Personnel, Mount Charlotte Thistle Hotels; F. Newstead, Personnel & Training Manager, Kentucky Fried Chicken; A. O'Carroll, Group Quality Manager, Jury's Hotel Group plc; G. Patchett, Group Personnel & Training Manager, Metropole Hotels; M. Pearson, Human Resource Director, Tom Cobleigh plc; S. Pridday, District Personnel Manager, Forte Posthouse; M. Purtill, Personnel & Training Manager, Chewton Glen; P. Purves, Personnel & Training Officer, Down Hall Hotel; C. Ramsay, Regional Personnel & Training Manager, Gardner Merchant Ltd; I. Rees, Managing Director, Cadogan; B. Roberts, Personnel & Training, Copthorne Tara Hotel; A. Robson, Personnel Controller, Butlins Ltd; B. Rosamund, Training & Development Manager, Novotel UK Ltd; D. Saunders, South East Regional Coordinator, Employment Service; C. Scott, Recruitment Officer, Mansfield Brewery plc; C. Sheppardson, Consultant, Portfolio International; J. Spencer, Director of Personnel, Leith's Good Food Ltd; T. Storey, Personnel Officer, Mansfield Brewery plc; J. Summers, Chief Personnel & Equality Officer, London Borough of Ealing; B. Sydney, Regional Manager, Catering Guild; S. Symington, Betty's Café Tea Rooms; A. A. Thibault, Chief Executive, Concord Hotels; J. Tinworth, Personnel Manager, Style Conferences; J. Tudor, Manager – Equality & Recruitment, European Passenger Services; B. Vitel, Personnel Manager, Sheraton Grand Hotel, Edinburgh; A. Walker, Research Director, Hotel & Catering Training Co.; J. White, Personnel & Training Officer, Russell & Brand Ltd; B. Worthington, Group Personnel Director, Friendly Hotels.

The following professional associations and government agencies also provided valuable information: Advisory, Conciliation & Arbitration Service; Institute of Personnel Management; British Institute of Management; Industrial Society; Tavistock Institute; Institute of Training & Development; Management Charter Initiative; Hotel Industry Marketing Group; BTEC; City & Guilds of London Institute; HCTC; HCIMA; British Institute of Innkeeping; British Hospitality Association; Confederation of Tourism, Hotel & Catering Management; UK Bartenders Guild; Low Pay Unit; Progressive Training; Personnel Management/Publications Ltd; Employment Department; National Council for Vocational Qualifications; Confederation of British Industry.

My apologies to any organisation or individual omitted from this list.

I would also like to acknowledge the support of my colleagues at Rotherham College of Arts & Technology, and sincere thanks to Trevor and Veronica Holland, who painstakingly corrected and typed this script.

INTRODUCTION AND
HOW TO USE THE TEXT

—

This text is designed to introduce students to the fascinating and challenging area of people management. It aims to provide a practical insight into the theories, practices and key elements of effective human resource management. With a wide range of case studies and examples of current practice from a variety of hospitality operators, the text will provide you with a positive overview of approaches and activities.

Commencing with an outline of the development of human resource management and key elements of current practice, the text describes, in detail, activities such as manpower planning and strategy, styles and methods of personnel management, leadership and motivation. Following chapters detail the role and functions of personnel departments and managers, legal aspects and effective approaches to recruitment and selection. Other chapters concentrate on the development of personnel in respect of training and progression and cover aspects related to appraisal, team and individual training. The final chapter looks in detail at the future role and function of human resource management.

Within such an introductory text it is not possible to cover all aspects to the depth some readers may require. However, by using the key points and questions listed at the end of each chapter, and exercises and assignments provided in Appendix A, readers will be able to extend their knowledge and skills considerably.

The text is aligned closely with NVQ Levels 3 and 4, GNVQ Advanced, and is appropriate for students on HNC, HCIMA and HND courses. Students currently studying on these programmes will be able to relate exercises and assignments to these programmes directly, which will help to achieve specific units and competences.

Research for the text was carried out over several years with a concentration of investigation in the months prior to its completion. The aim was, as in my other book *Marketing for the Hospitality Industry* published by Hodder & Stoughton in 1993, to provide a practical insight rather than a detailed explanation of more theoretical approaches.

The hospitality industry has not been without its critics over the years, particularly over the manner in which it has dealt with human resource management. Yet, similar to many other industries, it has faced a variety of social and economic factors which have created significant challenges. The rise and then decline in demand, the increased competition and the change in the nature of demand from increasingly sophisticated and complex markets have forced organisations to analyse closely their costs and operating methods. Businesses and organisations struggling to survive in a highly competitive climate are required to manage all aspects of their operation effectively. Staff often form the most expensive element.

The text is designed to take the reader through the background to human resource practice and then discusses more practical functions, systems and related practices. Each chapter is provided with:

- an introduction
- aims and objectives
- a summary or review
- key points
- related questions

By reading these points first, elements of each chapter should become clearer. The main elements are designed to provide the underpinning knowledge required for specific NVQ units in addition to the provision of more general information.

Additionally, in Appendix A, there are a number of assignments and exercises that relate specifically to topics raised in each chapter. Upon completion of a chapter the reader may wish to attempt either the assignment or one of the exercises. These are designed to provide additional learning, satisfaction and, in stated cases, written evidence for related NVQ elements or units. Readers with some degree of understanding of the subject may wish to undertake all the assignments and exercises provided in Appendix A. If they possess part responsibility for the Personnel and Training function within their workplace they will find completion will further enhance this important function. Lecturers or trainers using this text will quickly identify the sequence in which it operates and, whilst directing students to particular sections, can make good use of the exercises and assignments detailed in Appendix A.

Excluding the references to individuals within the industry, I have included no reference within chapters to other reading material. This is in no way a slight to the authors of other texts on human resource management.

Throughout the book certain human resource management terminology is used; whilst I have attempted to keep jargon phrases to a minimum, there is a definite need at times to include them.

Investment in quality personnel, the life blood of organisations, is increasing in importance. Whatever sector they reside in, all organisations will require appropriate personnel systems and procedures to manage and use their workforce effectively. The industry has not been slow to adapt to the new climate and increasingly leads the way in developing positive human resource management practices. Current practice is moving away from the purely functional aspects of personnel management into areas best described as quality partnerships. This text aims to identify the core framework from which such developments can occur. If, by providing this text, I assist the industry then I will have achieved one of its main aims.

I hope you enjoy reading and working through the text, obtaining knowledge, skills and insight.

CHAPTER 1

INTRODUCTION TO PERSONNEL AND HUMAN RESOURCE MANAGEMENT

—

All too often personnel and training is given a low profile in the hospitality industry, which is both sad and counterproductive. Resources of time, money and expertise in personnel and training should be allocated with similar priority to other industries, subsequently a lot of the problem areas of staff retention, low morale and skill shortages could be reduced.

CHRISTINE LLOYD, PERSONNEL AND TRAINING MANAGER

The vision which emerges when the changes of the past decade are extrapolated is one of scaled down 'leaner and fitter' organisations in both private and public sectors, new organisational structures made up of autonomous units, many more small businesses . . . a shift of emphasis from collectivity to individualism, increasingly sophisticated information and communication systems, production technology and a business climate which is customer driven, quality focused and fiercely competitive. It is against this background that the management of people needs to be considered.

'MANAGING PEOPLE – CHANGING FRONTIERS', IPM CONSULTATIVE DOCUMENT, *PERSONNEL MAGAZINE*, 1994

The personnel function is becoming more recognised as essential for the maintenance and development of the business.
We need to improve our profile and the contribution we can make to improving the business.
The hospitality industry is a people industry – therefore investing more in the personnel function is the only logical approach.

PERSONNEL AND TRAINING MANAGERS, HOTEL SECTOR

Everyone who works has the right to just and favourable remuneration ensuring . . . an existence worthy of human dignity.

UN UNIVERSAL DECLARATION OF HUMAN RIGHTS, ARTICLE 23(3)

The key aspects for the future are lean, efficient, flat structures with empowered employees who have responsibility and ability to react to customer demands – well trained, well rewarded (and) 'sharing the actions'.

M. WORTHINGTON, DIRECTOR OF HUMAN RESOURCES, FORTE POSTHOUSE

1.1 AIMS AND OBJECTIVES

By reading through this introductory chapter and completing the questions and related assignments, you will obtain an appreciation of the role of human resource management (HRM). Specifically you will be able to:

1   obtain a perspective on personnel and HRM within the hospitality industry;
2   understand the relationship between an organisation and its employees;
3   explain the importance of employee motivation;
4   identify approaches to leadership and management;
5   identify basic approaches to the management of quality through employees;
6   list and explain the key roles and functions of personnel and HRM.

1.2 INTRODUCTION

This first chapter will concentrate on introducing you to the background, key roles and functions of people management. Commencing with an overview of personnel and HRM, this chapter includes strategies and approaches to employee motivation, leadership and management. Additional reference will be made to quality management and descriptions provided on the actual job of personnel and HRM.

One criticism often levelled at personnel managers (in fact, managers in general) is that they often concentrate on 'fire fighting' rather than 'fire prevention'. It would be unrealistic to represent personnel and HRM managers in too idealistic a way and the pressures of today's industry create significant challenges for such individuals. 'Fire fighting' is a managerial skill like any other and the ability to respond rapidly to situations, at either a strategic or operational level, is a daily element of many personnel and HRM responsibilities.

HRM is often stated as a support function, assisting the achievement of business objectives; to do this it is necessary to understand what motivates employees and the range of other skills required in people management.

1.3 OVERVIEW OF PERSONNEL AND HRM IN THE HOSPITALITY INDUSTRY

Examples are provided throughout this text of current personnel and HRM practice, the majority of which are from medium to large size hospitality companies or businesses. The industry, however, is predominated by small catering businesses – the thousands of pubs, clubs, cafés, restaurants, bed and breakfast establishments, guest houses and takeaways which make up the hospitality industry. For the small business, often operated by an owner manager, a significant part of this text may appear inappropriate. In fact for businesses with less than six staff, many elements of current employment legislation are not relevant or applicable.

This text is therefore primarily focused on personnel and HRM considerations for businesses with reasonable levels of staffing. However, much is relevant to all businesses (remember Forte started with one small unit!). This section is aimed at providing you with an overview of:

- the basic structure of the hospitality industry
- descriptions of the various approaches to personnel and HRM
- examples of current strategy and practice
- views from personnel, HRM specialists and others on this function
- factors which affect the practice of personnel and HRM

By describing the structure of the industry you will gain a more detailed understanding of the reasons behind specific approaches to personnel and HRM. This will assist you in recognising the importance of the various elements described in further chapters and sections of this text.

If you discuss personnel, training, human resource development and management with specialists in the industry, a wide variety of viewpoints will be put forward. The views of such individuals are important and I make no apologies for making more reference to them than to academic studies of the HRM function. This is not to say that you cannot learn from such academic research, nor should hospitality managers neglect looking at other industries to identify effective practice.

The referencing to practitioners within the industry is an element you will identify throughout this text. The research for this text involved a variety of questionnaires, surveys, field research, interviews and periods of involvement and observation. A considerable part of these activities was targeted at personnel, training and human resource managers.

Questions ranged across the following areas: the existence of a manpower plan or strategy, recruitment and selection methods, the use of external or personnel consultants, predicted changes to workforce, training and development activities, areas of concern, involvement of NVQs, Investors in People, TQM, priorities for the forthcoming year, descriptions of the job of personnel, degree of involvement in strategic planning and predictions for the future.

From such research certain common themes, challenges and concerns were identified. However, it is important to recognise that hospitality organisations will approach personnel and HRM in different ways.

KEY POINT

Whilst all hospitality companies and businesses require a personnel facility (concerned with the administrative control of the function), they will differ in respect of their approach due to factors such as the size, style and culture of the organisation.

Before some of the differences in approach are described it is important to provide an overview of the structure of the industry.

Structure of the hospitality industry

It would be rather simplistic to describe the industry as one neat, homogeneous sector, and a considerable number of studies and textbooks have attempted to identify the various sectors within the industry. Additionally, the industry has often been classified as being concerned with the provision of food, drink and accommodation. This definition omits the growing leisure sector, so my classification of the hospitality industry includes this sector.

The term 'the hospitality industry' refers to *companies, organisations and businesses which have as their core (main) business the provision of food, drink, leisure, business facilities and accommodation.* Of course, some businesses will not provide all of these.

However, consider retail organisations and companies whose main business may be the sale of clothes and other merchandise, yet who provide restaurants, cafés, takeaways and snack bars within their premises. Also, what about service organisations like hospitals, prisons, the Post Office and Police? These are large, national operations which, although possibly organised on a regional basis, will possess significant catering and accommodation facilities. Whilst the privatisation of many traditional Government services is altering the structure of such organisations, they remain as major players in the provision of catering and other services.

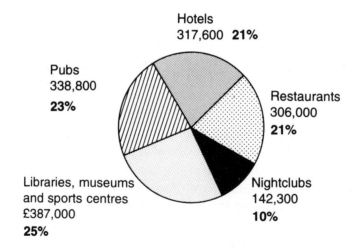

Total: 1,491,700 employees

FIGURE 1 *Employees in tourism-related industries in Great Britain, June 1990.*

This factor causes some problems with the definition of the industry I provided above and causes confusion with identifying the number of employees working within the industry. Figures ranging from 1.4 million to 2.6 million employees are commonly provided and this relates to direct employment and does not include the considerable number of people who work in companies or businesses directly supplying the industry. Figure 1 excludes the considerable number of employees in cafés, in-store catering, schools, hospitals and other hospitality-type organisations.

It was at one time possible to separate the industry into two distinct sectors, commercial and welfare. This was based on the assumption that welfare companies were subsidised in some way and, therefore, not profit orientated. As stated, the large scale privatisations of the 1980s and 1990s have significantly altered this picture.

KEY POINT

Today the hospitality industry is made up of a complex variety of organisations, companies and businesses, and their approach to personnel and HRM issues will relate to a considerable number of external and internal factors.

For anybody studying the industry, defining the structure becomes quite difficult and the question must be asked as to whether companies which have sections or divisions dealing with retailing, licensed premises, property and facility management should be included. This complexity is not in reality of great importance. Of greater relevance, certainly for this text, is how such companies approach the personnel and HRM function. The approach an organisation takes will relate significantly to the mission, culture, values, benefits, strategies and objectives it possesses (or proclaims to possess).

Organisational mission and values

Within this text a number of examples are provided of hospitality companies' mission statements, with additional statements on personnel policies and employment practices. To gain an understanding of a company's approach to personnel and HRM, such statements are often a useful starting point.

The 'mission' refers to a statement by a company as to how the company sees itself (or wishes to) and provides a brief description of its purpose. Such statements serve several purposes in that they:

- provide a focus on which to build the company or business
- provide the opportunity to make positive statements to employees, suppliers and customers about their purpose
- assist organisations to obtain the Investors in People standard

The company may also state publicly (and more importantly to its employees) what its values and beliefs are in relation to staff and employment practices. Such statements may indicate not only the way in which employees are viewed, but also the type of personnel policies that exist within the organisation.

─────────────────── KEY POINT ───────────────────

Positive statements on personnel policies and employment practices are a possible indication of the approach to HRM within an organisation.

Hospitality companies or businesses which value their employees and possess a belief that investment in employees is a benefit to the organisation rather than a cost, will of course need to demonstrate this in a variety of ways. However, their approach to personnel and HRM will be affected by a considerable number of factors.

Approaches to personnel and HRM

Hospitality companies and businesses will differ in their approach to this function due to the following:

- size, location and distribution
- style, culture, mission and values
- structure and hierarchy
- company or business traditions (accepted practices)
- strategic plans and business objectives
- the degree of recognition given to the function
- profitability (and ability or willingness to invest in the function)
- growth and change in technology
- specialist legislation which affects the operation
- owner's or senior management's beliefs and styles
- pressure and influence from professional bodies
- the skill and expertise of individuals with the personnel or HRM responsibility

Obviously the larger the organisation the greater its need for more formalised systems, the more geographically spread the greater the need to establish regional support units and the more complex the organisation the greater the need for personnel systems which allow for diversity within the organisation.

Consider a large company like Forte, with a brand range covering luxury hotels, medium hotels, Travel Lodge operations, event catering, airport services, motorway and specialist restaurants. Each brand is specifically geared towards a particular market segment and each, due to its operating size, will possess its own particular type of personnel and HRM approach.

For such diverse companies the challenge is to design personnel and HRM systems, policies, procedures and practices which suit the style of the company. Whilst at board level the chief executives will have a strategic view of the role of personnel, the actual style and approach will be designed to complement and support the type of organisation. The style and approach will also be affected by change within the organisation and changes in the environment in which it works.

For large hospitality companies specialising within an area, e.g. McDonald's, the problem perhaps is a lesser one. By specialising in one type of operation there is no need to have different personnel styles or approaches. The very strength of the personnel role could be the opportunity to take a uniform approach. The information outlined below will provide you with an indication of how McDonald's currently approaches personnel practices.

McDonald's Restaurants operates over 13,000 restaurants including 535 units within the UK, employing over 31,370 people. Its policy statement on employment practices is as follows:

- To recruit people who have a positive attitude towards customers, themselves and other employees and who are capable of delivering the highest standards of quality, service and cleanliness to our customers.
- To employ local people wherever possible.
- To ensure that employees and job applicants are selected, trained, promoted and treated on the basis of their relevant skills, talents and performance and without reference to race, colour, nationality, ethnic origin, sex, marital status or disability.
- To provide a clean, safe, healthy and enjoyable working environment.
- To provide training and development for all employees to enable them to achieve the highest level of skills possible.
- To provide career opportunities which allow employees to develop to their full potential.
- To provide challenging and rewarding work.
- To pay for performance.
- To communicate effectively with all employees via crew meetings, one to one discussions, in house publications and regular opinion surveys.
- To encourage the educational pursuits of employees through McDonald's Books, Education and Scholarship programmes which provide financial support to qualifying employees who are undertaking a recognised course of study.

As a member of the Opportunity 2000 campaign (to increase the quality and quantity of women's participation in the work force, which a number of other catering operators have joined) McDonald's has been one of the most progressive companies involved in a variety of initiatives to assist and develop employees.

McDonald's provides a full range of benefits for its salaried employees, ranging across PPP, BUPA Healthscreen, pension scheme, company car, clothing allowance, bonus scheme, President's award scheme, sabbatical, stock option scheme, stock purchase plan, company loan scheme, further education assistance and relocation assistance.

V. Arciniega, McDonald's Restaurants

Of course, some large and successful companies, whilst operating in a particular sector, possess a variety of units and services.

A second example is Novotel, which is a division of the Accor company.

Accor is a large international catering company with units and divisions in over 58 countries. With over 82,000 employees spread over a variety of operations, including hotels, restaurants, institutional catering service ... auxiliary services and railroad catering. In the UK, the main hotel division is Novotel. Such international expansion has been increasing over the past decade, especially in Europe with many UK operators developing operating, franchising and management links with European operators. With the emergence of such networks, the opportunities for personnel to work in other countries expand, and HRM management will increasingly seek to incorporate the varying personnel management styles and procedures that exist.

Novotel, similar to other international chains actively promotes the movement of personnel to other countries where it operates and offers a scheme for employees to exchange positions for short periods. The following statement comes from Novotel's employee handbook:

Welcome to Novotel,
I am delighted to be able to introduce you to Novotel and to the world of opportunity that is the Accor Group. Here at Novotel we believe that the success of our hotels is built upon TEAMWORK AND QUALITY. Like any successful team, we work closely together right from the start. Our managers and senior staff help individual employees bring out the best in themselves and each other. This is a belief we have always held to achieve quality.
This is because our employees are the key to our future. In return for their initiative, commitment and high levels of services, we offer effective personal training and skills development, and the opportunity to pursue a rewarding and satisfying career within a growing and highly successful organisation.
Starting a new job and integrating into a committed team is never easy. We hope that you will feel at home with us very soon.
"WELCOME TO THE TEAM ... GOOD LUCK!"

Novotel UK Ltd

Novotel is just one example of how hospitality companies are both expanding and consolidating their operations, especially in Europe. This, as stated, will have effects on the way such operations are managed.

QUESTION

What problems exist for hospitality companies when they commence operations in another country in respect of personnel policies and procedures?

Strategies, objectives and culture

The business strategies and objectives of hospitality organisations will obviously differ, as will specific strategies related to manpower planning, recruitment and selection, personnel policies and practices and training and development.

KEY POINT

A primary function of personnel is to assist the achievement of business strategies and objectives.

Whilst such aspects are directly related to the business, these objectives can only be achieved through individuals and a lot depends on the type of culture (the beliefs and ways of doing things) that a company possesses. An outline of developing a training and development culture is described in Chapter 5, page 240.

Additionally, the culture of an organisation will be supported by the way in which the organisation is structured. The structure refers to the way the company or business is organised, the lines of command or control, layers of staff, reporting procedures and decision-making processes.

Hospitality organisations have changed considerably over the past decade, with a flattening of structures and subsequent devolution of the personnel function. Certainly even within the larger organisations there are moves towards more open and participative cultures which seek to create wider ownership of company values and objectives. This can only assist the personnel and HRM function, although for organisations going through such change it is a process that causes considerable challenge.

Influences on personnel and HRM

The approach to personnel and HRM will also be affected by a variety of other influences, including:

- government social and economic policies
- pressure from professional bodies, e.g. HCIMA, Institute of Personnel Development, HCTC
- research bodies, e.g. Low Pay Unit
- government bodies, e.g. Commission for Racial Equality
- academic research, e.g. universities and colleges
- various industry groups, e.g. Hotel Industry Marketing Group, British Hospitality Association

Such bodies will attempt to influence the direction of national policies in respect of all aspects of the industry.

The Institute of Personnel Management has developed a series of codes of practice related to employment and personnel issues, which a significant number of organisations and personnel specialists acknowledge. The aims of these codes of practice are to encourage best practice within organisations. Currently these codes of practice cover the following areas: age and employment, career and outplacement consultants, continuous development, employee data, equal opportunities, employee involvement and participation, recruitment consultants, human resource planning, redundancy, psychological testing, training and development, recruitment, secondment, smoking, substance misuse, professional conduct and regulations, improving work experience, harassment at work and counselling. The IPM has now joined with the Institute of Training and Development to become the Institute of Personnel Development.

Professional bodies do a lot both to enhance the status of the industry and to promote positive training and development. Other research type organisations may concentrate their work on a particular aspect of employment, including equal opportunities, study of management styles or general employment conditions.

Studies on pay, salaries and working conditions have provided personnel specialists with a considerable amount of information. Whether they use this information is, of course, dependent upon both personnel and organisational beliefs.

The Low Pay Unit is an independent organisation established in 1974 in response to concern about the problems of the working poor.

Supported by the Joseph Rowntree Charitable Trust, various other charities, foundations and donations, it has earned a reputation for impeccable research and analysis. Campaigning to reduce levels of hardship and poverty it provides information, training and advice related to employment policies.

The Unit undertakes research to provide government, trade unions, employers and employees with expert advice. Additionally, it operates the Employment Rights Advice Service. This service deals with over 2000 enquiries per year, ranging from employers seeking advice on wage rates to individuals seeking advice on aspects related to pay and conditions.

In 1993, three out of every five enquiries were from women, whilst one in seven came from young people (under 21 years old).

Pay and conditions have always attracted a considerable amount of interest. With the abolition of the Wages Councils in August 1993, the hospitality industry entered a new era with regard to pay and benefits.

Because the hospitality industry comprises such a large range of different businesses – of various sizes and differing aims and styles – pay policies in hotels, restaurants and catering establishments need to be fair and equitable. Good employers will wish to offer a fair and realistic pay deal, create jobs and encourage their employees to progress by training and motivation. In return, their employees will give greater commitment to the business and stay, thus reducing staff turnover with all its attendant problems and expense.

Pay and Benefits Survey 1993, Greene, Belfield-Smith Division of Touche Ross Management Consultants

---

The hospitality industry requires ongoing analysis of pay and benefits if it is to remain competitive with other industries and attract appropriately skilled and qualified personnel. The pay and benefits survey referred to above was conducted by Greene, Belfield-Smith, a division of Touche Ross Management Consultants, in conjunction with the HCIMA and the British Hospitality Association.

The survey looked at the pay and benefits of over 18,000 hospitality personnel from across all sectors of the industry and covered the full range of positions. With analysis of national averages and regional variations, such a survey provides hospitality operators and the industry with sound information on which to base remuneration and benefit levels.

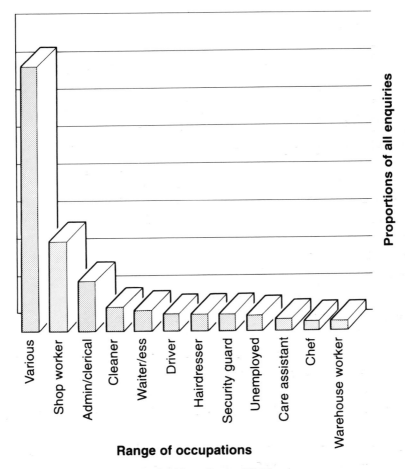

FIGURE 2 *Snapshot analysis of occupations held by callers to ERAS.*

Figures 2 and 3 indicate snapshot analyses of occupations held by callers to the Employment Rights Advice Service and problems causing people to contact them.

Conclusion: HRM in the hospitality industry

There is no doubting that this role has undergone considerable changes over the past few decades. The move towards more participative cultures with fewer layers of managerial staff has

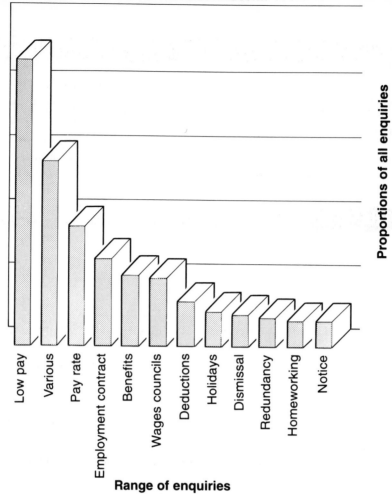

Figure 3 *Snapshot analysis of problems causing people to contact ERAS.*

accelerated this change, along with the effects of economic recession, the growth in competition, changes in technology and consumer demand.

The role of the personnel specialist has moved towards an advising and developmental service which, whilst retaining the functional side of personnel, is becoming a focus for change within organisations.

Before identifying specific elements of the job of personnel and HRM, it is important to provide an introduction to the aspect of people management.

1.4 INTRODUCTION TO PEOPLE MANAGEMENT

It is hardly surprising that the industry is currently preoccupied with issues that relate to the performance of its employees. The recognition of the importance of managing its most important resource – its people – is clearly evidenced by the amount of investigation, discussion and investment in effective personnel policies.

THE JURYS MISSION STATEMENT

'We at Jurys are a team dedicated to guest satisfaction, providing the highest quality of products and services, where employees develop as individuals and perform all tasks with great pride for the ultimate success of the company and its share holders'

Jurys Hotel Group plc

THE VILLAGE LEISURE MISSION STATEMENT

'We aim to delight all of our customers'

PEOPLE CHARTER

We will:

1 Be customer focused
   • Everyone will be expected to seek opportunities to delight their internal and external customers
2 Be committed to continuous quality improvement
   • Everyone will be expected to support the continuous improvement of quality in everything that we do
3 Communicate and listen
   • Everyone will be kept informed about the development of Village Leisure and changes in policies and procedures
   • Everyone's ideas, views and suggestions will be sought, listened to and a response given
4 Empower people
   • Everyone will be aware of what is expected of them
   • Everyone will be encouraged to take personal ownership of our business objectives and values
   • Team working will be encouraged to resolve problems and improve quality
   • People will be involved in the decision making process
5 Recognise and reward achievement
   • Career development will be encouraged with promotion based on merit
   • Training will always be given before promotion is actioned
   • Good performance will be recognised and rewarded
   • Everyone will be treated fairly with equality of opportunity
6 Promote learning
   • Everyone will be expected to be receptive to new ideas and learning opportunities
   • Everyone will receive regular training
   • Everyone will receive coaching on personal performance

Mission Statement, Village Leisure Hotels

People are the life blood of service industries and represent a large cost for all hospitality operators. This cost relates not only to the direct costs of pay and benefits, but also includes the costs of personnel administration, recruitment, selection, training and development, HASAWA, pensions, accommodation, clothing, staff facilities and so on. Such costs will, of course, vary from one organisation to another, but will be a major investment for all organisations.

The return on this investment is the contribution employees make to the provision of profitable services and facilities and consequently employees (people) are a resource that requires managing like any other organisational resource. What is different is the manner in which people can be managed; unlike machinery, plant, goods or facilities they are not inert units that can be moved or manipulated in mechanistic ways. Managers, therefore, require an understanding of the elements and factors which affect the performance of individuals and groups at work if they are to manage this resource effectively.

Thus, the management of people covers a wide range of interrelating factors and covers such aspects as:

- functional and administrational management
- strategic planning
- personnel policy formulation
- resourcing, scheduling and control

These aspects, whilst affecting directly the management of people, are in reality indirect management considerations. They are the strategic decisions a company or organisation makes to equip itself to meet its key business objectives. To manage people effectively, managers require an understanding of individuals, which covers such aspects as:

- *motivation* which affects an individual's ability and willingness to maintain and improve performance
- *individual perceptions* which will affect employees' attitudes towards work
- *leadership* which will impinge on the manner in which individuals accept direction and responsibility
- *team and group performance,* understanding that individuals also work as part of groups and teams within the organisation
- *organisational structure and culture* which will set the framework in which employees work

Additionally, you could add personal factors such as age, gender, skills, abilities and individual domestic issues.

KEY POINT

The management of people should not be concerned just with the functional tasks of ensuring that tasks and jobs are completed, but rather with consideration of all the factors which directly or indirectly affect individual employees at work.

A significant amount of research has been conducted on these elements, especially those relating to leadership, motivation and organisational structure and culture. Whilst following sections will outline specific elements of this research, it is useful to provide examples of general approaches to the improvement of organisations through effective people management.

Of the current management 'gurus', none has attracted more publicity than Tom Peters, whose books have sold in their millions throughout the world. After studying 43 companies that were considered to be excellently managed, Peters identified eight attributes of management style, all of which related to elements of people management. Whilst Peters was writing on organisations in general, there is no doubting the influence he and his co-writer have had on management thinking. (Whether this influence is justifiable is another argument.) The central themes running through their proposals were:

- the need to communicate and involve people in the business
- the idea that people work more effectively in smaller units
- a need for organisations to have uncomplicated structures and lines of management
- the need to establish a culture (way of doing things and managing people) that promotes shared goals and values

Many of the larger hospitality companies, accepting these concepts, have invested considerable time and resources in adapting their personnel policies to bring about major organisational change.

THE EIGHT ATTRIBUTES OF EXCELLENT ORGANISATIONS

1	Basis for action	preference for 'doing' rather than waiting for further analysis
2	Keeping close to the customer	
3	Autonomy and entrepreneurship	breaking up a company or corporation into smaller units, each thinking independently and competitively
4	Productivity through people	enabling all employees to appreciate the importance of their personal participation and enabling them to share success
5	Hands on, value driven	keeping all employees in touch with the main task of the business
6	Sticking to the knitting	remaining in the one area of business at which employees are good
7	Simple form, lean staff	uncluttered organisational structures with minimal levels of hierarchy and few people at the upper levels
8	Simultaneous loose–tight properties	a climate in which there is a dedication to the central values of the company combined with a tolerance for all employees who accept the values

T. J. Peters and R. H. Waterman (1982) *In Search of Excellence*

The Industrial Society conducted intensive research on over 50 of Britain's major organisations to pinpoint vital success factors. The Society identified the six corporate strategies that are most critical to an organisation's success. They were as follows:

- high quality leadership
- creating an opportunity culture

- communicating and involving
- growing by learning
- building better working relationships
- working towards a common future

The research also identified specific objectives for each of these corporate strategies. Whilst all have particular relevance to the HRM function, key aspects directly relate to create a positive HRM culture.

Access, opportunity and personal development are key elements in motivating people to minimise their contribution and commitment to any organisation. To unlock this asset, the organisation must:

- have explicit guidelines on recruitment, training and promotion, which remove barriers based on race, gender, disability, religion, age and class
- provide a working environment which encourages the personal development of all employees
- regularly review the progress and development needs of all employees and set personal targets and development plans
- train individuals fully in the skills they need in order to operate effectively within and for the organisation

Industrial Society, 1993

The goals of effective people management

To survive in today's highly competitive hospitality market, operators require to maximise the return on all their investments and, as stated, the investment they make in staff is considerable. Effectiveness in the management of people is, of course, not a guarantee of business success which is, in itself, reliant upon a variety of factors and considerations.

Accepting that a company or business is concerned with managing its human resources effectively (and, unfortunately, there still exist businesses where this is not the case), then it is important to identify why this is considered so important.

Employers could be said to require:

- a stable, appropriately skilled workforce
- motivated employees who perform to the best of their abilities and potential
- accurate forecasts on staffing costs (both direct and indirect costs)
- minimal disruption to working patterns
- a quality of care and service which meets the needs and expectations of customers

The organisation and its managers need to understand which people policies, procedures and practices will positively assist the achievement of these goals. As mentioned, these include:

- motivation of employees
- the effect individual employee perceptions and attitudes have on work
- the effect that various styles of organisational structure, culture, leadership and management have on employee performance
- the role of teams in respect of individual and team performance

---

KEY POINT

In the management of people, the organisation has to consider not only the individual employee with specific needs and expectations, but also how the function of the organisation will affect the level of performance of the individual.

The management of people is concerned then with an understanding of the individual and an understanding of how organisational factors affect individuals within the workplace. However, it must not be forgotten that hospitality operators, similar to all businesses, seek to run their operations in the most cost-effective way, returning appropriate levels of profit. The investment made in its people by an organisation is reliant upon adequate levels of business, yet the success of the business is heavily reliant upon the effectiveness of its employees. This circle of reliance has been increasingly recognised as an element of hospitality management and is stressed throughout this text.

Hospitality operators rely on their staff to satisfy the needs of the business and to do this they need to design personnel practices which will assist this aim. (This aspect is dealt with more fully in Chapter 3.) In developing such policies, operators need to satisfy two main criteria:

1   The establishment of functional personnel systems which allow for the fair and effective management of people: *Administrational Need.*
2   The establishment of policies and practices which allow for the many influences on employee behaviour: *Cultural Need.*

Within such development there is a requirement to match the needs and expectations of individual employees with the needs, demands and objectives of the business.

The needs and expectations of the employee

Individuals will, of course, vary in respect of their expectation of work and how they will react to the different tasks and responsibilities set them. Consider for a minute why you are studying your present course, or why you are working at your present place of employment. For your course it might be to gain a qualification, obtain a job or worthwhile career or maybe even because it seemed a good idea at the time! For a job you are currently undertaking, it may be for financial return, because you could not get another one or because you obtain a high degree of personal satisfaction from it. The majority of individuals would possibly place financial reward as the main need, but consider the following:

- job security
- status
- recognition
- challenge (or lack of challenge)
- overall job satisfaction
- opportunity to travel

─────────────────── K E Y   P O I N T ───────────────────

To manage people effectively you have to have an understanding of what motivates individuals and, conversely, an understanding of what elements of the working situation act as demotivators.

In addition to possessing varying needs and expectations of work, individuals will vary in relation to their physical ability, personality, characteristics, capacity, capability, intelligence, aptitude and values. Their potential to perform effectively will be affected by such personal aspects and will also be affected by the nature of the job and the manner in which they are managed.

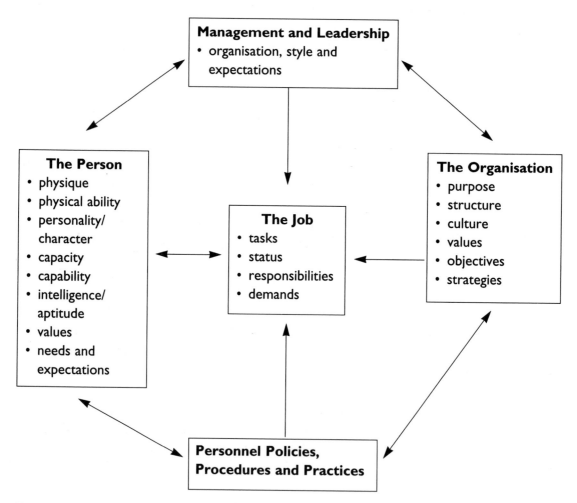

FIGURE 4 *The interrelation between the individual and the organisation.*

Figure 4 provides an outline of the interrelation between the individual, the job, the organisation and management policies and styles.

Increasingly employers seek to establish strategies and policies which minimise the potential for conflict between the organisation (its goals and objectives) and the individual. The developments in people management over the last decade have seen a move towards:

- increasing involvement of employees in the decision-making process
- improvement in employee communication in an attempt to facilitate the sharing of goals and objectives
- more open and informal styles of management
- personnel practices which more openly recognise the contributions employees make to the success of the business
- the development of organisational cultures which support positive working relationships

If I can instil a sense of pride in the job, a love of the craft and a commitment to the profession, I will have gone a long way in motivating my staff who often work long hours under considerable pressure.

EXECUTIVE CHEF, LARGE 4-STAR HOTEL

The chef quoted above, like many others in similar positions, invests considerable time and effort in encouraging his staff, providing effective training, opportunities for advancement, assistance with entering competitions and attempts to provide positive leadership through a professional commitment to his work and employees.

Yet many in the industry do not work either for such enlightened managers or in organisations which value their contributions. *The Hospitality Industry Employment Survey 1994*, sponsored by the *Caterer & Hotelkeeper*, analysed levels of pay, willingness to relocate, working hours and aspects of motivation and found that 'The most important aspect of a job was that work should be challenging. Job security, responsibility, recognition and career prospects were all rated as very important' (*Caterer & Hotelkeeper*, November 1994).

A similar survey entitled *Employment in the Catering and Hospitality Industry – Employee Attitudes and Career Expectations* by the Hotel and Catering Training Company, carried out on more than one thousand employees, reported that 'about a third of respondents were dissatisfied with promotion opportunities, perks and pay, whilst a quarter were unhappy with the opportunities available to obtain qualifications; 67% of respondents were happy with the hours they worked and more than three quarters were generally satisfied with their job' (*Caterer & Hotelkeeper*, November 1994).

Such surveys, of course, represent the findings on a very small sample of the industry's workforce. However, the reports provide a reasonable appraisal of overall attitudes towards jobs, organisations and status. Whilst surveying staff attitudes towards their current employment is commendable, it cannot provide all the answers in respect of what motivates employees.

─────────────── **KEY POINT** ───────────────

Organisations need to identify all the factors which affect the level of behaviour, motivation, competence and performance of their employees. In doing so they will be able (where practicable) to amend personnel policies and practices.

The current fascination with aspects of employee motivation and performance is hardly surprising given the challenges which have faced the hospitality industry over the last few decades. Rising costs, increased competition, changes in customer expectations, continued shortages of skilled labour, the drive to flatten structures, coupled with periods of economic up and down turn, have all made operators analyse much more closely not only their staffing levels, but also the productivity of employees.

In looking at employee costs and productivity, employers will analyse such aspects as staff retention, customer satisfaction and employee capability. In this respect they will seek to attract, recruit and retain appropriately skilled employees who will contribute positively to the organisation or business. A detailed explanation of the recruitment and selection process is described in Chapter 4. In reality, the employer requires personnel policies and management practices which actively support the objectives of the business. To this end employers need to understand the factors which affect employees' contributions to the business.

Motivation

Management theorists and academics have been studying this aspect for some time, attempting to identify and define models by which managers can gain more understanding of what motivates individuals to perform well. As with all such models, there are weaknesses for, whilst they can assist the general understanding of organisations and managers, they often, in practice, are limited in their relevance to the hospitality industry.

In looking at the aspect of employee performance, you will need an understanding of the basic terms which are associated with it. The brief explanations below relate to the individual employee:

- *Motivation*: response to varying work conditions, pressures and rewards; a willingness to work well
- *Performance*: level of work and degree of task and responsibility completion; also to do with consistency and quality
- *Capability*: innate potential and ability to complete tasks at different levels
- *Capacity*: ability to undertake a number of tasks and responsibilities, e.g. serve 5 tables, clean 10 rooms, handle 20 key accounts, or capacity to learn new skills
- *Competence*: ability for a certain task or tasks, e.g. being a competent sales person

Traditionally, managers have focused only on the aspect of employee motivation, an element you will recognise in reading other texts on people management. Unfortunately, there is no one simple answer to the question of what motivates people to perform and work well.

Whilst a number of theories of motivation exist, their direct relevance to the hospitality industry is, as already stated, questionable. Possibly their value is that they help to highlight the many factors which influence work behaviour and performance. If they are to develop an effective approach to people management, organisations and managers need to bring together their understanding of such aspects as motivation and performance as well as capability, capacity and competence.

A more sophisticated argument may be that if managers can understand what initially motivates individual employees, then they can identify the relevance of such aspects as capability, capacity and competence to maintaining employee motivation.

So what factors do influence an employee's work, behaviour and performance and what components of jobs and roles act as motivators and demotivators (Figure 5)?

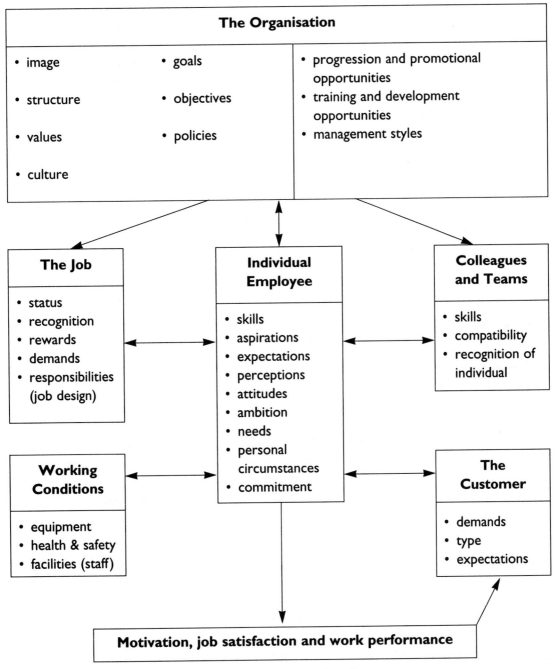

FIGURE 5 *Interrelation of motivating factors on the individual employee.*

Hospitality operators have looked at this aspect in more detail of late and have been concerned with identifying all components of a job, the aim being to design out elements of jobs that are demotivating or attempt to minimise the effect of them.

Job design

Job design is basically the way a job is structured and what it contains in terms of tasks, responsibilities, status, reward, recognition and value. It is an approach that is relevant to all areas, however; where it has seen most effect is in situations where jobs are repetitive, requiring little skill other than initial training.

Fast food operators like McDonald's and Kentucky Fried Chicken (amongst others) have developed a range of elements in such jobs, including reward and recognition for competence and service, in addition to job rotation schemes and career development programmes. What they seek to do is add value to a job in order to maintain job satisfaction and enhance employee motivation. Such approaches can minimise the effect of repetitive work and low status but not eradicate it, and employers can often do little more than accept high levels of staff turnover.

────────────── KEY POINT ──────────────

When designing jobs, employers will need to provide a package of components which focus not only on the tasks and responsibilities, but on all the elements which may influence behaviour, performance, job satisfaction and employee motivation.

Motivation can be said to be important at three levels:

1 motivating appropriate individuals to apply for vacancies;
2 motivating existing employees to perform well;
3 motivating existing employees to remain within the organisation and contribute effectively to the aims and objectives of the business.

The importance of effective recruitment and selection is covered in Chapter 4; however, it is important to recognise that companies and businesses require appropriate personnel and, therefore, need to encourage (motivate) suitable individuals to apply for vacancies.

If you are a student coming towards the end of your course, or an employee in industry thinking about a job change, consider what will attract you to apply for certain jobs. It could be any of the following:

- the job itself
- level of pay
- additional rewards and benefits
- status and image of the company
- challenge

- location
- training and development opportunities
- career progression possibilities

or even a basic need just for a job! Your reasons for applying may also be affected by your:

- level of skills, qualifications and experience
- personal circumstances, i.e. ability to relocate
- personal perceptions about a particular company or job

Employers use a variety of methods in both direct advertising and in respect of personnel policies to promote themselves actively to potential employees. Figure 6 is an example of one company's national advertising and it is a good one in respect of identifying benefits to potential employees. See if you can identify the benefits (some are obvious, some less immediately apparent, and others may depend on the individual applicant).

Singapore Sam is a rapidly expanding concept in Oriental food and due to this growth, we are looking for the following people to join our management team:

GENERAL MANAGERS: London & South-East

This position is ideal for an experienced restaurant manager who has worked in a high volume fast food restaurant and is now seeking a more demanding role at a more senior level. This position demands a wide range of skills and experience which could only be gained in the fast food industry. This includes setting and achieving budgetary targets, managing your management team, advertising, training and implementing marketing and promotional ideas.

At Singapore Sam we are committed to Quality, Customer Service and Cleanliness. As a general manager you must possess excellent communication skills as well as operational standards. In return for your experience and commitment we offer:

- Salary around £16,000 to £18,000
- Result related bonus
- Company pension scheme
- Leisure club membership
- Private medical plan

SINGAPORE *Sam*

MANAGEMENT TRAINEES:
London/Sheffield/Bristol/Norwich/Stoke-on-Trent

Applicants for this position should be aged between 20 and 25 years with a catering background or degree in Hotel & Catering. We offer a structured three month training programme to provide you with the key operational and managerial skills to assist you in your first managerial position. Salary will range from £10,000 to £12,000.

If you would like to know more about these opportunities please send your CV including current salary details.

FIGURE 6 *Job advertisements to attract potential employees.*

Motivating employees to perform well

Naturally some of the elements which will attract employees will assist in influencing levels of performance, e.g. status, level of pay and benefits. However, once attracted to a particular job or role, the level of performance and behaviour of an individual will be influenced by a variety of other factors. These include:

- perceived fairness of pay and working conditions
- personnel policies, procedures and practices

- range of additional benefits
- ability of co-workers
- relationship with co-workers and supervisors
- recognition from supervisors and peers of work performed
- opportunities for progression and development
- personal circumstances, i.e. health
- ability to complete tasks and responsibilities

Consider employees new into a supervisory position, who find themselves working with uncooperative colleagues in situations where complaints are high, important equipment is not working, working hours are extended due to staff shortages, promised training does not occur and management are critical of the employee. Sound familiar to anyone?

The above was a list of complaints I received from an ex-student who had recently joined a large hotel group. Charged with the responsibility for food and beverage within one hotel, the student, who had other supervisory experience prior to joining the company, stated: 'What really was the final straw was the criticism that I was not meeting my targets. How could I when the management itself was so ineffective? Each day I would receive new responsibilities, many of which were not in my job description and, to be honest, outside my experience. In the end I left, completely disillusioned with the company and the industry.' Luckily this individual found another job with a company which delivered what their advertising had stated and has since progressed to a senior management position.

In assisting employees to perform well, employers need to:

- reward at a level appropriate to responsibilities
- monitor stated personnel policies, procedures and practices
- set a level of responsibilities appropriate to an individual's capability and capacity, or provide training to allow additional responsibilities to be undertaken
- ensure that working conditions are conducive to supporting performance required

--- KEY POINT ---

Assisting employees to achieve appropriate levels of performance and behaviour is linked to a number of factors, all of which, in turn, relate to the manner in which the organisation supports a positive working partnership between themselves and the employees. The better the partnership, the higher the motivation and performance of the employee.

Motivating employees to contribute effectively to the aims and objectives of the business

The turnover of staff within the hospitality industry has always been high. The ability of a company or business to retain its key personnel is, of course, dependent upon a wide range of factors, many of which have already been identified. An employee may stay with an employer due to:

- fear of not getting another job
- inability to relocate due to personal circumstances
- the level of pay, reward and benefits
- possibilities for promotion and development

Additionally, employees may stay due to a number of reasons related to the company itself, such as:

- enjoyment, the 'feel good' factor
- sense of loyalty
- a belief that the company cares for them as an individual and values their contribution

It is this group of factors on which many companies have been concentrating. Having developed a sound base of personnel policies and procedures, attracted appropriate personnel and supported individuals in performing well, they seek to further enhance working relationships in a variety of ways. Positive working relationships appear to develop best when there is:

- effective, ongoing communication between the organisation or business and its employees
- a culture which recognises the contribution of individual employees
- a reduction in hierarchy, allowing personnel access to senior management
- a structure which allows individuals of all levels to share in decision making (what some companies refer to as empowerment)
- a flow of open information in the organisation, assisting individual employees to understand (and share) company objectives

This approach has many supporters in the industry and it is a recognisable management strategy to get the employees on board, sharing the vision, goals and objectives of the organisation. Companies such as Harvester Restaurants, Scotts Hotels, Gardner Merchant, Compass, Sutcliffe and Holiday Inns, amongst others, have all developed approaches which involve employees more in the organisation. This is in recognition that to retain key personnel, organisations have to implement wider ownership of the business. Such development may go on quietly within the organisation, with senior managers implementing strategies which support and assist employee investment. Additionally, the company may seek to publicise such an approach in as many ways as it can through informal and formal meetings, employees newsletters and in public statements, such as those in the box overleaf from Cala Hotels.

The Investors in People standard identifies the following statement as relevant to this approach: 'an Investor in People makes a public commitment from the top to develop all employees to achieve its business objectives'.

Chalmers Cursley, Managing Director of De Vere Hotels Ltd which employs 2700 people working in 26 hotels across England and Jersey, recently stated: 'We wanted to establish a single process which would link the demands of the business identified at board level and from customer feedback with the training and development of all our employees' (*Employment News*, October 1994).

The Investors in People standard is, of course, one scheme amongst many to assist the commitment of individuals by promoting positive investment in them by the organisation.

HOW EVERY EMPLOYEE CAN CONTRIBUTE TO THE SUCCESS OF THE COMPANY

Contributions will be specific to each individual/team but will focus on the following key areas:

1 Product knowledge
2 Customer care
3 Appearance
4 Enthusiasm
5 Standards of performance
6 Communication and teamwork
7 Cost control
8 Development of self/others
9 Adaptability

MISSION STATEMENT

'To invest in our people and build a team motivated to meet customer expectations'

Cala Hotels

WHAT IS I.I.P.?

I.I.P. is a national programme which matches training needs to business requirements and where appropriate is linked to national qualifications.

SOME OF THE BENEFITS TO YOU

- The opportunity to work towards formal qualifications
- The chance to improve your career prospects
- You will help to decide your training needs
- Improving your skills will give you more confidence to do your job
- Knowing what is required of you will give you more job satisfaction
- It will improve communications between you and your supervisor/manager
- You will be encouraged to express your views
- You don't necessarily have to go to college – qualifications are obtainable in your workplace
- These are national qualifications and you can take them with you if you change employers
- You will be working for a company that is committed to training and development

Cala Hotels

BASS PEOPLE COMMITMENT

To offer the highest standards of customer service and remain closely attuned to customer needs.

To be the first choice for those people seeking a career in pub retailing.

To train and develop our staff, giving them the skills they need to be the best in the business.

To meet both business and personal goals through real teamwork and excellent communications.

To involve all our staff, enhancing job satisfaction by empowering people to improve the business.

To share the rewards of our success with all those who have helped us achieve it.

To extend people's abilities, helping them to succeed by building an environment based on high integrity, strong and consistent values and continuous improvement.

Bass Taverns

Scotts Hotels, a subsidiary of Scotts Hospitality Incorporated, has over 2000 bedrooms within the UK at present. Part of their mission statement provided to all employees states:

We recognise the value that each and every one of our people has in reaching our purpose and we will develop them, empower them and recognise and reward their unique contribution. . . . We recognise that, in a people business, our people are No.1. The growth of Marriott Hotels in the UK depends on the loyalty, interest and team spirit of our people.

In describing their management style, the organisation states:

Unwavering commitment to Total Quality results in an organisation with a feeling of human warmth. It transforms the 'parts' into one large 'whole' when individuals work in synergy with each other. . . . We also believe in making business fun for everyone. Hence our people at every level are encouraged to fully participate in the running of the business, to think objectively, use their initiative, take responsibility and, above all, enjoy their work.

Scotts Hotels Ltd

The motivation of employees, then, cannot be considered solely in respect of job satisfaction, but also in respect of aspects related to the:

1 employment of individuals;
2 levels of behaviour and performance;
3 maintenance and retention of key staff who, by involvement in the organisation, will contribute positively to the values, goals and objectives of a company or business.

So far descriptions have been provided which, along with other material in this text, will identify for you possible blueprints of effective personnel and human resource management strategies.

KEY POINT

Recognising the employment strategies which will assist employee motivation is crucial to the organisation. However, organisations must also recognise that people are individuals with varying wishes, needs, expectations and attitudes. In addressing such issues organisations need to implement management styles which actively support the achievement of organisational goals and objectives and promote positive working relationships.

The key point here focuses on the need for a positive management style, which is described briefly in the following section.

1.5 LEADERSHIP, MANAGEMENT AND QUALITY

KEY POINT

Personnel management and human resource management is concerned with the direct and indirect management of people and both the style and manner of leadership and management will influence employee behaviour and motivation.

Studies of both leadership and management have created certain common assumptions, as follows:

- leadership is easily definable
- leaders are born, not made
- all managers are leaders (and vice versa)
- there are styles of leadership (autocratic, charismatic, etc.)
- participative leadership and management styles are better at improving organisational effectiveness
- autocratic leadership and management styles predominate in the large, more formal organisations
- individuals (employees) need to be managed or led

Such assumptions can, of course, be challenged by experience, although this does not appear to reduce the fascination of academics with this subject. The inclusion of this area is not to provide a detailed explanation of leadership and management theories, rather it is designed to provide you with a basic understanding of how leadership and management can influence employee behaviour and motivation.

To assist this explanation, it is useful to provide some basic definitions:

- *Definition of management:* succeed in doing, be in charge of, administer, handle, control. Most people would define management as being concerned with activities which sustain tasks. Managers therefore concentrate on such elements as strategy, structure and systems. Management is the formal side of employee organisation, setting tasks, schedules, instructing, directing and telling.

- *Definition of leadership:* providing leadership which relates to a capacity to influence people and generate a desire to complete activities or tasks. Leadership can be said to be concerned with style, people, skills, shared goals and values.

QUESTION

When does the need for leadership take over from the need for management if, in fact, it is required at all?

This is, of course, an almost impossible question to answer. You might like to take a few minutes to list the qualities or personal characteristics of someone you have enjoyed working for. It could be a manager or supervisor or a tutor in your college. You may find it useful to keep to brief statements like 'caring' or 'skilful'. Your list may also include statements like 'charismatic', 'thoughtful', 'commands respect' or even 'works employees hard but is fair'.

Now reverse the task and compile a list of characteristics of an individual you have not enjoyed working with. Your second list may include comments like 'unfair', 'demanding', 'bossy', 'disorganised' or even 'lacking in authority'.

Taking the exercise a little farther, you may wish to get a work colleague or friend to complete the same task (on the same people) and compare notes.

This sort of exercise is quite common in the analysis of preferred leaders or managers and many organisations use forms of personality testing in an attempt to identify leadership or management style. Such exercises or tests, whilst useful, are coming under criticism and at best they provide indications of style or approach, not definitive answers. The important element to recognise is that, despite countless studies and increased use of leadership style tests, a clear definition of leadership is not available (and perhaps not particularly useful).

Returning to the list of assumptions on leadership and management outlined earlier, you may wish to identify which of these statements you agree with. Most people would state that, in general, they prefer managers (leaders) to be consultative (that is talking things through) or democratic. I have tested this proposal on a number of occasions with groups of trainee managers. Generally almost all stated they preferred such 'fairer' styles of management; however, on closer questioning related to organisational efficiency (getting things done), many of the individuals changed their preference to management styles which focused on tasks, control and organisation.

So let's make another assumption – leadership and management is achieving tasks *through other people.*

KEY POINT

Managers (leaders) need to achieve the goals, objectives and tasks of their organisation. To achieve this they must obtain the cooperation of employees and 'manage' their performance. Note: In respect of motivation, managers must know how to influence employees to gain cooperation and performance.

You may now recognise that managers (leaders) have a role to play in:

- directing
- controlling
- administering
- organising
- and influencing employees

Styles of management and leadership

The manner in which individual managers (leaders) undertake these roles is affected by a number of factors, including:

- personality
- skills and experience
- type of organisation, i.e. formal, informal, large, small
- number of staff
- status in organisation and level of responsibility

This aspect of managerial or leadership styles has been studied for some time with various descriptions and definitions being identified. These can be separated into two main types:

1 *Task orientated* where the individual focuses in on tasks and responsibilities as the driving force; consultation with staff is minimal;
2 *People orientated* where the individual focuses on employees (subordinates or colleagues); consultation takes place and is seen as assisting in gaining the cooperation of employees to complete tasks.

You might like to complete a small research project of your own on this aspect (with the cooperation of supervisors or managers in the industry).

───────────────── QUESTION ─────────────────

How do your supervisors or managers spend their time during an average working week?

Request they record time spent on such things as:

- paperwork (by themselves)
- informal meetings
- formal meetings
- consultation with employees
- directing others
- telephone calls (internal and external)
- forward planning

Analysis may provide you with a picture on *what* the manager does (perhaps not *how*). Such a study may help you in understanding the manner in which individuals manage. If there are a number of you studying for a course, it can be useful to compare notes.

Professional bodies like the HCIMA and the HCTC have conducted similar studies for some time. However, research on managers has been reduced over the past few years and it is an area worthy of more study. Certainly, up-to-date research on managers in respect of style, skills, qualifications and work patterns would allow improved understanding of the job of management and leadership in the hospitality industry and, perhaps, be of more use than current reliance on existing theories in respect of style and behaviour.

Table I Styles of management leadership

DESCRIPTION	CHARACTERISTICS	
Autocratic	Expects and demands compliance, works within formal structure	
Dictatorial	Expects compliance, controls, dictates and directs; little time for consultation or negotiation; formal type	possibly task-orientated managers
Paternalistic	Expects compliance; works from a base of directing and seeking obedience; organisational structure less formal	
Democratic	Seeks compliance via consensus, belief in sharing ideas. Formal structure which supports the organisation. Reasonable levels of consultation and communication.	
Consultative	Shares information, emphasis on communication and joint problem solving; organisational structure and hierarchy relatively formal to support idea of common goals	possibly people-orientated managers
Charismatic	Leads others in hoped for compliance, sets example, works from the front; consultation minimal	
Empowering	Shares problems and issues, allows individuals to solve problems and make decisions within agreed framework	

Table 1 provides some possible descriptions of management style. However, it is important to recognise that individual managers may exhibit elements of all or some of these styles (or others), although perhaps not at the same time.

A final exercise you may wish to complete is to identify the style of management appropriate to given management situations. Consider the following list and note separately the style you think best fits the situation.

1   Opening a meeting for the management team of a new hotel.
2   Formal presentation of new quality system to heads of department.
3   Formal disciplinary interview.
4   Counselling session for junior member of staff experiencing difficulties with responsibilities.
5   Training session for group of unit managers in company personnel procedures.
6   Team building session for banqueting staff.
7   Appraisal interview for assistant manager failing to meet targets.
8   Meeting of supervisors to set up a quality improvement group.

Of course, management and leadership style may have little to do with organisation effectiveness and may have more to do with relationships. One way of identifying an appropriate style is to relate the degree to which consultation takes place (or should). Put in another way, management and leadership style may relate to the degree of telling or selling.

KEY POINT

Managers will all possess their own style, which will be affected by factors such as organisational structure, task, personal skills, experience and attitudes. Possibly the style of management or leadership is less important than the ability to achieve objectives in a manner which assists employee motivation and performance.

This section has provided you with an introduction and overview of the elements of motivation, management and leadership. A deliberate omission has been repetitions of models of motivation and theory from such writers as Maslow, Herzberg and McGregor. This is in no way criticism of their work as they have been extremely influential in the development of approaches to people management. (You will find explanations of such theories in many of the standard text books.) There is no doubting the need to obtain a basic understanding of such models in relation to the effective management of people. I hope that this section will have helped you begin to understand.

I will leave the last comment to a Director of a regional catering company:

It is vital we train and motivate our staff, thereby improving standards of service and customer care. A happier, contented, well-managed and motivated staff assists an organisation to retain its competitive edge and meet its goals and objectives. With the increasing demand for quality we rely on staff, through our managers, to deliver this quality. If they are not motivated they won't.

These have been evidenced by the move towards Quality Systems which, whilst initially concentrating on the process of production and delivery (*BS 5750/IS 9000*), have begun to concentrate on the contribution of people to quality improvement. The effects of quality management methods on HRM are considerable and worth describing in detail.

Management of quality through people

The drive for quality via initiatives such as quality assurance, control and Total Quality Management has been a predominant factor in organisational development over the last few years. The hospitality industry has not been slow in adopting these initiatives into their operating systems and culture. Whilst the benefits of such systems have been well documented, the changes to human resource management processes and the installation of such approaches have created significant challenges for hospitality operators.

Total Quality Management, which can include many of the initiatives developed over the past fifteen to twenty years, is an approach which involves all employees within an organisation. Based on the considerations that:

- quality is the responsibility of everyone
- quality is not just the relationship between the organisation and its customers, often focused via customer care systems
- quality management requires effective communication between the organisation and employees, and participation by employees in quality improvement

Therefore, organisations developing TQM and other quality systems need to adapt their human resource management strategy to one based upon:

- clear and effective communication
- employee involvement and empowerment
- lack of hierarchical and structural barriers between the organisation and its employees
- concept of internal customer, i.e. quality between employees and between the organisation and its suppliers

For both large, formal organisations and small, independent businesses, the challenge is to accept alterations to their style of people management. At one end of the scale this might include alterations to the structure and organisation of the company, whilst at the other end it will require alterations in the way in which employees work.

CASE STUDY. HARVESTER RESTAURANTS

Harvester Restaurants, in developing quality, identified radical alterations to the status and role of its unit managers and supervisors. With a strategy of developing a team approach, unit managers lost their traditional role and job title. Managers became team coaches and team managers, with the emphasis of teams sharing the responsibility for problem solving and quality improvement.

Work within the units was based on team involvement with the emphasis on 'empowering' individuals to identify quality improvements and deal directly with problems. Extending the involvement of employees, Harvester built into their organisation a number of initiatives related to removing the traditional hierarchical structure. Having operated an annual conference for personnel, they identified a need to alter the emphasis with the focus being an elected representative from each unit. This was a deliberate change in recognition of the need to involve all levels of staff.

With the title 'Winning Teams Means Business' Harvester, which at that time operated over 80 units throughout the United Kingdom, developed the conference theme 'guest delight through the delivery of quality' and identified that 'the quality of our people determines the success of our people'.

The investment Harvester has made in both quality improvement and alterations to the style of its people management has been considerable.

Participants were elected by their units and were responsible for sharing the outcomes with colleagues back at their specific units.

The annual conference was then aimed at sharing ideas, reviewing progress and identifying the way forward – an approach to people management that pervades the whole organisation.

Information courtesy of Harvester Restaurants Ltd

Harvester is, of course, only one example of many hospitality operators who, identifying a need to imbed quality approaches within their organisation, have recognised that *quality improvement is delivered by the people of an organisation and, to affect quality, alterations in the approaches to people management are required.*

Table 2 identifies current quality methods and approaches and perspectives on the role and practice of people management. In developing quality, organisations will identify the need to focus on the customer. This does not just mean the external customer who purchases goods, services or facilities, but also the internal customer – the employees and the suppliers who form part of the chain for quality delivery.

KEY POINT

In developing quality the organisation will have to alter both structural and cultural approaches. This will have a direct effect on the style and manner in which the people are managed.

The management of people in an organisation developing a TQM structure is characterised by:

- the move away from more traditional, formalised styles of management to more open consultative styles
- the recognition of the contribution all employees can make to the benefit of the organisation and its customers

Obviously the comparisons shown in Table 3 are generalisations; however, the main elements to recognise are the ways in which individual employees are valued and involved.

Table 2 Quality management approaches to human resource management

METHOD	APPROACH	HRM PERSPECTIVES
Quality Circles	Groups of people meet on a voluntary basis with direct line manager — internally assessed	Development of team structure and loosening of formalised lines of management
Quality Assurance (e.g. BS 5750/IS 9000)	Improvement by product specification, based on procedure manual, with quality checked by internal and external auditing — externally assessed	Teams and individuals charged with responsibility for adhering to procedures; continued use of formalised job descriptions and tasks
Total Quality Control	Quality improvement based on specifications, procedures and cost reduction; concept of internal and external customer — internally assessed	Training of employees in procedure and systems; commencement of team approach to Q/A; formalised structure remains
Investors in People	National initiative providing benchmarks and measurable performance criteria for quality and effectiveness of investment in employees — externally assessed	Improved communication and consultation required; individual employees perceptions analysed
TQM (Total Quality Management)	Strategic approach incorporating other quality methods; no end result; emphasis on ongoing quality improvement — ongoing assessment by all parties	Flattening of structure, sharing and caring organisation; recognition of contribution of all employees

---

KEY POINT

The concept of quality management is one which will be around for some time to come and hospitality managers need to recognise the link between quality systems and the management of people.

Table 3 Comparisons between traditional and TQM organisations

	TRADITIONAL ORGANISATION	TOTAL QUALITY MANAGEMENT ORGANISATION
Values	Focused on profit motives and performance; employees seen as costs	Focused on the customer (internal and external); employees valued as an asset, not cost
Culture	Focused on right of managers to manage and the importance of the organisation	Improvement comes from all within the organisation; a learning culture
Structure	Hierarchical and formalised — clear lines of management and responsibility; decision passed down the line	Less formalised flatter structure, lines of management responsibility and decision making in existence, but based on shared approaches and teams
Leadership styles	More formalised and autocratic; emphasis on control and direction; employees seen as deliverers of decisions	Less formalised and more consultative; emphasis on empowering employees to share responsibility
Employee involvement	Maintained at level of employee; little or no contact between employee and senior management; minimum of involvement by employees in decision and policy making	Medium levels of contact between employees and senior managers; focus for changes (operational) of employee level — opportunity for involvement in decision and policy making high

In a survey of hospitality operators in late 1994, senior, personnel and human resource managers were asked to identify current and forecasted involvement in Quality Management and comment on such aspects as benefits of Quality Management approaches in respect of the company, the employees and the customers.

Further responses were sought in respect of management, training and involvement of employees in the development of standards, identification and correction of problems. Of the 75 hospitality companies and businesses which responded:

- 17% were involved or had obtained BS5750 (IS9000)
- 65% were committed to or had achieved the Investors in People award
- 15% were involved with TQM
- 32% operated company devised quality schemes

- 8% used other quality measure methods
- (17% of the total had no involvement in Quality Management developments)

Generally companies reported a relatively high level of staff involvement in such developments and all identified positive links between Quality Management initiatives and employee management.

Quality Management was seen as a continuous process, not a single event. As one manager stated: 'Quality is an ongoing process ... it is important that we communicate to all our employees why it [QM] is important and how standards can be continually improved in order that we not only meet, but exceed our customer expectations.'

A senior manager in a hotel chain commented: 'Higher standards are achieved through better trained and informed staff. Thorough training [in QM] provides better training opportunities for staff, increasing their skills and employability and giving greater understanding and feeling of involvement in the business.'

The general manager of a luxury hotel commenting on the benefit of QM and, specifically, IIP to employees stated: 'Employees know that they work for a reputable company which is interested in them as individuals and [a company] which recognises the contribution they make to the business.'

J. Roberts (Oct 1994) Quality Management in the Hospitality Industry,
Rotherham College of Arts and Technology

In conclusion, the management of people is a key element in the overall function of human resource management in that:

- people management is important as people are the deliverers of the service, product and facility
- the investment in people is a recognition of both the contribution people make to an organisation and the costs involved in employing people
- organisations (and managers) need to understand what methods of people management are the most effective and appropriate
- people management concerns both functional, administrative tasks and aspects related to the understanding of people
- hospitality organisations require well managed people if they are to achieve their objectives
- in managing people a balance has to be struck between the needs of the organisation and the needs and expectations of individual employees
- the development of quality management systems has more to do with the effective management of people than with production-type processes

People management relates in practice to the manner and style in which individuals and teams are managed within the organisation. HRM can be said to deal with wider strategic issues, an aspect dealt with in the following section.

1.6 ROLES AND FUNCTIONS OF PERSONNEL AND HUMAN RESOURCE MANAGEMENT

Personnel directors have to behave as general managers with personnel specialities rather than as personnel people with general management tendencies.

NVQ PERSONNEL STANDARDS LEAD BODY, DISCUSSION PAPER 1993

In researching the role of personnel and human resource managers you will quickly identify that there are possibly as many definitions as there are personnel specialists! This apparent confusion is perhaps quite understandable given the increasing complexity and range of functions such individuals undertake. This debate will no doubt continue and, as the industry itself changes as it adapts to global markets, so too will the nature and role of personnel and HRM. One aim of this text is to describe for you details of current and future practice, which will provide a reasonable picture of the key roles and functions of this vital component of hospitality management.

Within the preceding section on people management, it was identified that all organisations require systems and methods for the management of employees. The complex company or business of today requires not only systems but specialists who can take a central role in advising on and designing personnel management policies.

This section will concentrate on identifying the key roles and functions of personnel and human resource management specifically related to the hospitality industry and include reference to both strategic and operational issues. Before identifying these functions it is important to recognise two key points:

KEY POINTS
---

1 The role and function of personnel and HRM will vary in respect of the size, style and culture of a company or business.
2 There is a growing acceptance that all supervisors, managers and department heads have a personnel role to play, which is directly affecting the role and status of personnel and human resource management specialists.

Obviously you cannot compare the HRM requirements of an independent hotel operator to that of a large multi-site contract caterer. Additionally, each company and business will develop its own approach to people management based on the beliefs, values and culture it possesses.

As one director of a large hotel chain commented recently: 'We believe all managers should be personnel managers and deal more directly with personnel issues – any other approach just does not make sense.'

You will recognise in your reading and research that the current debate about the role, function and contribution of personnel and HRM is increasing, with many of the traditional, more functional tasks being replaced by other more strategic roles.

In studying the returns from various surveys conducted during 1992–94 on personnel practices in the hospitality industry, covering some 360 companies, one aspect to emerge was the varying titles given to individuals with some form of personnel responsibility. Whilst there remained a predominance of the use of the title 'Personnel and Training Manager', others included 'People Manager', 'People and Quality Manager', 'Manager of Employee Resourcing', 'Quality and Human Resource Manager (Director)', 'People Empowerment Manager', plus a reasonable number of 'Human Resource' directors and managers. Whether this retitling has more to do with modernising the title than with a deliberate policy to realign personnel management into a more strategic and developmental role within organisations is debatable.

Appreciating such a debate exists should not dissuade you from identifying the common roles and functions of HRM, as it is the understanding of these that is important, not an academic debate on titles and interpretations.

In the surveys conducted during 1992–94, aspects studied were the degree of involvement of individual 'personnel' managers in strategic planning, the various priorities they were targeting, definitions of their job role, main challenges for personnel managers for the next year and identification of specific concerns that would affect their role.

Any statistical survey possesses weaknesses. However, following analysis of the raw data, certain factors did become clear.

1 There was a general move away from emphasis on the functional role of personnel to one which was concentrating on the development of strategy.
2 A general concern existed amongst the majority of 'personnel managers' that whilst the emphasis of their role was changing, there were still major problems to tackle.

The above factors were particularly evidenced by returns from line and unit personnel managers. For personnel directors and human resource managers in more senior positions, concerns were centred on the need to adapt organisational culture to the changing nature of the market. A significant number of these senior managers also identified that the emphasis for HRM was moving away from operational matters and there was a move to the development of the concept of the HRM manager as an internal consultant.

J. Roberts *Personnel and Human Resource Management Training Surveys 1992–1994,*
Rotherham College of Arts and Technology

Key roles and functions of HRM

Before looking at these key roles, it is important to consider the factors which have and will affect them.

ORGANISATIONAL FACTOR

As organisations change and develop in response to economic and market changes, their approach to the management of their people will obviously need to change. Whilst the hospitality industry is still dominated by small independent businesses, the major players, such as the large hotel chains, contract caterers and restaurant and leisure groups have gone through major restructuring in the past ten years. This change has been in response to a variety of factors, including:

- the boom and recession periods of the late 1980s and the early 1990s
- rebranding of sections of the larger companies which has generated particular approaches to HRM due to reorganisation
- 'delayering' or flattening of organisational structures which has increased the role of the line manager in respect of front line personnel activities
- growth in competition both nationally and globally, with increased focus on the customer and the need to improve quality

There is no doubting that as hospitality companies redefine their strategies and policies for the next decade, the role of HRM will need to figure centrally in the planning and decision-making process. What is not so apparent is to what degree HRM policy will dictate other strategic plans and policies.

FIGURE 7 *Organisation and strategy.*

In organisational and strategic management terms, HRM policies will often be seen as deliverers of the overall strategic plan. Policies and plans, including manpower planning, recruitment and selection, and training and development practices, will be geared towards the achievement of specific corporate objectives (see Figure 7). The human resource plan will aim to integrate with other policies and plans and seek to achieve the stated company objectives.

KEY POINT

The human resource function is affected by the nature of the organisation, its structure and objectives, and exists primarily to support the business and its aims.

This approach to the role and function of HRM supports the argument that HRM is in essence a support service (albeit a vital one) and not an instigator of changes to organisational structure or objectives. This is not necessarily true, as evidenced by the emphasis many hospitality companies are placing on their personnel policies. Certainly within the past decade there has been an increase in positive statements relating to investing in people. How far such statements go in identifying a major change in the influence of HRM as an organisational strategy is again debatable.

Analysis of the roles of senior board members and executives of the major catering companies might identify individuals with a specific HRM remit, but this is generally not the case. As the strategic plans stem from such corporate bodies, the lack of HRM representation again indicates that such a function remains a supportive one. This, however, does not weaken the role, and the contribution HRM can make to the business is described later in this section.

To recap, the organisation will affect the status, role and function of personnel and HRM activity in the following ways:

1   The size, style and culture of an organisation will set the key roles of the HRM function.
2   The status of HRM within the organisation is dependent upon the perception of its contribution to the achievement of company plans and objectives. One aspect of this latter point is the emphasis being placed by some observers on the need to 'sell' HRM to senior managers.
3   The manner in which the organisation is structured and the degree to which the personnel function is passed down to line managers, will define the parameters of any central HRM role.

In previous sections descriptions were provided on common approaches relating to the management of staff. For personnel managers the need to recognise how the company is organised, functionally, is as important in understanding its underlying culture and values.

Expanding companies seek to redefine management functions and activities in line with revised structure. Alongside this they also seek to ensure that cultural values and philosophies are integrated into new units and their employees. This aspect has certainly created problems in the last few years, with the increasing numbers of take-overs and acquisitions.

Consider the problem facing employees in the school meals service who have often found themselves with new employers. Whilst legislation, such as the Transfer of Undertakings, has provided partial protection in respect of employment conditions, such employees still face the trauma of major organisational change. The personnel or human resource role in such a situation is a crucial one, and one that deserves further attention in the future.

Additionally, consider the position of employees in a business being operated by managers appointed by receivers, or hotels which become managed by another company. Potential conflict exists between the organisational demands of the new management and the need to ensure a reasonable stability in working practices.

Conflict can arise from a variety of factors, including changes in:

*   reporting systems
*   financial control systems

- employment conditions, personnel policies and practices
- status of individuals
- organisational structure, e.g. the existence of additional levels of management
- purchasing systems
- standards
- perceived and stated organisational culture and values

As the line in Arthur Hailey's book *Hotel* states: 'the first thing we do when taking over a hotel is to reassure everyone that nothing will change; the next thing we do is start sacking people.' Whilst this is a fictional representation of an hospitality operation, there is no doubt that changes in structure and ownership do create significant problems.

Adapting to the organisational element is not restricted to the larger companies and similar problems exist in smaller businesses. Individual employees will possess their own preferred organisational style and, whilst some will prefer the more formalised hierarchy of a larger company, others will perform better in a more informal working environment. This aspect was discussed with a group of students undertaking a day-release management programme. Several had recently changed their jobs, including moving from large hospitality companies to smaller ones and vice versa. Whilst reasons varied, the one common factor in all the moves was a desire to join an organisation which more closely matched their idea of a positive organisation. This element is described in more detail later in this section.

Whatever the style or size of the organisation, management, in particular personnel and HRM specialists, will have to be aware of the environment in which they work.

ENVIRONMENTAL FACTOR

The hospitality industry faces an increasingly competitive market, with the present pressure for cost reduction being balanced against the need to maintain and improve quality. If the recession of the early 1990s provided the opportunity for hospitality operators to flatten their organisations and reduce levels of staff, then the improvement of the economic climate of the mid to late 1990s will create other opportunities and challenges. In periods of economic upturn, competition increases and with that the demand for improved services and skilled labour. How fit the British hospitality industry is to take advantage of more favourable environmental conditions relies heavily on the skill and expertise of its managers.

--- **KEY POINT** ---

Adapting to economic and environmental opportunity is a role in which HRM can play a positive part. Yet it will, itself, be affected by the changing environment around it.

Catering operators require personnel and HRM policies that are flexible enough to deal with such change. However, the flattening of structures and the partial demise of the traditional personnel function has weakened many operators' ability to adapt to changing circumstances.

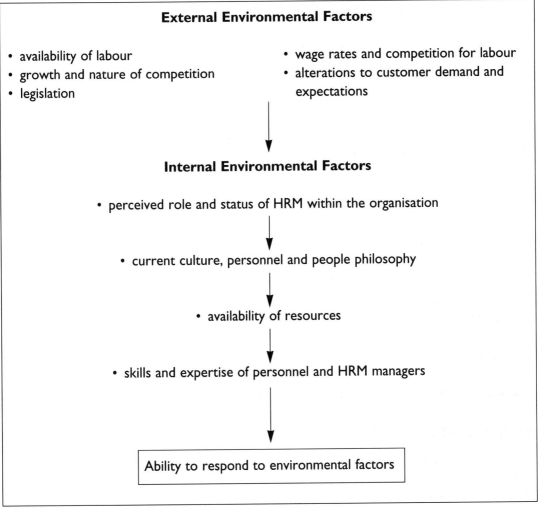

External Environmental Factors

- availability of labour
- growth and nature of competition
- legislation

- wage rates and competition for labour
- alterations to customer demand and expectations

Internal Environmental Factors

- perceived role and status of HRM within the organisation

- current culture, personnel and people philosophy

- availability of resources

- skills and expertise of personnel and HRM managers

Ability to respond to environmental factors

FIGURE 8 *Environmental factors affecting human resource management.*

The need for personnel and human resource managers to be aware of environmental factors has never been greater and in this respect it is important to recognise that both internal and external factors exist (Figure 8). External factors include the

- availability of labour
- prevailing wage rates and competition for labour
- alterations to employment legislation
- the growth and nature of competition
- alterations in customer demand, especially the current trend towards quality and value for money

Internal factors include the

- perceived role HRM plays within the organisation

- current culture, personnel and people philosophy of the organisation
- availability of resources to allocate to personnel and human resource activities
- skills and expertise of the personnel department and management in developing and managing effective people policies

So, individuals charged with personnel responsibility require an ability to respond to the nature of the environment in which they work. An inability to forecast and react to both negative and positive changes in the environment leaves the organisation in a potentially weak position. The effect on the staff of such organisations can be severe and another major factor to consider is that of people.

PEOPLE FACTOR

If current examples of articles in professional journals and academic studies are anything to go by, the interest in employee motivation, communication and empowerment has never been higher. The need to improve both employee relations and general conditions of employment is being increasingly recognised. Yet many would argue that the industry has been lacking in this vital area.

The make up of any workforce will be dependent upon a variety of factors, including:

- scale and attractiveness of pay and benefits
- status and image of the company or business
- competition for labour
- effectiveness of advertising, recruitment and selection
- general conditions of employment
- training and development opportunities

All these are affected by the overall image of the industry. In attempting to attract individuals into the industry, companies, professional associations, catering journals and colleges have achieved a lot over the past few years. Yet, despite all these attempts, the image of the industry is still relatively poor compared to many others. Having possibly attracted individuals (trained or untrained), many operators fail to retain workers due to ineffective personnel policies, poor management and unrealistic working practices and conditions. This element is covered in more detail in Chapter 3.

As the demographic make up of the UK alters, companies will need to address more closely the people factor, investing in improved liaison with schools and colleges, careers teachers and job centres. This element is covered in more detail in Chapter 2.

The ability to address these vital issues will, of course, be dependent upon both organisational structure and environmental factors. The skill in people management is to take account of discrepancies in personnel strategies, policies and practices and compensate for such shortfalls whilst ensuring the achievement of company objectives.

KEY POINT

The performance of employees is linked to a wide variety of influences and, having planned staffing levels and attracted appropriate employees, the personnel department's role is to retain effective employees appropriate to the needs of the business.

All managers require knowledge and skills in relation to employee relations. Their job will be affected by their ability to recognise how both external and internal factors influence their ability to manage.

Following this brief description of some of the factors which affect the role and function of personnel individuals and departments, we can now identify the key elements of this particular responsibility.

Key roles and functions

It is possible to separate these into two main areas, although there is obviously an overlap between them:

1 *strategic*;
2 *operational.*

The strategic role can be said to include:

- manpower strategy and planning, in respect of the company's strategic plan and objectives
- personnel policy formulation, in respect of advising and designing appropriate policies which assist the company or business

The operational role can be said to include:

- personnel administration, e.g. payroll, absence, pensions, legal aspects
- recruitment and selection
- appointment and induction
- training and development
- promotion and succession
- discipline and grievance
- employee motivation
- retirement, redundancy and 'leavers'
- provision of legal advice

The majority of these functions are dealt with in this text. Additionally, it is important to recognise the contribution HRM can and is making to the development of the culture, values and beliefs of the organisation itself. If the organisation recognises this contribution, then the role becomes increasingly central to the development of the business.

KEY POINT

It is important to recognise that the role and function of HRM/personnel within organisations will vary. Part of management strategy should be to define this role clearly.

There also exists an important role in respect of advice and development. This involves the personnel and HRM department, manager or specialist in researching potential trends and business developments, especially where they could impinge on any aspect of people management. By analysing pay scales, labour availability, legislation, training developments, competitors and customer needs, the personnel specialist can provide vital information to senior management. Within the larger hospitality companies this role is becoming increasingly important and is, in part, recognition of the contribution personnel and HRM can make to strategic development. Personnel and HRM, then, operates at both the strategic and operational level and supports the organisation in a variety of ways.

Figure 1.7 identified how the human resource policy and plan fits into the basic strategic planning of a company or business, regardless of size or style. This element is worthy of further explanation as the role personnel or HRM plays in the organisation is of increasing importance.

Well established companies or businesses will possess an existing base of personnel policy and practice. Pay scales, benefit packages, recruitment and selection methods and training and development programmes will be operating on accepted lines. Whilst external and internal factors may encourage adaptations to well established practices, the organisation will often be making only minor amendments. The role of personnel and HRM could then be seen as one of maintenance and repair with the personnel specialists acting as minders of the system.

This, of course, ignores the role that HRM plays in the strategic development of a hospitality company, an aspect referred to previously. The HRM function can also be said to include the roles of system adaptation and system design. The extent to which the redesign of human resource strategy can affect the strategic and business objectives is dependent again upon the status of HRM within the company or business.

KEY POINT

Human resource management in reality is concerned with providing advice on strategic decisions, not on directing overall company policy.

Whilst the role of personnel and human resource management has changed significantly over the past few decades, its ability to force company direction will remain limited to the role of advisor and deliverer.

Role of personnel and HRM in business improvement

The personnel function is becoming increasingly recognised as essential to hospitality organisations, especially in relation to such initiatives as Investors in People, NVQs and levels of staff performance and motivation. Hospitality businesses rely on their staff to deliver the quality of service our customers require. We just cannot survive or compete without appropriate personnel, they are at the heart of every business, or should be.

PERSONNEL DIRECTOR, NATIONAL HOTEL CHAIN

We are only as good as our weakest employee.

PERSONNEL MANAGER, NATIONAL RESTAURANT & PUBLIC HOUSE COMPANY

Of all the functions which exist to support the organisation, the personnel and human resource function is one whose contribution to business performance and improvement has been constantly undervalued. The value placed on personnel and HRM was (and still is in some organisations) related to functional administration – a type of caretaking role. You will recognise by reading this text, and the many examples of current positive personnel practice, that this attitude has changed over the past few years. Yet many companies and businesses still see the personnel and HRM function as a cost, rather than an investment (and an investment which actually returns profit).

Can a service which is primarily concerned with administration and planning actually contribute to business performance and improvement? The important definition to make is how the function *indirectly* contributes. Whilst not directly generating revenue or cash from its activities, it is a service which has the potential to reduce costs in respect of:

- recruitment and selection, training, manpower levels and strategy, staff turnover and absence
- possible risks of prosecution in respect of employment and HASAWA legislation
- misuse of equipment, facilities (and associated waste)

Performing an integrating mechanism between the strategic, functional, operational and administered activities of an organisation, it additionally provides a focus for the organisation's objectives and policies. Figure 9 provides a diagrammatic outline of this statement.

Personnel and human resource management acts as a focus for all the functional aspects of the organisation and seeks to provide appropriate support to the meeting of organisational strategies, values, culture, plans, objectives and operational requirements.

Excluding situations where the personnel and human resource management function can attract external funding or revenue (e.g. government grants or by the sale of training material), the service does not directly generate cash inflows. It is for this reason more than any other that it has traditionally been seen as a cost to the organisation.

The role personnel and HRM plays in possible cost reduction has also seen many senior managers put emphasis on cutting costs, especially related to direct labour costs. Such an approach is, of course, quite understandable and a legitimate management objective. Yet to see the personnel and HRM function solely in this light is a short-sighted view.

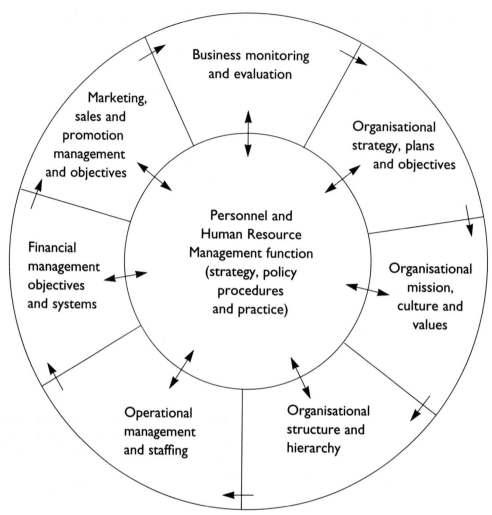

FIGURE 9 *Personnel and human resource management as an integrating mechanism in business management.*

KEY POINT

The improvement of business performance is linked directly to the performance, quality and effectiveness of an organisation's employees. Whilst market demand, quality of products, services and facilities, marketing and sales activities, financial and operational management affect business performance, it is the employees who deliver these aspects. Therefore, the effectiveness of the HRM function will directly affect the ability of a business to meet its business objectives and customer expectations.

The maintenance and improvement of profitable business can be said to rely on the following:

- identification of market trends, expectations and demands
- the satisfaction of customer needs and expectations (profitably)

- maintenance of plant, machinery and facilities in respect of suitability and safety
- provision of appropriately skilled and experienced personnel
- management of administrational functions enabling the business to operate in an appropriate and efficient manner
- development of an organisational culture and structure which supports achievement of organisational strategy and objectives

All of the above in turn rely on the efficiency and effectiveness of the organisation itself which, as stated, relies on individual employees. It is a circle of events and elements which makes any company or business operate. Whilst the personnel and HRM function assists the organisation to achieve its business objectives, it also acts as a respondent to many external and internal factors.

Costing of the personnel function

In one way the cost of the personnel function is quite easy to establish, for example:

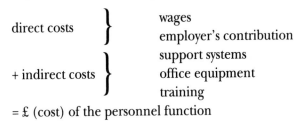

direct costs } wages
employer's contribution

+ indirect costs } support systems
office equipment
training

= £ (cost) of the personnel function

Such a simplistic costing model, whilst useful in establishing the cost to the organisation, ignores costing methods which seek to identify the cost benefit of possessing a personnel function, or, looking at it another way, what the cost is of *not* having an effective personnel function. The costs of *not* possessing an effective personnel function could be:

- high staff turnover and absence rates
- demotivated staff (unhappy customers?)
- wastage in terms of management time spent dealing with personnel issues
- ineffective training and development
- prosecution (HASAWA, employment legislation)

─────────────── K E Y P O I N T ───────────────

The organisation has to decide what type of personnel function will best fit its structure, culture and business objectives.

Large hospitality companies may decide that the best type of personnel management will be one based on regions – removing the direct personnel and training role from the unit and providing support and advice from a regional team. Certain hotel groups have developed this approach over the past few years. Seeking to reduce costs and identifying improved standards, such groups saw the contribution of personnel and HRM to business improvement as one of an advice, support and delivery unit. With particular targets set in respect of staffing levels, employee costs, training and development for the region, tied into national plans and objectives, their contribution towards business improvement was born (perhaps) in the recessionary period of the early 1990s. Whilst such a strategy can be quite legitimate, whether it is one which allows regional personnel specialists to really contribute towards long-term business improvement is debatable.

For small hospitality businesses the contribution of the personnel function to business improvement is just as important, yet it is often a function the owner or manager cannot afford. In such circumstances the role can be undertaken in two different ways:

1 as part of the owner's or manager's job;
2 contracted out to a personnel consultant.

Note that the second approach is one that is becoming increasingly popular even in medium-sized companies. Whatever the size of the company or business, the personnel role is a vital one and one that cannot be overestimated. Table 4 below provides examples of how personnel can contribute towards key elements of the business. The contribution personnel can make to business improvement is therefore considerable.

Table 4 Contribution of personnel to specific organisational challenges

CHALLENGES	RISKS	CONTRIBUTION/ROLE
Staffing levels and costs	High staff turnover and absence rates	Manpower planning; recruitment and selection system
Employment legislation	Prosecution, e.g. HASAWA, equal opportunities	Development of positive personnel policies, practices and procedures
Employee motivation	Demotivated staff will not share organisation's beliefs or values and do little to contribute towards business improvement	Setting of pay scales, employment conditions, induction, management style
Succession and promotion planning	Costs of seeking staff externally, demotivation of employees who see no opportunities for improvement	Staff planning, appraisal systems, training and development
Customer care and satisfaction	Profit reduction as dissatisfied customers move elsewhere	Design and delivery of effective training and development
Organisational control	Lack of control results in management inefficiency (see below)	Assisting creation of a participative organisation with shared problem solving and decision making
Management efficiency	Inefficient managers will create waste and demotivated staff	Design of management training programmes, contribution towards positive organisational beliefs, values and culture

The following section in this chapter will look in more detail at the job of personnel and HRM.

1.7 THE JOB OF PERSONNEL AND HUMAN RESOURCE MANAGEMENT

I feel the personnel and training function needs to go a long way within the industry – it is the key to success. Yet many do not recognise this; I could do so much, however I have to help run the hotel, leaving no time to concentrate on personnel and training. I almost play at it!

PERSONNEL AND TRAINING MANAGER, NATIONAL HOTEL CHAIN

My job is both easy and difficult to describe, at one level I retain responsibility for the administration side – wages, contracts and the like – whilst at another level I am required to advise senior management on future human resource issues. Mix into this aspects of staff welfare and counselling, recruitment and selection, grievance handling, devising, delivering and evaluating training and contributing to the staff newsletter, then you will gain some understanding of such a role. But then, is there a common description for such a position?

PERSONNEL AND TRAINING MANAGER, LARGE LONDON HOTEL

The example quoted above, whilst representing an individual's particular view of her job at one point in time, does indicate that the job of personnel can mean many things. Comparing the job of personnel and training managers is, of course, difficult – for instance, can you reasonably compare the job of a regional Personnel and Training Manager for a large multi-site contract catering company to that of a Personnel and Training Manager in a medium-sized hotel? What of the differences between that of the Human Resource Director at a large company with different branded operations (e.g. Whitbread) and that of the Personnel Director of a small chain of restaurants (e.g. Richoux)?

The nature of the job is dependent upon the size and style of the organisation and the position the job holds in the hierarchy of the organisation. A reasonable assumption to make is that the level of the position in terms of seniority will dictate the level of responsibilities and tasks undertaken. Yet the size of the organisation does not in itself provide a definitive guide to the nature and activities of the job. Consider again this concept of level. As a Personnel Director of a medium-sized restaurant chain pointed out to me recently: 'my previous job was Personnel Manager for a chain of hotels abroad and, within that role, the emphasis was on implementing board and senior management decisions. In reality I had little influence on strategic personnel and human resource issues. My present job allows me direct daily access to the Managing Director and the other senior directors – my involvement in strategic decision-making has increased considerably and I feel I am able to contribute positively to the business in a variety of ways.'

KEY POINT

The level of the job of personnel has a lot to do with access to senior management and the degree of influence the post holder has in respect of both strategic and operational matters.

In 1968 the Institute of Personnel Management in its Jubilee statement concluded: 'it is not the personnel manager's job to manage people, but to provide specialist services that can assist the management team to make the most effective use of their human resources.' The IPM definition provided an indication that the job of personnel was changing radically and, since then, the perception of the role has continued to be redefined. Before describing some of these definitions it is important to outline the main characteristics of the job of personnel and human resource management within the hospitality industry.

Table 5 Scope and role of people management

LEVEL	MAIN ACTIVITIES
National level	• Promotion and development of personnel standards • Image of industry, qualifications • Image of role of personnel and HRM
Company level	• Manpower planning and strategy • Personnel policies, procedures and practices • Auditing, monitoring and reporting • Budgeting and resourcing • Recruitment and selection
Unit level	• Staffing and resourcing • Monitoring, evaluation and reporting • Unit training and development plans • Budgeting control • Pay and personnel administration • Performance monitoring
Team level	• Motivation and performance • Team building • Resourcing and scheduling
Individual level	• Motivation and performance • Discipline and behaviour • Advice and counselling • Career progression • Skills identification and training • Pay and benefits • Monitoring of delivery and performance

The previous section identified that personnel management related to key levels – strategic and operational. Table 5 provides an outline of some of the potential functions of personnel and human resource managers related to the level of activity.

Further definitions of the job of personnel include:

- *Organisational Personnel Manager*
  Characteristic of the late 1950s and 1960s. The job of personnel was seen as delivering senior management decisions.
- *Industrial Relations Manager*
  The 1960s and early 1970s saw a rise in industrial disputes, something which partly affected the hospitality industry. The personnel manager was seen as the negotiator between management and staff.
- *Staff Welfare Manager*
  Such a role was characterised (and in some organisations still is) by involvement in staff welfare and counselling. In some companies this manifested itself into the organisation of social activities.
- *Administrator*
  As organisations grew in size, personnel took on an increasingly administrational type role. The emphasis was on the maintenance of personnel systems.
- *The Trainer/Facilitator*
  As investment in training and development increased, personnel concentrated on the design and delivery of training. Personnel managers were seen as facilitators of employee development, albeit training that had been identified elsewhere.
- *Internal Advisor*
  The late 1980s and early 1990s saw the emergence of the role of advisor. Organisations reduced staffing levels and flattened structures. Computerised personnel systems had alleviated many of the administrative tasks and responsibility for operational personnel issues was devolved to line managers. In larger multi-site organisations, regional personnel managers were appointed. Fortes, during its rebranding in 1993–94, removed the post of personnel and training manager from many of its hotels.
- *Strategic Advisor*
  A feature again of the larger hospitality companies. The personnel or human resource directors, working at head office level, involved themselves in advising on long-term strategies and policies with little day to day contact with operational staff.

The job of personnel and human resource management is a diverse one, covering a range of variables depending on the organisation or business.

Additionally, you have to recognise that the job of personnel has changed and, no doubt, will continue changing as organisations adapt to the market challenges of the new millennium. Over the past few years relevant issues have included:

- equality of opportunity
- violence or harassment at work
- appraisal

- employee counselling
- organisational change
- pay, benefits and pension issues
- new methods of training, e.g. NVQs and competence
- methods of recruitment, e.g. psychometric or personality testing

Equal opportunities

The personnel manager's job in relation to equal opportunities has been largely governed by the increase in legislation in this area. Possibly the responsibility for setting up an equal opportunities policy, with additional responsibility for the monitoring of the policy, initially created significant problems for hospitality operators. As stated, for the personnel manager of the mid to late 1990s the job will largely be centred on ensuring compliance with the legislation and organisational policy. However, there remain issues related to the employment of both younger and older workers and individuals with disabilities or special needs. In this respect the job of personnel is more problematical and touches on some quite sensitive areas.

The Disabled Persons (Employment) Acts of 1944 and 1958 require employers of more than 20 people to adhere to a quota system, in that 3% of the workforce should be registered disabled. In reality the enforcement of this law has not been aggressive and, of course, many individuals with special needs are not registered disabled. Recent changes to this legislation may see improvements in such schemes. Charitable organisations such as Mencap and SCOPE (previously the Spastics Society) amongst others operate schemes to encourage the employment of such individuals and slowly organisations are reconsidering their position in this respect. The job for personnel managers in respect of the employment of disabled persons is a difficult one – should it be to actively promote positive discrimination, as many would perhaps justifiably argue, or should it be to concentrate on employing individuals who can 'perform' at the highest level?

Violence and harassment at work

According to a report conducted by the *Caterer & Hotelkeeper* in May 1994, incidents of violence in the workplace are increasing. Three out of ten people have been physically attacked by customers and 13% of respondents stated they had been subjected to physical abuse by work colleagues. In respect of sexual harassment, 22% of women and 3% of men claimed to have been sexually harassed at work.

Lifestyle Survey 1994, *Caterer & Hotelkeeper*, 30th June 1994

The job of personnel and human resource managers in respect of such issues could (and should) concentrate on:

- objective recording and reporting of such incidents
- design of personnel policies which attempt to minimise such incidents
- counselling of staff involved

- discipline of staff involved
- provision of training of staff in dealing with aggressive or violent customers
- developing a confidential helpline for staff

This latter activity is one which several of the major catering companies have set up, often through professional employee counselling organisations. Again the job of personnel in such situations is a sensitive one; however, it is a job that is increasingly being recognised as important for organisations to undertake.

Appraisal

The move towards employee appraisal schemes has seen some major alterations over the past few years. The annual one-to-one interview with a line manager has been superseded by a variety of more effective methods. Whatever the type of scheme, the personnel and HRM manager has a specific role to play in developing, implementing and monitoring the scheme.

If appraisal is concerned with effective communication, problem solving, development of individual objectives and progression, then it can be seen that the personnel specialist should be involved. For such schemes to work, they must be accepted and understood by the employees and part of the personnel or HRM manager's role is to work with employees and senior management in obtaining such commitment. Appraisal is described in more detail later in the text (page 205).

Employee counselling

Mention has already been made of EAPs (employee advisory programmes). Such schemes form an important and positive element in respect of employee management and motivation. In companies where such schemes do not exist (and unfortunately these are in the majority), the provision of both formal and informal counselling to employees remains an important element in the management of people.

Personnel specialists or line managers and supervisors with personnel responsibilities could be involved in:

- designing, implementing and monitoring a formal counselling facility or process
- provision of training in counselling of staff (although training should be provided by appropriately qualified professionals)
- conducting formal and informal counselling sessions

Counselling should not be confused with grievance-type interviews, although counselling may form a major element of such a situation.

Organisational change

As identified previously, many of the UK hospitality companies and businesses have gone through some major structural, organisational and cultural changes over the past few years. In such situations the personnel specialist has a specific role to play in:

- advising senior management of methods and approaches that will minimise the 'traumas' of such change
- assisting in the communication of changes to employees
- monitoring (along with others) the effects of organisational change in respect of employee motivation, performance and retention

Pay and benefits

The package of pay, benefits and rewards forms an important part of the level of employee motivation. Whilst the personnel specialist may not set the levels of pay and other types of reward, they are involved in respect of:

- administration, monitoring and reporting
- researching and advising senior management on possible additions and alterations to policies

For instance, performance related pay (PRP) has been gaining wider acceptance, yet it is a system with many variances and difficulties. Traditionally PRP was targeted at senior levels of staff; however, many hospitality companies are introducing such schemes to other levels. Whether such schemes will become more widely accepted remains to be seen; it is, therefore, part of the job of personnel and HRM to obtain increased understanding.

New methods of training (competence)

Many personnel managers have responsibility for training and development, an aspect some would say can cause conflicts of interest. Whilst training and development is described in detail in Chapter 5, it is important to identify possible responsibilities in this area. Such responsibility may include:

- identification of training needs (company, unit, team and individual)
- development of training plan
- commissioning or delivery of training
- monitoring and evaluation of training and development
- recording of individual outcomes

With the increased utilisation of NVQs and competence-based training, responsibilities may be increased in respect of communicating new methods to both employees and senior management and advising on implementation, strategy and policy.

Methods of recruitment and selection

The responsibility that the personnel and HRM manager has for this function will, of course, depend on the size and style of the organisation. Within the area of HRM the recruitment and selection of staff is a vital function and is dealt with in Chapter 4.

At this stage responsibilities can be identified as:

- design and implementation of recruitment and selection policy, procedures and practices
- training of other staff in recruitment and selection techniques and skills
- direct recruitment and selection

In respect of personality or psychometric testing, the personnel manager's job may be to research and appraise potential material or agencies, or act as the qualified administrator and deliverer of such recruitment methods.

As you can see, the job of personnel and human resource management contains many functional and operational elements. Whilst the preceding section described the role and function of such a position, this section has provided you with additional detail on what the job may involve on a day-to-day basis.

─────────────── **KEY POINT** ───────────────

The job of personnel and human resource management is a varied, complex and challenging one. The exact nature and responsibilities of the job will be directed by the size, style, culture, goals, vision and objectives of the organisation.

1.8 SUMMARY AND KEY POINTS

This introductory chapter has provided you with an overview of the role, function and job of personnel and HRM. By identifying the need to manage people and manage such 'resources' in a positive cost-effective way you should now recognise the importance of personnel and HRM to hospitality organisations. What should be clear is that all employees are individuals, an element which all managers must recognise.

The change from a functional approach to personnel to a more employee-centred approach is in part a recognition of the challenges hospitality companies and businesses face. However, the industry is made up of a wide variety of organisations, all with different styles, values and cultures. Arguably HRM development should be a central focus for any hospitality company, with the HRM function acting in support of strategic and business objectives. Whilst differences in approach to people management will occur, the key roles and functions of HRM remain relatively constant.

The skills required of personnel and HRM specialists in today's hospitality industry are considerably different to those of a decade ago. Yet such specialists must operate from a firm base of personnel systems.

The next chapter looks in detail at the first and perhaps most important element of personnel and HRM – manpower planning.

KEY POINTS

- People management encompasses a wide range of management functions and activities, of which personnel is only one part
- The role and function of HRM and personnel is changing rapidly in the hospitality industry in response to a wide number of factors
- Obtaining greater understanding of what motivates employees, creating improved job satisfaction and improved performance is part of all managers' roles, and it is an area where HRM specialists can provide invaluable support
- Ensuring a sound base of personnel policies exists, which assists the organisation in achieving strategic objectives, forms the core of effective HRM
- In the competitive market in which the hospitality industry operates, the contribution effective HRM can make to business improvement is considerable
- Whilst the core job of personnel and HRM remains fairly constant, the approach will vary according to the style, size and culture of an organisation
- As the industry is a people industry and relies, in the main, on the quality of its people to maintain service standards, then the effective management of employees is of vital importance

---

QUESTIONS

1 List and explain the various activities involved in the management of people.
2 Define the terms 'personnel' and 'human resource management' and explain possible differences between them.
3 Describe two approaches to the motivation of employees within the industry and compare these to a theoretical approach.
4 Discuss the statement 'all managers in today's hospitality industry require personnel skills and should have personnel responsibilities'.
5 Identify the key roles and functions of personnel and human resource management in relation to the hospitality industry.
6 Discuss how HRM managers can improve the involvement of individuals and teams in the development of the business.
7 Explain how the culture, size and style of hospitality businesses can affect the approach to people management.

CHAPTER 2

MANPOWER PLANNING, STRATEGY AND PRACTICE

———

Hotels and Catering have witnessed fast job growth in recent years, with over half a million jobs created in the past two decades. During the 1990s the rate of increase is projected to slow as productivity growth speeds up. Nevertheless, direct employment is still expected to increase by 250,000 to 1.6 million by the year 2000.

DEPARTMENT OF EMPLOYMENT (1994) REVIEW OF THE ECONOMY, INSTITUTE OF EMPLOYMENT RESEARCH

Decentralisation, delayering and downsizing are all words that pepper the management language of the 1990s, and are likely to do so well into the 21st century. But dramatic structural changes are only the starting point; the goal must be a more effective style of management which is responsive to customer needs.

'MANAGING PEOPLE AND CHANGING FRONTIERS', IPM CONSULTATIVE DOCUMENT, PERSONNEL MANAGEMENT, NOVEMBER 1993

85% of 180 hospitality operators surveyed reported that they had no formalised manpower or recruitment plan. Of these 85%, over 95% identified lack of skilled staff or high staff turnover as a significant problem.

J. ROBERTS (JUNE 1994) HUMAN RESOURCE PRACTICES IN THE HOSPITALITY INDUSTRY SURVEY, ROTHERHAM COLLEGE OF ARTS & TECHNOLOGY

The changes taking place in the labour force, particularly the decline in the number of young people, are likely to make recruiting and retaining new employees increasingly difficult. To help meet and overcome these difficulties, it is important for employers to have a human resource plan.

ACAS (1994) RECRUITMENT POLICIES FOR THE '90s

2.1 AIMS AND OBJECTIVES

By reading through this chapter and completing the related questions and assignments, you will gain knowledge and appreciation of the role manpower planning plays in assisting business survival. Specifically you will be able to:

1 define the terms manpower planning and manpower strategy;
2 understand the reasons and methods for monitoring, analysing and controlling absence and labour turnover;
3 identify and understand the factors which affect and influence manpower planning and strategy;
4 recognise that such activity is an ongoing process requiring review and amendment to match changes in business circumstance;
5 identify the basic elements of manpower audits and design an audit for a sample operation;
6 identify basic methods of manpower planning appropriate to various styles of business.

2.2 INTRODUCTION

All businesses regardless of size and style will need to give careful consideration to how to identify and plan for appropriate levels of staff. An activity which extends far beyond the recruitment and selection process, as all businesses need to identify not only the members of staff required, but the skills, levels, qualifications, location, attributes and availability of staff to match business plans and objectives.

2.3 IMPORTANCE OF MANPOWER PLANNING

As the hotel industry developed in the latter part of the 19th century and early part of the 20th century, staff planning was characterised by the availability of a large workforce, albeit that skills were generally of a low level. In today's terms catering companies were fairly small and, excluding the need to cosset certain levels of personnel, managers undertook little in the way of planning staff. Emphasis was on maintaining levels of staff in an industry dominated by long hours and low pay. The huge increase in catering operations over the past thirty years, with the growth in large multi-site national companies alongside changes in customer demand, has led to operators developing more comprehensive approaches.

Manpower planning in the 1990s is being recognised as a vitally important function in assisting business survival. Even though the industry is still predominated by small, independent operators, there exists considerable understanding and acceptance of its role. Yet it is not an activity which is undertaken as effectively as it should be – a statement which could partly explain the high levels of staff turnover in some sectors and specific units.

Generally personnel managers, senior managers and owners have approached this activity in an ad hoc fashion. As critics have identified, they have been fire-fighting when they should have been concentrating on fire prevention!

Annual staff turnover in the Catering and Hotel industry more than halved in the last decade, but the industry still has one of the highest turnover rates of all. With over 2.4 million employees and an annual turnover of 27%, the cost of replacing staff who leave is £430 million a year.

Hotel & Catering Training Company Research Department (1994) *Employment Flows in the Catering and Hospitality Industry*

The *Caterer* reports (1994) that recruitment is taking off again in the mid 1990s. Advertisements are up, indicating an increase of 31% in the number of jobs on offer. However, vacancies for chefs are up by 44% and for waiters by 70%. Salaries have risen by 7.6% but poor wages and bad working conditions still mean higher turnover rates. Far-sighted employers are now attempting to do more to attract and keep employees, especially young people.

Definition of manpower planning

Manpower planning has received considerable attention recently as companies have recognised the key role it plays in assisting business success. Whilst manpower planning primarily concentrates on activities related to identifying requirements and setting up processes to ensure effective staffing, it also, in my opinion, relates to other key personnel and human resource management tasks including budgeting and costing, labour turnover monitoring, absence control and employment practices. Therefore, manpower planning is a fairly complex activity and one which is affected by a large number of factors.

Whilst a number of definitions exist, my preference is as follows:

- *manpower planning*, a strategy for the identification, acquisition, effective utilisation, improvement and retention of an organisation's human resources appropriate to its needs

Manpower planning, then, is concerned not only with ensuring appropriate levels of staff, but also with the development, implementation and monitoring of effective personnel policies, to satisfy the business skill and development needs of the future.

It is an activity which occurs at both the strategic and operational level.

--- KEY POINT ---

Manpower planning must be closely linked to the business plan and objectives if the company is to assist its chances of survival and growth.

Operationally, the company has to put in place policies and procedures which assist the effective implementation of its plan, in a way which allows for continuous monitoring and adaptation to meet changes in circumstance.

Whilst the primary function of manpower planning is to create a framework for effective use of human resources, it is also used in the day to day operation of a catering unit. Personnel managers, owners and departmental heads will have responsibility for ensuring appropriate levels of staff are available to service the needs of the function, event or facility. Scheduling or rotating staff is an ongoing challenge for such individuals. Considerations are not related to national trends or increase in competition, rather they are concerned with the practicalities and realities of staffing the front line. So, manpower strategy and planning covers a wide variety of tasks, including:

- identification of staffing requirements
- development of a strategy to meet the requirements of the business
- recognition of the factors which will affect the need for and availability of staff
- design, implementation, monitoring and adaptation of personnel policies which will assist the achievement of plans and objectives
- acceptance and understanding of the plans by those who have to implement them
- day to day operation of a unit in respect of its staff scheduling and resourcing

Strategically the operator will need to consider:

- influences or the availability of labour (this aspect will be dealt with later in this chapter)
- the plan the business has for the future and how this will affect its manpower needs
- the changing nature of the market (an aspect covered in this chapter and in the final chapter)

At the operational level the considerations are:

- employment policies and procedures (Chapter 3)
- recruitment and selection (Chapter 4)
- systems for the monitoring of absence, retention and turnover (dealt with later in this chapter)
- training and development (Chapter 5)

As stated, the approach to these activities will differ depending upon the size and style of the operation. What is of key importance is the recognition that effective personnel and human resource management does not start with recruitment and selection. Effectively identifying staffing requirements through the function of manpower planning and matching these plans to clear business objectives is of increasing importance and one which forms the framework for an operator's employment policies and practices. Figure 10 sets out this framework.

Following this overview of manpower planning and strategy, the role this activity plays in assisting business survival is explained.

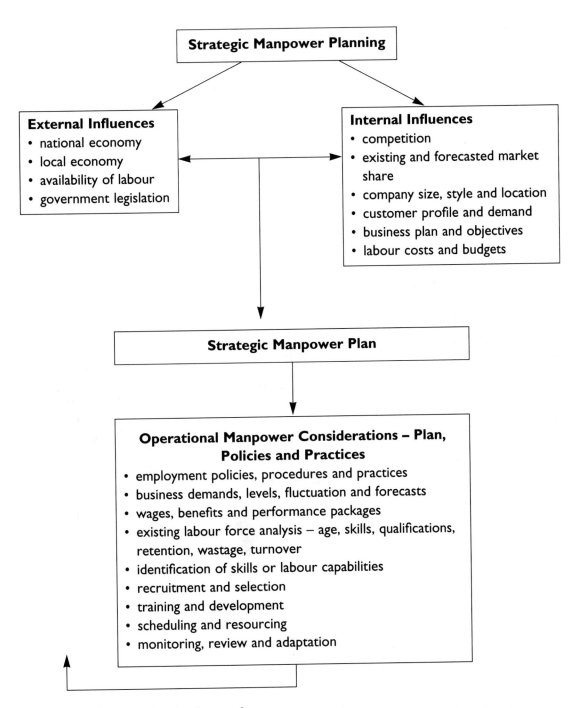

FIGURE 10 *Manpower planning framework.*

2.4 KEY ELEMENTS OF MANPOWER PLANNING

It is important to describe in more detail the contribution manpower planning makes to the success of businesses and what factors influence its effectiveness. As stated, manpower planning assists organisations in:

- identifying and assessing recruitment needs
- anticipating alterations to recruitment needs
- formulating appropriate employment policies
- identifying training and development needs
- developing career advancement policies
- reducing staffing costs

As a function it operates at both strategic and operational levels. Hospitality operators need to understand what factors exist which will affect the business, now and in the future (Figure 2.1 identified some of these factors). Companies will seek to develop strategic plans based upon analysis of the environment in which they operate, as the environment will affect the manner in which it can operate successfully.

Factors which influence and affect manpower planning

THE ECONOMY AND ITS INFLUENCE ON MANPOWER PLANNING

Regardless of the size or style of the company or business, its potential for success, profitability and growth is dependent in part upon the condition of the economy. In the boom period of the mid to late 80s, hospitality operators experienced significant growth, skilled labour was in relatively short supply, customer demand was high and prices and wages rose as companies attempted to take advantage of growth economy. The sharp recession in the early part of the 1990s, with reductions in demand, witnessed the reversal of growth. Organisations responded by slowing down expansion plans, reducing staff levels and holding down wages. Whilst the hospitality industry has always had a high level of bankruptcies, these trebled in this period. Manpower plans based on the boom period were quickly adapted in response to the change in demand. Generally speaking it was those organisations with inflexible plans and overstaffed units that suffered the most. Operators who had correctly analysed the environment and who possessed more flexible manpower policies were in a better position to manage such change.

The commercial hospitality sector saw an overall loss of over 94,000 jobs in the period 1990–92.

Employment Forecast Update, Hotel & Catering Training Company

---

The performance and stability of the economy exerts considerable influence on industry, and service industries are, in turn, affected by the trends in business and tourism spending. Of course, there are variances in the way the economy operates, and whilst national trends may exert overall pressures, operators will also need to be aware of regional and local economic performance. Whilst national economic performance affects all companies, businesses concentrating on a local market will need to more closely analyse the factors which directly affect it, e.g. development of local tourist attractions.

KEY POINT

Decisions related to manpower planning are directly influenced by national, regional and local economic performance.

The economy will affect the nature and level of demand which assists the operator in identifying staffing requirements.

THE HOSPITALITY MARKET AND ITS INFLUENCE ON MANPOWER PLANNING

As the economy will directly influence a company's plans and potential for survival and growth, so too will the market or the demand for goods, services and facilities. However, it is not just the level of demand that hospitality operators have to consider, it is the type and nature of demand.

Hospitality operators need to undertake the systematic gathering, recording, analysis and utilisation of information related to customer demands, needs and expectations.

J. Roberts (1993) *Marketing for the Hospitality Industry*, Hodder & Stoughton

---

If the company is to meet the demands, needs and expectations of its customers, it will require appropriate levels of skilled labour. Having identified a demand for a new unit, facility or service, the operator will need to ensure that recruitment, employment and training policies will satisfy this demand. Additionally, when demand reduces or alters significantly, the operator will need to possess the ability to respond effectively. In response to the market, the operator, when manpower planning, will need to:

- analyse the nature, level, type and location of demand and respond to such demands
- forecast the type and level of staff required
- develop recruitment and selection policies which support business plans and allow for flexibility
- identify training and development activities

LEGISLATION AND ITS INFLUENCE ON MANPOWER PLANNING

As manpower planning involves the design and implementation of employment policies, procedures and practices, it will obviously be affected by the type of legislation that exists. When setting up manpower plans and policies, the operator will be involved in:

- ensuring adherence to the laws and regulations that directly affect its plans, policies and procedures
- analysing possible changes in legislation that will affect its business in the future
- providing training and development that covers such legislation

The HASAWA, Food Hygiene and COSHH regulations have been prime examples of this.

THE AVAILABILITY OF LABOUR AND ITS INFLUENCE ON MANPOWER PLANNING

The people in the labour force and their skills are of major significance to the British economy in an increasingly competitive world. The UK labour force is undergoing marked changes, which will affect its size and composition. The Employment Department reported in 1993 that the key features of the labour force by the end of the century will be:

- much slower growth in labour supply than during the 1980s; the labour force will grow by 700,000, reaching 28.8 million in the period to 2001; this is less than half the increase witnessed in the 1980s
- women will account for over 85% of the labour market growth; by 2001 they are expected to make up 45% (12.8 million) of the total labour force
- the labour force will have a greater proportion of older workers
- the numbers of young people in the workforce will continue to decline between 1992 and 2001; the numbers of people aged 16–34 will fall by 1.3 million, whilst numbers in the 35–54 age group will rise by 1.9 million
- the reducing numbers of young people will focus attention on the need to develop the skills of the existing workforce and to use the potential of special groups in the labour force

For employers, major implications of such features, alongside other economic factors, will include the need to:

- develop and retain the existing workforce to make the best use of their abilities
- make greater use of the skills and potential of groups who are currently underused in the workforce
- develop links with students, schools and colleges to compete effectively in the reduced labour market

The Hotel and Catering Training Company Employment Forecast Update 1992–2000 reported an expectation of around 156,000 new jobs for the period 1995–2000, with a requirement for over 13,000 people per week to meet the hospitality industry's demand for labour. Whilst general unemployment is forecasted to remain high, the industry, as stated, faces specific challenges in ensuring it possesses the most appropriate staff. These challenges include:

- competition from other industries for skilled labour
- the continuing poor perception of the hospitality industry (despite all the initiatives undertaken to improve its image)

- the levels of pay, reward and benefits which for some observers still remain low in respect to other industries
- the nature of the industry itself, in that it operates as a service to others

There is no doubt that the industry is addressing such challenges; however, personnel and human resource specialists will need to adapt to a changing workforce and one that has increased expectations of its employers. Therefore, manpower planning operators will be involved in:

- analysing and forecasting labour supply (Tables 6 and 7)
- developing employment policies and practices which attract the type of personnel required
- developing training and development plans which increasingly concentrate on upskilling existing workers
- developing employment practices which assist the retention of skilled employees
- targeting recruitment campaigns at particular sectors of the workforce

Thus, several external influences exist which directly affect the manner in which businesses operate. For manpower planners there are other influences related to the company itself.

Internal influences on manpower planning

No two companies are the same, even if they operate in similar sectors or markets. It is the differences which exist that will influence specific approaches to manpower planning. Obviously a national fast-food operator will require different levels and types of staff to that of a travel lodge company or a specialist leisure facility operator.

Figure 2.1 identified the framework for manpower planning and the internal policies, procedures and practices which are required. Whilst these are common to all catering operators,

Table 6 Employment forecasts: commercial sectors 1990–2000

	1990	1992	1995	2000	1990–92 No	1990–92 %	1992–95 No	1992–95 %	1995–2000 No	1995–2000 %
Restaurants	304	295	315	368	−9	−3.0	+20	+6.9	+53	+16.7
Pubs	332	329	337	356	−3	−0.9	+8	+2.4	+15	+4.5
Clubs	145	137	139	142	−8	−5.5	+2	+1.0	+2	+2.1
Hotels	309	271	305	317	−38	−12.3	+34	+12.4	+12	+4.1
Contract catering	148	118	133	154	−30	−20.3	+15	+13.0	+21	+16.1
Self-employed	167	160	165	180	−7	4.0	+5	+3.1	+15	+9.1
Commercial Sectors	1404	1310	1394	1513	−94	−6.7	+84	+6.4	+119	+8.5

Source: *Hospitality*, Oct 1993, p. 10.

Table 7 Employment forecasts: catering services sectors excluding and including domestics and housekeepers 1990–2000 (thousands)

	1990	1995	2000	1990–95		1995–2000	
				No	**%**	**No**	**%**
Excluding domestics & housekeepers							
Education	88	93	96	+5	+5.0	+3	+3.7
Medical	77	78	80	+1	+2.0	+2	+2.0
Industrial	89	79	72	−10	−10.9	−7	−8.4
Retail	41	42	45	+1	+2.4	+3	+7.7
Recreation and culture	30	32	36	+2	+3.1	+4	+16.6
Public administration	27	27	28	0	+1.5	+1	+1.9
Travel	19	19	20	0	+0.4	+1	+1.3
Total	371	370	377	−1	−0.3	+7	+2.0
Including domestics & housekeepers							
Education	279	293	304	+14	+5.0	+11	+3.7
Medical	321	327	334	+6	+2.0	+7	+2.0
Industrial	240	214	196	−26	−10.9	−18	−8.4
Retail	45	46	50	+1	+12.4	+4	+7.7
Recreation and culture	33	34	40	+1	+3.1	+6	+16.6
Public administration	43	44	45	+1	+1.5	+1	+1.9
Travel	20	20	20	0	+0.4	0	+1.3
Personal	100	105	130	+5	+5.0	+25	+24.0
Total	1081	1083	1119	+2	+0.2	+36	+3.3

Source: *Hospitality,* Oct 1993, p. 10.

the approach will differ, as stated. The main internal influences on manpower planning, strategy and practice are:

- size, style, type and location
- market and client base
- probability and ability for internal investment
- 'age' of the company – new companies will obviously be concerned with setting up effective systems
- culture that exists within the company and its commitment to the human resource function
- management skills available, especially in connection with the personnel and human resource management function

For small, independent businesses all these considerations may be dealt with by one individual, the owner or manager. For new, medium-sized companies, the responsibility may lie with a small management team or personnel specialist, whilst in a large company with a considerable number of units, the function may be addressed via regional or branch managers assisted by personnel specialists and trainers. (The Thresher case study on personnel and training in Chapter 5 provides an excellent example of a larger company's approach.)

--- KEY POINT ---

Effective manpower planning is concerned, not only with detailed analysis of the external environment, but also with the whole business.

CASE STUDY. HAVEN LEISURE: MANPOWER PLANNING IN PRACTICE

As part of the Rank Organisation, Haven Leisure is one of the largest leisure and caravan park companies in the UK with 52 units employing, at the height of the season, over 6000 staff. Of this total, approximately 900 are permanent staff based either at head office or at one of their sites.

With the need to ensure a level of skilled, experienced and appropriate staff, the company has developed particularly effective recruitment, selection and training strategies, policies and practices. Their manpower planning follows a fairly standard system based upon historical data and business forecasts for specific sites. With discussion and site budgets identified, each site is then provided with a budget for specific facilities and cost units (bars, catering, maintenance, etc.).

Heads of department within each site can, therefore, plan their specific staffing requirements. To put this in some perspective, a large site would have about 38 permanent staff and a requirement to recruit approximately 300 seasonal staff to provide service and facilities to a site capacity of 10,000 guests at peak times.

Owing to its investment in training, and other personnel policies, a high percentage of seasonal staff return and recruitment for permanent staff is often from such seasonal staff. (This has resulted in the turnover of permanent staff being less than 10%.) The heads of department recruit and select directly for their specific areas, using a variety of methods, including local and national advertising, local agencies and job centres.

The company has used assessment centres for more senior positions, an activity which, while relatively expensive, is recognised as an invaluable recruitment method. With such large numbers of staff, effective training and development programmes have been developed for all staff, including a career and personal development programme for senior site staff, on site induction and specific skills training, together with the piloting of the NVQ Level IV programme for deputy managers.

The personnel and training team annually reviews the support service it provides to site managers and staff and sets specific objectives for the forthcoming year. For 1994–95 these were:

- strategy for customer care improvement
- development for strategic recruitment

- enhancing communication
- improving long-term succession planning
- management development
- further development of career and personal development programme

Regular visits to the sites by the personnel and training team assist the recognition of the team as a vital support service related to all personnel matters.

The mainly seasonal business results in complex problems for such an operator and the company recognises that effective manpower planning does not just result from generating an annual manpower plan but relies heavily on ongoing personnel and training support.

Trevor Norgett, Personnel and Training Manager, Haven Leisure

---

Manpower planning priorities

The underlying priority for hospitality operators is to ensure that they possess the right levels of staff to satisfy demand. Expressed in simple terms, this means ensuring that the business can provide the goods, services and facilities it offers. Despite changes in technology and deskilling, the hospitality industry is a people business and it relies heavily on the availability and skills of its staff to deliver such services.

From the introductory section of this chapter you will have realised that manpower planning covers a variety of functions and activities. The priorities for companies and businesses are to:

- identify the level of staffing required
- identify the skills, attributes, qualifications and experience required
- forecast the level of demand for staff in relation to factors such as seasonal variances, labour turnover, customer demand and business objectives

The analysis of this information will result in a projected staffing plan, which can be costed, resourced, implemented and monitored.

Whatever the size of the company or business, the operator can project forecasted staffing requirements and costs and analyse these against projected demand, revenue and profit. For businesses in the process of setting up, projecting such needs and costs are a key consideration. For existing businesses the priority is to keep staffing levels and costs at a level appropriate to existing and forecasted business. Large, multi-site national companies will possess detailed information on staffing needs and costs, with a blueprint of the set-up and operating costs of any new units.

Companies such as McDonald's, Harvester, Little Chef, Travel Lodge and Pizza Hut, who operate branded operations, will have comprehensive operational cost data. Backed up by regional or national personnel and human resource departments, manpower planning forms an ongoing but well-established part of management practice.

───────────────────── **KEY POINT** ─────────────────────

The first priority for companies is to establish a staffing profile or plan, identifying the staffing needs and associated costs.

For a company with 15 similar units across the country, operating with a management couple, deputy, two assistants and five other staff, staffing needs and costs can be easily identified. However, this is to presume that things will not alter, either in respect of the staff itself, the level of demand or the opportunity for expansion. It is within this area of change that operators will identify other priorities. These include the need to:

- monitor labour turnover and absence (dealt with later in this chapter)
- monitor and analyse staffing profile (dealt with later in this chapter)
- monitor and analyse staffing costs
- develop systems which allow for flexibility in managing the levels of staff (Chapter 2)

These priorities require an operator to develop a strategic approach to manpower planning which identifies short, medium and long-term priorities and actions.

Strategic manpower plan (the human resource plan)

All companies require detailed plans for all aspects of the business. Whether it is financial planning, marketing, market share or market position, restructuring or alterations to the company culture, senior management will want to identify what these objectives are and how best to achieve them.

───────────────────── **KEY POINT** ─────────────────────

A strategy for the managing of a company's human resources is a vital part of a company's overall business and strategic plan.

Whilst we recognise that not all hospitality operators will generate such plans, it is important to re-emphasise the importance of plans in the overall success of the company or business. Figure 2.1 identified the framework for manpower planning and identified the main considerations.

Having conducted both external and internal analysis, the operator will have identified an overall staffing profile. The strategic manpower plan will further identify:

- the range of employment policies, procedures and practices required (see Chapter 3)
- the level of wages, benefits and performance packages
- potential short- or long-term gaps in existing workforce
- the range of skills and qualifications required

These will identify the level, range, style and methods of recruitment and selection and will allow the company to plan, deliver and monitor staff, training and development.

This basic explanation of manpower planning priorities and tasks, whilst providing you with the framework of human resource planning, ignores some of the complexities of the task, a task which grows with the size and distribution of a company. Many factors exist which will affect the ability of a company to manpower plan effectively:

- trading patterns may alter radically
- individual units may suffer from sudden and high staff turnover
- business takeover may seriously affect the nature of the company
- restructuring may radically alter the operator's requirement for certain types of staff
- lack of appropriately skilled labour may restrict a company's ability to expand or develop additional services

Furthermore, however detailed the strategic plan, if weaknesses exist in the areas of personnel policies, wages and benefits, recruitment and selection or training and development, then the planning will have been a fruitless activity.

For hospitality operators, manpower planning is an increasingly important element in development. If you observe some of the major companies within the UK, you will recognise the alterations and developments they go through and how these affect their manpower needs. When Trust House Forte, as it was then known, went through major restructuring in the late 1980s and early 1990s, significant alterations were made to the staffing profile of some of its units, particularly in the hotel division. Queens Moat, which went through a serious financial and structural problem in 1993–94, faced considerable pressure from financiers and shareholders, resulting in the sale of properties, reductions of staff and the centralising of operations and control.

The recession of the early 1990s saw a large number of hospitality businesses fail, whilst others struggled to maintain profitability. Manpower plans developed in the pressurised years of the late 1980s were rapidly discarded with reduction and survival strategies replacing expansionist strategies.

KEY POINT

For an operator to survive in today's competitive market, manpower plans are required to be increasingly flexible, allowing the business to adapt to sudden changes in demand.

For a business to be able to plan effectively, it requires information about its current position. This means conducting regular and ongoing monitoring of its staffing profile. The next section will identify the reasons and methods for undertaking such analysis.

2.5 MANPOWER AUDITS

To really understand the nature of an existing workforce, the operator will need to carry out regular audits. Such audits will provide vital information in respect of human resource planning and it is an activity increasingly used to assist the achievement of business objectives.

Basically, a manpower audit is a detailed analysis of the staffing profile of an organisation. It could identify, analyse and include some or all of the following:

- total numbers and location
- age and gender profiles
- length of service
- staff turnover and absence rates
- qualification and training profile
- costs of labour by position, department or unit
- ethnic monitoring
- staff productivity
- attitudinal survey

The aim is to establish an accurate profile of the staff within a unit or company. Once this has been identified, the company has a benchmark on which to evaluate performance and plan more effectively. What is important to realise is that such an activity should not be completed as a one-off.

─────────────────── KEY POINT ───────────────────

Effective manpower planning is reliant upon an ongoing and comprehensive analysis of staffing profiles.

With the advent of computerised personnel records, such information gathering is becoming easier to obtain. However, it is the type of information all hospitality operators should possess. The areas identified for analysis will provide the operator with different types of information.

1 *Total numbers and location* will assist operators of multi-site operations in:

- targeting resources
- evaluating unit cost differences
- targeting recruitment and selection activities

2 *Age and gender profiles* will assist the operator in:

- identifying individuals nearing retirement
- succession planning
- monitoring equal opportunities policies
- targeting recruitment
- identifying styles of training and development

3 *Length of service* will provide operators with:

- a measure of the quality of human resource management
- identification of individuals for promotion or development
- possible indication of weaknesses in career progression paths

4   *Staff turnover and absence rates* will:

- indicate effectiveness of human resource management
- identify potential problems in relation to staff motivation and retention
- possible identifications of Health and Safety issues

5   *Qualifications and training profile* will identify:

- potential gaps in training plans
- individuals requiring training and development
- effectiveness of training and development activities
- individuals with potential for promotion

6   *Costs* will provide the operator with:

- direct costs of labour, e.g. wages, national insurance
- individual costs of labour, e.g. overtime, benefits, personnel administration
- indices of performance of department in relation to income or contribution

7   *Ethnic or equal opportunities monitoring:* there are specific pieces of legislation and codes of practice which provide for the monitoring of the workforce. (For more details on this aspect refer to Chapter 3.)

8   *Staff productivity analysis* will provide the operator with:

- an estimation of the productivity or value of specific groups of employees, departments or units

9   *Attitudinal survey:* these are growing in use and are undertaken either directly by the organisations or by external consultants. Additionally, the emergence of Quality Management systems, Total Quality Management and the Investors in People initiative has encouraged employers to investigate the perceptions of its employees towards a variety of aspects. These could include individuals' perceptions and observations on:

- new procedures
- existing policies and procedures
- training and development
- career progression and advancement opportunities
- operational structures
- ethnic and equal opportunities

--------------------------------- KEY POINT ---------------------------------

As part of the process of implementing Investors in People, companies are encouraged to undertake a survey, on two levels, of managers and employees. Individuals are commonly asked to comment on access to training; information on company mission and objectives; attitude of either group towards training and level of effectiveness of communication.

Certain common sense guidelines exist for the use of such surveys.

1   They should be seen to be confidential – providing the employee with protection.
2   The survey should ask questions that are relevant to the organisation and the individual.
3   All employees should be involved, with special consideration for those for whom English is not their first language or who possess other physical barriers to the completion of the survey.
4   The questionnaire and the questions should be prepared with expert assistance to ensure clarity, ease of understanding, fairness and responses which will assist the organisation.
5   Management should be prepared to accept the findings of the survey, accepting the fact there will also be a margin of error in questionnaire-based surveys.
6   The survey should be voluntary and no coercion or pressure attached to its completion. Legitimate encouragement is acceptable and several hospitality companies have offered various types of incentives to encourage fuller participation. (As an example of the use of attitudinal surveys, see the case study on Village Leisure, page 243.)
7   The survey should result in some form of identifiable actions.

Surveys can also be used in a before and after comparison, attempting to identify the real value or effectiveness of changes to policies, procedures and practices. There are certain limitations to attitudinal surveys, including the degree of accuracy of response. However, increasingly, employers are using such methods to identify the effectiveness of their human resource policies. It should also be clarified that confidential attitudinal surveys are substantially different from more standard employee response documents. These will include employees' comments on training and development and appraisal schemes, often referred to as 'smiley forms', and their use in identifying employees' perceptions is limited.

─────────────────── K E Y   P O I N T ───────────────────

The detailed analysis of the workforce can provide the employer with a significant amount of information relating not only to the employee profile but also to their perceptions on the human resource policies of the company.

As stated, for medium to large hospitality companies such analysis is relatively easy to collect; for small or independent operators the need is not so important. The following case study provides an example of such an audit, giving basic information on a hospitality operator. It should identify the difficulty and risk involved in the analysis of basic statistics.

CASE STUDY. A MANPOWER AUDIT

THE BACKGROUND

This company operates in the hotel and leisure sector and currently owns and manages six units in the Midlands. The company commenced trading 15 years ago with one hotel (20 bedrooms) and has progressively expanded to a situation where the units now comprise five hotels and a leisure complex.

The units are operated fairly independently with managers appointed in each unit, overseen by a Chairman and Board of Directors.

With a policy of continued investment in the upgrading of units and the slow development of group procedures, the company has performed well despite the difficulties of the early 1990s. Marketing, promotion and merchandising activities were undertaken regularly, were well planned and productive. Customer satisfaction points were high and rising and the company had a well established customer base with a high level of returning customers. Overall the company was performing well and poised to expand further.

THE MANPOWER AUDIT

This was conducted over a two-week period and comprised analysis of personnel records, analysis of labour costs, turnover and absences. Additionally, individual confidential interviews were conducted with a cross-section of employees to ascertain their perceptions of certain aspects and to identify potential gaps in the management information. All this information was collected, analysed and used to assist the development of revised company structures, policies and objectives.

The information below sets out part of the research and survey findings:

- total number of staff   285
- full time   117
- part time   168
- percent of full time
  employees in head office capacity   3.5%

Breakdown by Unit

	Unit A	Unit B	Unit C	Unit D	Unit E	Unit F
Total staff (numbers)	50	52	28	65	48	40
Full time (numbers)	15	38	12	30	12	10
Part time (numbers)	35	14	16	35	36	30
Female (%)	85	70	65	28	55	32
Male (%)	15	30	35	72	45	68
Supervisory (%)	20	10	10	15	8	10
Management (%)	2	4	2	1	2	5
Average length of service management supervisory (in years)	15	6.5	7	3	9	4.5

Breakdown by Unit – *continued*

	Unit A	Unit B	Unit C	Unit D	Unit E	Unit F
Average length of service full-time staff (in years)	12	4.5	6.5	4	10.5	2.5
Percentage of supervisory & management staff with appropriate qualifications	30	100	85	70	65	55
Annual turnover of staff in previous year (all staff) (%)	25	20	12	66	10	70
Annual absence rates* (%)	8	10	12	15	32	28
Percentage of full-time personnel (not supervisory) with appropriate qualifications	20	22	60	55	65	45
Average age of supervisors/managers	45	24	20	22	32	23

* Absence rates refer to percentage of hours lost against annual total hours. As indicated, other information was obtained.

OBSERVATIONS

Accepting the fact that certain information has been omitted, what conclusions would you make on the employee profile of this company in respect of:

- training and development
- succession planning
- staff turnover and absence
- comparisons of units
- specific companywide issues?

Clearly there were imbalances and issues for the company to address (which they did). However, from such a statistical analysis only observations and assumptions can be made. The company, of course, had access to more detailed information, analysis of individual questionnaires and also its knowledge of the individuals, teams and units. Additionally, as can be seen from the statistics, the units varied in size with Units E–F being the most recent acquisitions.

Validity of manpower audits

Manpower audits can provide a company with a detailed profile of the workforce in respect of a wide variety of factors. Their effective use is dependent upon ensuring all the necessary and relevant information is available. Used alongside other types of management information, such as the outcome of appraisals, guest comments and business forecasts, they can form a vital ingredient in formulating future personnel strategy and policy.

Information about personnel is an increasingly important aspect of human resource management. The following section deals with the aspect of labour turnover and absence, and addresses the factors which affect this element.

2.6 STAFF TURNOVER AND ABSENCE

If there is one factor which demonstrates the effectiveness of personnel policies and practices more than any other, it is the levels of staff turnover and absence. The hospitality industry has, unfortunately, always been characterised by depressingly high levels of staff turnover and absence. Other studies by professional bodies, the Department of Employment, the HCTC and industry itself, all report on levels of staff turnover based upon a variety of factors.

However, the rate or level of staff turnover is, at times, a misleading figure. Taken as a base statistic it simply recognises the movement of personnel in and out of the sector, a particular company, unit or department. Other factors have to be considered before deciding that levels are inappropriate or an indication of ineffective management.

Employees will leave employment for the following reasons:

- resignation, either voluntarily or due to incapacity
- dismissal (including redundancy or constructive dismissal)
- retirement

Additionally, promotion or movement within a company, if not taken into account, will also affect basic labour turnover rates.

Obviously the more comprehensive the personnel system, the greater the ability of the operator to analyse labour turnover in detail. Large companies will be able to collect and evaluate statistics on all aspects of staffing – labour turnover being one of these. Also they will be well placed to identify potential problems and implement strategies to solve labour turnover issues.

Before looking at possible methods for reducing high levels of turnover and absence, it is important to understand the relevance of this element to effective human resource management.

Labour turnover

COSTS OF HIGH LABOUR TURNOVER

The actual cost of labour turnover is difficult to estimate as it depends on what elements are included in the calculation. Most commonly, the cost of replacement is the first element, which will concentrate on the cost of advertising, recruitment and selection.

However, the actual cost will be more than the cost of the advertisement or payable applicants costs, as the cost of management time and resources required has to be put into the calculation.

Additional or hidden costs could possibly include:

- training of replacement staff
- overtime payments to cover for absent staff
- lost or delayed production
- interruptions to work flow
- increased production costs, wastage
- increased risk of accidents due to inexperienced employees undertaking new tasks

Obviously not all of these will occur for every employee leaving and a lot depends on the particular position vacated. The problem may become serious for an employer if particularly high levels of labour turnover exist. In such situations the effect on both the employer and remaining employees can be extreme, with loss of morale, productivity and performance. Lacking the support of a stable workforce, standards drop, quality suffers and customer dissatisfaction increases. As standards drop so staff morale decreases with the result that standards continue to decline. It becomes a vicious circle which only drastic action can remedy.

KEY POINT

The overall cost to a hospitality business faced with high labour turnover can be much more than just the replacement of staff, if replacement is possible. High labour turnover indicates a serious problem for the operator and one that requires considerable management skills to correct.

The key considerations for employers in respect of staff turnover are to:

- identify patterns or trends of labour turnover, wastage or absence
- identify the factors which are causing such problems
- develop personnel systems, policies and procedures which reduce levels of turnover

It is these three areas that industry has recently begun to tackle more effectively. Before describing the methods currently used, it is important to recognise that there is a positive side to labour turnover.

Leaving employees create opportunities for the operator to:

- restructure a department or unit
- re-evaluate the vacated position in terms of strategy for replacement

- provide promotion or development for other employees
- reduce labour costs if the strategy is for non-replacement
- appoint someone with better skills or experience

KEY POINT

Labour turnover, whilst creating problems for hospitality operators, also provides a variety of opportunities. All vacated posts should be evaluated in respect of replacement strategy.

IDENTIFYING AND ANALYSING LABOUR TURNOVER

Unless an operator can identify actual rates of labour turnover and furthermore identify the reasons for turnover, the ability to manage its workforce effectively is seriously reduced. By identifying rates and causes the operator can:

- control the level of staff, establishing and managing one of the most costly elements of the operation
- forecast manpower needs more accurately
- control direct and indirect labour costs

There are a variety of ways such an analysis can be undertaken. In its most simplistic form, companies will measure labour turnover as number of leavers in a period as a percentage of the total number employed:

Therefore: $\dfrac{\text{number of leavers}}{\text{average number employed}}$ $\times 100$ = turnover rate (or separation rate)

Example: $\dfrac{25 \text{ leavers}}{135 \text{ employed}}$ $\times 100 = 18.5\%$ turnover rate

The separation rate approach has a number of inherent weaknesses, especially if the figures are for the whole company or unit. It ignores the reasons for staff leaving, and indications of particular problems with a unit, department or cohort of employees. It is a relatively crude method, but one that is useful for comparing annual rates. Industry uses more sophisticated models which take into account other factors, such as retention or survival.

Stability index
This method analyses the retention of staff over a period, as follows:

$\dfrac{\text{Number of employees with 1 year or more of service (present)}}{\text{Number of employees 1 year ago}}$ $\times 100$ = stability index

For example:

$\dfrac{30 \text{ (more than 1 year's service)}}{150 \text{ (number of employees 1 year ago)}}$ $\times 100 = 20\%$ stability index

The measure or indicator of stability provides information relating to the retention of staff. This approach also raises the question of what a company should be measuring.

Increasingly employers are attempting to identify what factors assist the retention of staff, rather than attempting to identify why they left. This is a proactive method rather than a reactive approach and can be undertaken by attitudinal surveys, via staff appraisal and in regular performance review meetings. This stability or retention rate is often referred to as the survival rate – rather a negative term in relation to current human resource practice. Measures of labour turnover can also include:

- seasonal variances
- length of service
- geographical variances – especially useful for companies operating sites spread around the country
- comparison of units
- comparison of departments
- cohort analysis, e.g. receptionists, chefs, housekeeping personnel or unit managers

COMMON FEATURES OF LABOUR TURNOVER

Traditionally, labour turnover rates have been high in:

- first six weeks of employment (the induction crisis)
- larger more centralised hospitality organisations
- large urban areas
- fast-food operations, especially those operating in urban areas
- certain groups or cohorts of employees including trainee managers, hotel receptionists, chefs, licensed premises staff, housekeeping personnel, kitchen porters and unit managers

Note: The current shortage of skilled chefs is resulting in increased movement of those with the right skills and experience.

─────────────────── **KEY POINT** ───────────────────

Identifying the factors which cause high staff turnover is a major priority for hospitality operators.

───

The operator facing increases in costs, reductions in quality and lack of continuity in service, will recognise fairly quickly the need for corrective action. Whilst some managers and personnel officers used to accept high turnover as representative of the industry norm, current accepted thinking centres on the recognition of the real cost of losing staff.

The need, therefore, is to identify the reasons behind turnover and seek methods to reduce it. Personnel and human resource specialists, along with external bodies, have been analysing these factors for a considerable period. Obviously they differ in respect of the sector, region, season, company and position. The main reasons for staff leaving employment include:

- terms and conditions differ from those expected

- induction process failing to create the right working relationship
- dissatisfaction with the job or company
- inadequate or ineffective management
- lack of challenge or job satisfaction
- individual appointed over their skill level
- pay and benefits
- promotion to another company

Studies have shown time and time again that a problem with pay is rarely the reason for employees leaving an organisation.

In addition to all the above, the reason for leaving could be lack of training and development opportunities, forms of harassment or inequality, personal health, family or domestic problems or stress.

ESTABLISHING THE CAUSE OF LABOUR TURNOVER

There are two basic ways of identifying the cause of employees leaving:

1   *Exit interview*, where employer, personnel manager or manager attempts to solicit reasons from the individual. Such interviews are normally conducted on a one-to-one basis or by requesting the employee to complete a brief questionnaire. Whilst such interviews are useful, certain problems exist:

- they are reactive and often have minimal effect on the employee who is dissatisfied
- if the employee is dissatisfied and demotivated, discussions concerning the reasons could result in further conflict
- the reason may be the manager involved

As a basic practice, the use of exit interviews can be of assistance to an organisation, but as stated here has certain limitations. For larger companies facing high turnover in specific areas the answer may be for such interviews to be conducted by an impartial consultant who, possibly, could more accurately identify the main cause or reasons.

2   *Attitudinal survey*; mention has clearly been made of the use of such surveys in identifying employees' attitudes and perceptions related to their employment, the basic benefit being that such surveys are proactive and seek to identify problems before they become unmanageable. Certainly work and studies completed over the past five to six years on the quality of work is leading operators to review employees' attitudes and feelings more regularly.

Whilst I have identified the main reasons for turnover, operators will commonly look at three aspects of their policies and practices:

- recruitment and selection
- induction
- training and development

'Manpower planning is concerned with balancing all the factors which affect the business.'

These aspects are described in detail in Chapters 4 and 5. However, in respect of labour turnover, the operator will want to identify whether any aspects of these elements are responsible for employees leaving.

The induction crisis referred to earlier in this section is a problem for the whole industry and, despite major improvements, still remains as a problem for employers. It is during the first few weeks of a job that employees feel most at risk and are most likely to react to perceived unfair treatment or demands. The relationship between employee and employer is set within this period and it is a process which employers are constantly trying to improve.

Whilst companies have looked in detail at recruitment, selection and induction, many have ignored the other stages employees will go through during their period of employment with an organisation (Table 8).

You will see that there are a wide variety of factors which affect labour turnover; overall it remains the responsibility of the organisation to identify and minimise adverse factors.

KEY POINT

Labour turnover continues to cause hospitality operators major problems, even in times of recession. Whilst a degree of turnover can be perceived as 'healthy', the nature of the industry indicates that continued efforts must be made to reduce it to acceptable levels.

Absence

If employees leaving an organisation for reasons of dissatisfaction is an indication of human resource problems, so are levels of absence, an aspect which causes the industry major problems. Similar to labour turnover, employers need to identify the rates of absence and possible reasons and seek to minimise these to an acceptable level. Again the advent of computerised personnel systems has allowed companies to more easily identify trends and statistics.

As a starting point, any hospitality operator requires a system for identifying and tracking absence rates. This in itself can assist operators to reduce absence. In individual cases where an employee is not completing his/her work contract, then the employer has obvious recall to the normal employment legislation, i.e. disciplinary procedures. Accepting that there will be a number of inappropriate employees, it also has to be recognised that employee absence can be due to factors created by the employer. These include issues related to:

- health and safety
- equal opportunities
- stress
- general employment conditions
- harassment
- responsibility or position related problems

The industry has been undertaking a proactive analysis of the reasons behind absence and many of the larger companies have created positive practices for dealing with absence. Individual

Table 8 Common problems related to stages of employment

STAGE	PROBLEMS	POSSIBLE SOLUTIONS
1 Recruitment, selection and induction	• Job does not match individual's perception • Terms and conditions are altered • Incorrect appointment • Induction process fails to create working partnership	• Improve job evaluation procedure • Ensure job evaluation description appropriate • Amend person specification process • Establish interviewing and selection training • Evaluate recruitment, selection and induction process
2 Settling and transition, where employee has begun to settle into position and organisation	• Honeymoon period of induction is over and nature of position becomes clearer • Company culture, values at odds with individual aspirations • Individual becomes dissatisfied with promotional opportunities	• Implement ongoing evaluation, appraisal and review • Improve consultation and communication with employees • Clarify career and promotional paths and put on equal basis
3 Acceptance, where individuals have commenced on possible progression path, or established themselves in a particular position	• Career paths become blocked • Changes in structure and position create problems for individuals and groups of staff • Position lacks challenge and interest	• Analyse quality of work; develop revised team working • As changes in structure are unsettling, effective consultation and communication is required • Reanalyse positions and attitudinal surveys • Restructure training and development

appraisal schemes, availability of employee counselling, private health care schemes and employment legislation all assist employees to manage specific individual problems related to their work.

For the employer the aim must be to identify, reduce or alleviate reasons for absence related to working conditions. This is, of course, easier for the larger operators and despite the major restructuring of the industry over the past five years, there is still a large number of small catering businesses which lack the organisation to operate such schemes.

However, whatever the size of the business, absent employees create additional cost, disruption to production and service and increased pressure on other employees. It is a problem that will only be minimised by constant analysis of staffing statistics and positive action on behalf of the employer.

The final section in this chapter will look briefly at particular approaches to manpower planning by the various sectors of the hospitality industry.

2.7 APPROACHES TO MANPOWER PLANNING

This section will describe the various approaches to manpower planning undertaken by the sectors of the hospitality industry. An important aspect to recognise is that, whilst certain factors remain constant and applicable to all types of operations, each sector will need to consider and plan for specific factors which affect them.

KEY POINT

Whilst the common factors exist which affect a company's approach to manpower planning, each operator will require an approach which is relevant to their particular organisation.

Licensed trade

This sector has undergone significant changes over the past decade. The effects of the Beer Orders on major brewery companies has seen large scale restructuring with significant numbers of public houses coming onto the market. Additionally, the nature of the industry has been altering with a movement towards food-centred premises and themed public houses. There has also been a move towards branded food operations and significant numbers of small licensed house companies have emerged, examples being Tom Cobleigh in the Midlands and J. D. Weatherspoons in London.

Traditionally, the larger breweries such as Whitbread's, Vaux and Bass operated on three levels:

1 *tenanted houses,* where pubs were operated by couples who leased the property from the brewery and had certain degrees of freedom;
2 *managed houses,* where the company employed a manager or management couple and all staff were employees of the company;
3 *free trade,* where the brewery supported privately owned premises, often gaining the contract for the sole supply of beers, spirits and other beverages.

'Managers need to establish effective means of monitoring staff absence.'

The larger breweries organised their premises on a regional basis, with regionalised support for purchase, operations, finances, personnel, facilities and development. Excluding the free trade, manpower strategy was characterised by:

- centralised manpower planning and strategy development
- regionalised personnel support
- regionalised and local recruitment

Whilst the company set a particular budget for a unit, it was often left to the individual licensee to recruit his/her own bar staff, often on a part-time or casual basis.

The restructuring of the breweries and the development of branded operations has led to a change to this approach, with the emphasis on increased head office control and targeted national recruiting. Traditionally, recruitment was targeted at management couples and whilst many breweries still operate with significant numbers of 'landlords/landladies', the move is towards management structures similar to hotel and restaurant companies. Such changes have affected the manner in which breweries and licensed house companies are approaching all aspects of their manpower management activities.

One licensed trade company has developed a manpower strategy based, in part, on computer analysis of the possible customer base for new units. In identifying the characteristics of the locality, they further identify not only the style of the unit, but also a personnel profile.

Hotel sector

The diversity of this sector makes generalisations difficult. For example, there are considerable differences between a large hotel chain operating 3–4 star properties throughout the country and an independent operator in the luxury country house hotel market. Can you compare Forte Crest with le Manoir aux Quat' Saisons? It is, therefore, necessary to break down this sector into types of organisations.

LARGE HOTEL CHAINS (E.G. FORTE, STAKIS, SWALLOW)

Similar to other sectors within the industry, the hotel chains have gone through some major restructuring over the past few years. The predominant company in terms of number of units and bedrooms (Forte) has restructured into several specific branded operations, including Forte Crest, Heritage, Post House and Travel Lodge. Whilst other companies have developed new brands, e.g. Holiday Inns, Court Hotels. New entrants to the market have included Radisson and Ramada with companies such as Scotts repositioning themselves within the market.

Traditionally, the hotel companies have operated on a national basis with manpower strategy and policy being set by head office. Individual hotels would have been allocated a manpower budget within the overall operating budget and unit managers would have had little or no freedom to deviate from set company guidelines. Whilst recruitment for operative staff would have been on a local basis, managers and trainee managers were recruited on a national basis and companywide progression plans were common.

FIGURE 11 *Example of branded licensed premises.*

The increase in branding has led companies to more closely identify particular types and levels of staff for specific operations. Common characteristics and trends of the larger hotel chains include:

- decline in school leavers encouraging companies to target other age groups
- partial increase in the use of agency staff or contracting out aspects of the operation – certain major London hotels commenced this strategy in the late 1980s, especially for housekeeping or function personnel

- regionalisation of personnel function with individual units being supported by local offices
- deskilling of positions and encouragement of flexibility amongst employees – the traditional hotel kitchen with large brigades is no longer the norm, only remaining in the larger 5-star hotels
- manpower policies and practices encouraging the greater utilisation of personnel across a range of duties becoming increasingly common
- centralisation and regionalisation of support services, such as personnel, training, sales and marketing, finance and control affecting the range of staff within the units

MEDIUM-SIZED AND INDEPENDENT HOTEL COMPANIES

With growing competition for skilled labour and lacking the status of the larger groups, this sector often has more difficulty in attracting appropriate levels of staff. Career progression and development opportunities are more limited than in the larger companies and this size of company will, additionally, lack the scale of support available to companies such as Forte or Swallow.

Increasingly these smaller companies are recognising that their image as an employer is of vital importance to their ability to plan manpower effectively. Manpower strategy is then linked partly to the creation of a positive image, identifying for potential employees the advantages of working with a more personalised style of organisation.

For specialist hotel operators at the luxury end of the market, this problem is diluted as individuals will be attracted by their reputation and status. For the thousands of small hotels the main problem is attracting and retaining staff of the right calibre. One solution identified was for groups of hotels to merge in respect of recruitment, training and development. An experiment initiated by a group of hotels in the Cotswolds in the late 1980s, whilst not dictating the manpower requirements of individual units, allowed the operators both to reduce manpower recruitment costs and attract higher levels of applicants.

RESTAURANT SECTOR

The huge growth in high street retail-type restaurants operating under various brands over the past decade has both increased the competition for labour and resulted in gaining an image of a sector which mainly attracts young, unskilled or semi-skilled employees.

Whilst there are thousands of small, privately-owned restaurants which still offer the tradition of silver service, the growing emphasis is for fast, friendly, informal service. Companies, such as the Bright Reasons Group, which operate Bella Pasta, Pizza Piazza and Pizzaland, have developed improved training and development policies with clear career paths. Such multi-site organisations will develop manpower strategies which, whilst setting clear establishment personnel levels, will also allow them to reduce labour turnover.

Recognising that a degree of deskilling has occurred, such operators have invested considerable effort into customer service skills and schemes which assist the retention of staff. An important factor to consider is the type of customer who forms the main market for such restaurants, the nature of which will dictate in part the style of manpower. Berni Inns, which operated in the 1960s and 1970s, were for a period a highly successful steak bar-type operation. Their market was predominantly couples with families and older couples and food service staff were predominantly middle-aged females.

In the late 1970s and early 1980s the high street restaurant companies were fighting hard for a younger market and manpower strategy was to operate with a predominance of younger staff. The mixing of the market has, in part, led restaurant operators to redefine their manpower needs. The larger companies again are assisted by their national position, with access to well developed personnel and human resource departments.

Contract catering

This sector has experienced significant growth over the past twenty years and has become highly competitive. Companies, such as Gardner Merchant, Sutcliffe, Compass, Russell and Brand and BET, all operate large numbers of sites across the country. Initially concentrating on the provision of staff needs for other companies, these groups are now diversifying into schools, colleges, hospitals, the forces and involving themselves in other support services such as maintenance, cleaning, security and overall facility management.

Traditionally seen as the lower end of the catering market, companies have invested considerably in delivering high quality services and have become an attractive proposition for employees. Often operating on a regional basis, such companies have well developed effective manpower strategies with clear progression and development opportunities for their employees. Individual units are supported by local and regional head office services with recruitment and selection being operated at a local and national level.

The success of these companies has, in part, been due to the match between manpower planning and the delivery of quality services. They have often been in the forefront of initiatives designed to attract and retain quality staff with comprehensive training and development facilities.

With sophisticated establishment and unit models, backed up by local and regional support, such companies face minimal problems related to manpower planning.

Leisure sector

The growth of the leisure sector has, similarly to contract catering and high street restaurants, been a major feature of the industry over the past few years. Within this sector I would include:

- theme parks, e.g. Alton Towers, Blackpool Leisure, American Adventure, Chessington
- holiday centres, e.g. Center Parcs, Haven, Pontins
- visitor and heritage centres, e.g. Longleat, National Trust Properties
- miscellaneous operators, providing operated small centres, garden centres, animal sanctuaries, mansions

The range of these is impressive and they attract considerable numbers of visitors. For the majority of these, their origins were not, traditionally, in the provision of catering. For many they were considered peripheral to the main product and personnel planning was geared towards other services. Whilst some leisure companies and businesses have contracted out their catering services, the majority have now integrated such provision completely with their other products. For this sector particular problems exist, including:

- often seasonal nature of the business
- location, which is normally well away from large urban areas and available labour

(See the case study on Haven Leisure, page 69, for an example of a manpower planning approach to this sector.)

Historically, such organisations would have retained a small nucleus of permanent staff and recruited large numbers of personnel for their peak season (April–September). Manpower strategy was developed to recruit, select and train large numbers of staff within a short period, relying in part on employees returning for several seasons. Staff were predominantly young, with significant numbers of students. Personnel systems and practices were geared towards this influx of staff with, in all honesty, little thought given to long-term retention. Whilst such companies will have to increase numbers in the peak period, increasingly they are developing manpower strategies which stabilise numbers of staff across the year. This sector has also been affected by the need to train staff more effectively.

Consider also, amongst others, the following sectors of the industry:

- travel lodge-type operators
- cruise companies
- motorway service companies
- in-store caterers
- school meal or direct service organisations

All will have specific approaches to their manpower planning which create challenges, problems and opportunities. If you study any of the sectors you will quickly identify the manner in which companies approach this important element. The style of recruitment, advertising, company statement and communications will need to represent their particular philosophy and approach. As hospitality continues to diversify, so too will approaches to both manpower strategy and practice.

2.8 SUMMARY AND KEY POINTS

Manpower planning is, as you can see, more than just the acquisition of appropriate levels of staff for a company. It is an important management function which encompasses a variety of elements, including the identification of needs, levels and location of demand and recruitment and selection. Additionally, it is not a function which stops once a company has commenced operations.

A major overlap exists with other aspects of personnel and human resource management and an employer has to possess an understanding of how external, environmental factors, such as demographic trends and skill shortages, will affect the ability to provide appropriate levels of staff.

The increasing competition for skilled personnel will affect the policies and practices of hospitality operators, and strategies will need to be developed which, again, assist companies to obtain skilled personnel. Even the small, independent operator will require a strategy for its workforce if it is to remain competitive in today's market, whilst the medium to large hospitality operators will require detailed plans to assist the maintenance of performance and market position.

Manpower planning is, then, a dynamic function and one that is becoming increasingly important. Without appropriate strategies, plans and policies, operators will face a difficult task, especially in an industry characterised by high labour turnover and absence rates.

KEY POINTS

- Manpower planning, including the development of strategy, is becoming increasingly important for all hospitality operators
- The effects of demographic trends and the availability of skilled staff will put increasing pressure on hospitality businesses to deskill in all aspects of their operations
- Manpower planning involves developing strategies, policies and practices which assist the identification, acquisition, effective use, improvement and retention of an organisation's human resources appropriate to its needs
- Manpower planning is an ongoing process and involves the operator in constant analysis of the business and its employees
- The improvement in rates of labour turnover and the reduction in absence is reliant on a variety of factors; effective manpower strategies will seek to target directly such elements as the cost of labour increases
- The hospitality industry, with its image of long hours and low pay, has a major task in attracting the level and calibre of staff required

QUESTIONS

1   Explain the importance of manpower planning for a hospitality operator.
2   Discuss the possible effects of demographic changes on the hospitality industry over the next decade.
3   Identify the internal factors which may inhibit an operator in developing an effective manpower strategy.
4   Describe the possible differences in approach to manpower planning in respect of a multi-site contract caterer, an events caterer and an independent 4-star city centre hotel.
5   Explain the benefits to an operator of conducting a detailed manpower audit.
6   Outline various approaches currently used in the industry to reduce labour turnover and absence.

7   The element of stress is often cited as a major cause of high labour turnover and staff absence; describe personnel policies and practices which could reduce levels of stress within a hospitality unit.

8   Identify and explain potential problems and challenges for a hospitality operator with minimal staff turnover.

CHAPTER 3

PERSONNEL POLICIES, PROCEDURES AND PRACTICES

Our people are what makes Quadrant the successful dynamic organisation that you see today. We are totally committed to recruiting, developing, rewarding and retaining our most important resource in order to stay ahead in a very competitive market.

QUADRANT CATERING

People are crucial to the success of any organisation. Finding and keeping the right people with the right skills is therefore a major concern for all employers.

ACAS ADVISORY BOOKLET

. . . to ensure that through efficient and effective liaison, communication and consultation we facilitate the provision of a carefully recruited, well motivated, properly educated, instructed and trained workforce, allowing our employees, at all levels, to work and develop within a caring, professional environment for the benefit of the company, the client and themselves.

MISSION STATEMENT OF THE PERSONNEL & TRAINING DEPARTMENT,
COPTHORNE TARA HOTEL

3.1 AIMS AND OBJECTIVES

By studying this section, reviewing key points, answering the questions and completing exercises and assignments in Appendix A, you will be able to:

1 appreciate the role such policies and procedures play in effective personnel and human resource management;
2 list the key personnel policies and procedures required;
3 understand the differences between a policy, procedure, practice and system and list examples of each;

4   describe methods of good employee communication;

5   have an understanding of the various approaches to such activities across the range of the
    industry.

3.2 INTRODUCTION

This chapter will concentrate on aspects which are traditionally seen as the core of personnel
management, i.e. the policies, procedures and practices which form the functional base of HRM.
Considerable numbers of textbooks, guides and leaflets exist on these topics, including many
targeted at the hospitality industry. Whilst explanations will be provided on the key practices and
procedures, the emphasis, similar to other chapters, will be on providing examples of how
industry approaches and undertakes such activities.

Throughout this text I have attempted to identify the need to match the functional aspects of
personnel management to the need for a more strategic approach. Chapter 1 outlined such
strategic approaches and developments, therefore it is now important to detail the key functional
tasks of personnel management.

3.3 ROLE AND FORMULATION OF PERSONNEL POLICY

Whatever the size and style of the operation, the employer will require a full range of rules,
regulations and guidelines to satisfy both legal requirements and the needs of the business and
its employees. ACAS in its advisory booklet on employment policies states: 'Every organisation
depends upon the effective use of its available resources – money, machinery, materials and,
above all, its employees – to achieve its objectives.'

Special care and attention are needed to develop employment policies which are both
effective and fair. An effective employment policy will contribute to the achievement of the
organisation's overall objectives, but this is unlikely to be effective unless it is also accepted by
employees and compatible with their interests.

Role of employment policies and procedures

Employment or personnel procedures form the functional base for effective human resource
management. Effective policies will:

- ensure the satisfaction of various aspects of legislation
- assist the creation and maintenance of systems which can be effectively managed
- protect both employer and employee in respect of employment issues
- reduce risk of waste or duplication in respect of both management and operational tasks

- minimise potential conflict between employer and employees
- allow managers to be more effective in respect of company objectives and the general policy framework within which they operate
- assist employees effectiveness

Consider the company which has no clear procedures for grievance situations, or whose policy exists but has not been communicated to its employees. Even a minor grievance may result in considerable disruption and demotivation of the parties involved. (In Exercise 8 in Appendix A, you will identify such a situation and recognise how the existence of effective policies would assist an effective outcome.)

The historical development of the personnel function has seen both a move towards the standardisation of employment and personnel policies and the emergence of human resource strategies based upon such functional aspects. A key element to consider is that without effective employment policies an organisation cannot hope to operate successfully.

Employers and employees will require, then, a set of rules, regulations, policies and practices which will ensure positive working practices. In addition to reducing risk of prosecution and providing protection for both parties, the nature and approach of employment policies help to set the style and culture of an organisation. Many personnel policies have their base in law and exist primarily to ensure adherence to specific sections of employment legislation. The interpretation of such legislation and the freedom to adapt to business circumstance is minimal. For example, the law related to sick pay, trade union representation, sex and race discrimination, health and safety and maternity leave is fixed and the onus is on the employer to adhere to specific statutory requirements.

However, many employers will use such legislation as a minimum requirement, enhancing policies to provide improved benefits or services for their employees. Examples of these have been the general move towards a no-smoking working environment in advance of health and safety legislation, and the granting of paternity leave. Enlightened employers may include a variety of positive personnel practices which are not based on legislation, but are considered vital in assisting the development of a well motivated workforce.

Personnel and training examples:

The following Case Study describes, in detail, the McDonald's operation and, specifically, their approach to human resource management. The inclusion of McDonald's in part represents the respect other hospitality companies have for McDonald's, which is mainly due to the well developed personnel, training and human resource policies they possess. Many in the industry would wish to emulate this company's success, especially in relation to its market share and effective systems.

CASE STUDY. MCDONALD'S RESTAURANTS (UK)

BACKGROUND

McDonald's opened its first restaurant in the UK in 1974 and currently operates nearly 500 units, employing in excess of 31,000 people. Of this figure, over 28,000 are employed as restaurant crew and over 2000 as restaurant management. The breakdown of staff is approximately 63% aged 16–20 years, with over 25% having more than two years service. Crew ratio between male and female is 53:47. Annual payroll and related costs for the Company operated restaurants were in the region of over £130 million.

With a target of opening 40 new restaurants annually to a forecasted level of 1000 units, the Company has a major human resource challenge. This Case Study will provide you with information about the structure of the Company and specific approaches to personnel and training.

STRUCTURE

Operationally, the Company is split into three regions – London and the South; the Midlands, East Anglia and Wales; the North of England, Scotland and Northern Ireland. The Company's senior management consists of a President, a Chief Executive Officer with five Vice Presidents.

Within each region there is a regional head office with a regional manager and vice president. Additionally, there are senior market managers responsible for a number of operational areas. Each of these areas is overseen by an operations manager. The regional areas also have support functions, such as personnel, human resource, financial, supplies and maintenance.

Each region possesses a purpose-built training unit, which provides on and off the job training for all staff within the region, with additional backup from the main headquarters in Finchley (London). The training is overseen by McDonald's Chief Training Officer who works in conjunction with regional human resource managers and operations managers. The breakdown of McDonald's training programmes is detailed later; however, to put it in some perspective, by the start of 1993 over 48,000 employees had received off the job training at the three centres.

Individual units come under specific areas and comprise standard high street units, drive-thru's, in-store units, small kiosk type units and franchised units. The units, whilst varying according to the size and style, will usually follow the structure shown in Figure 12.

Units usually employ an average of 55 hourly-paid employees and four salaried managers. With a policy of internal promotion, the majority of staff will have commenced either as crew members or as trainee managers. For all these levels of staff, comprehensive training and development schemes are available.

EMPLOYMENT PRACTICES

With such large numbers of staff spread over the UK there is obviously a need for coordinated policies and procedures. Mirroring the parent company in the USA and its particular philosophy, such policies cover the full range of employment practices.

Since opening in 1974, McDonald's UK has developed effective policies in respect of equal opportunities; setting up a group in 1992 to evaluate existing policies and develop action programmes.

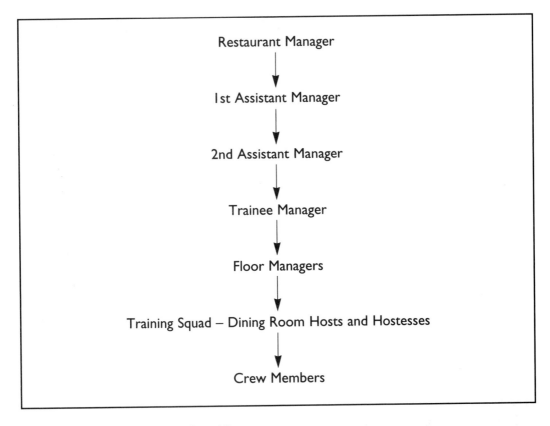

FIGURE 12 *Staff-structure in McDonald's.*

During this period the Company joined 'Opportunity 2000', a scheme to improve opportunities for women in work. Additional developments have been: improvements to maternity benefit and a part-time management scheme for salaried employees. A member of the Employers' Forum on Disability (which helps companies recognise, recruit and develop disabled people), McDonald's operates pre-recruitment schemes for disabled people and the long-term unemployed, which enable such individuals to join customised training schemes. Other activities include disability leave, a scheme to protect the jobs of newly disabled employees who must take time off.

EMPLOYEE BENEFITS

With slight variations, according to the level of the job, employee benefits include: private medical plan, pension scheme, clothing allowances, bonus scheme, sabbatical leave, stock option scheme, stock purchase plan, company loan scheme, relocation assistance and further education assistance. Additionally, there are the President Awards, related to a bonus for selected individuals.

EMPLOYEE COMMUNICATION

As can be expected of such a Company, employee communication is highly organised. In addition to regular restaurant meetings, Operation Supervisors regularly visit the restaurants. A variety of internal newsletters are produced, including 'McNews', published every two months for all crew members,

'EFT' (East Finchley Times), published quarterly for all office staff, 'High Levels' published quarterly for all management staff, plus a franchiser newsletter and regional newsletters.

TRAINING AND DEVELOPMENT

As indicated previously, the Company has a comprehensive training policy and programme which covers all employees. This ranges from in-store training for all crew members, in such aspects as Food Hygiene, HASAWA and standard operating procedures, to a wide range of off the job courses and programmes.

Promotion within the Company is geared towards advancement through results and all employees follow laid down training and development programmes. For employees seeking management positions, there are two main routes:

1 Trainee Management Scheme;
2 Junior Business Management Programme.

The overall management development programme contains four specific programmes which relate to the position the individual employee holds.

Figure 13 provides the range of courses leading up to area supervisor. For trainee managers entering the scheme, the regional office orientation day is followed by a 16-week programme in the selected restaurant.

On the orientation day I attended, 23 newly-recruited trainee managers received a thorough briefing on the history and structure of McDonald's, details of conditions of employment and detailed information on their training and development programme. All trainee managers are provided with a comprehensive manual for the first of the programmes (Management Development No.1). As they progress through the programme, achievement is assessed and recorded. As stated, promotion and pay increase is dependent upon successful achievement, and the development programmes are supported by regular formal reviews.

RECRUITMENT AND SELECTION

Whilst the majority of crew members are recruited locally, trainee managers and applicants for the Junior Business Management programme are recruited regionally. After completion of the initial application, selected individuals are invited to spend one to two days working in a restaurant undertaking on-job experience. The individuals follow a specific programme which allows joint assessment of suitability. (The majority of trainee managers on the orientation day had undertaken this experience; the others were individuals currently working in the Company.)

Such a scheme, although time consuming, allows the applicant to gain a feel for both the job and the Company, whilst allowing recruitment managers the opportunity to assess the individual's potential.

FINAL POINTS

With such a large Company, it is recognisable that comprehensive and effective employment policies and training and development programmes exist. Investment in People is a key part of their strategy. The need to open up progression routes for employees via training and development is matched by the need to create flexible working opportunities for crew members.

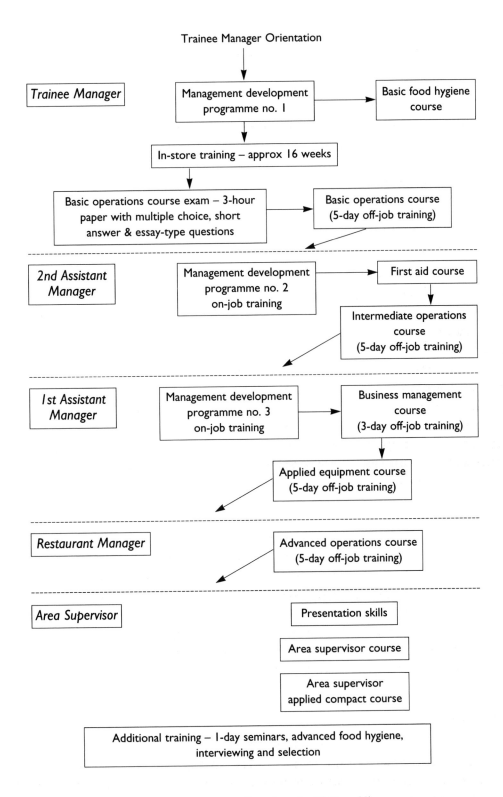

Figure 13 *Management development programme flow chart for McDonald's.*

This Case Study will have provided you with an insight into the manner in which such a company approaches these human resource challenges. Whilst McDonald's is not alone in developing such effective policies and practices, its success can be judged against the quality of its HRM activities.

McDonald's Restaurants Ltd, with assistance from Manchester Regional Office and Victor Arciniega, Senior Human Resources Officer.

Having read through this Case Study, consider the following questions:

- What elements of McDonald's HRM practices contribute most effectively to the retention and development of employees?
- What are the benefits to the individuals of the training and development programmes?

McDonald's, of course, is not alone in providing enhanced personnel policies and such policies are not restricted to the larger companies. A considerable number of schemes exist, ranging from subsidised holidays, employee exchanges, discount schemes and sabbaticals, to flexibility in dealing with employee leave or domestic difficulties.

Generally speaking, personnel policies fall into two specific groups:

1 policies and practices required by law;
2 policies and practices related to employee motivation and development.

The manner in which such policies are developed is dealt with in the next section.

─────────────── **KEY POINT** ───────────────

Whilst personnel policies form the functional base to human resource management, they have an additional role which is to assist the implementation of positive employment practices.

─────────────────────────────────────

The formulation of personnel policies and practices

Figure 14 identifies a simplified flow related to the formulation, development and communication of personnel policies. The development of policies will be influenced by other external and internal factors.

EXTERNAL FACTORS

- *Legislation*, which places responsibility onto the employer (for example, Health and Safety)
- *Codes of Practice*, developed by professional bodies and associations within the industry related to employment issues; whilst not legally binding, they exist to exert pressure on employers to adhere to various guidelines

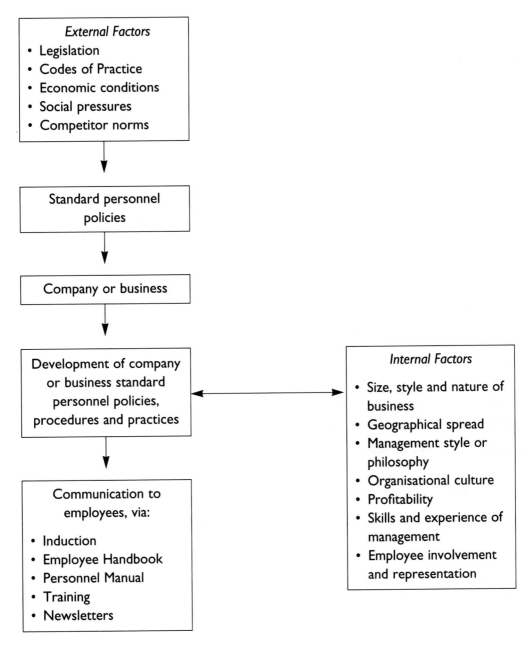

FIGURE 14 *Development of personnel policies.*

- *Economic conditions,* prevailing or forecasted economic or market trends resulting in employers amending policies or practices, e.g. in times of recession or reduced profitability certain employment benefits may be withdrawn; in the late 1980s and early 1990s access to training and development suffered in this way
- *Social pressures,* the demand for amendment to policies in light of social change; again, during the 1980s and the 1990s several social issues resulted in changes in policies; these included a

move towards non-smoking policies, green issues, which altered some companies' approach to sub-contracting and employment practices, and the recognition of the need to involve employees more in the business or company

- *Competitor norms*, for companies operating in similar markets or sectors, there will be pressure to normalise or standardise policies, especially with regard to employee pay, benefits and working conditions

Such external influences do exert considerable pressure on companies and business, as do influences from within the operation. These can include the particular culture or management style of an organisation, the make-up of the workforce, trade union influence and the size and style of the operation itself. This last factor has particular relevance. Within larger, more formal companies, policies and procedures are in the main clear and well communicated. Their formality may also cause some inflexibility. Smaller less formal operations, whilst possessing policies common to others, will often be more flexible in their approaches.

INTERNAL FACTORS

The nature and style of the company or business will have a major influence on policy formulation and practice as will the:

- geographical location and spread of units
- management style and philosophy
- management skills and experience
- degree of employee involvement and representation
- overall performance and profitability of the business

Whilst employee participation and involvement is increasing, the degree of their influence is limited to the degree to which the employer can and will amend policies. Even in the most empowered workforces, the influence they can exert on standard policies is minimal.

The development of policies and practices is finally dependent upon their effective communication to all employees, an aspect which has improved over the last decade. This aspect of employee communication is dealt with later in this chapter.

─────────────────── **KEY POINT** ───────────────────

The way in which an operator develops and communicates its policies will have a direct influence on their effectiveness.

Before looking at the role and importance of employee communication, it is necessary to provide an outline of the key personnel policies.

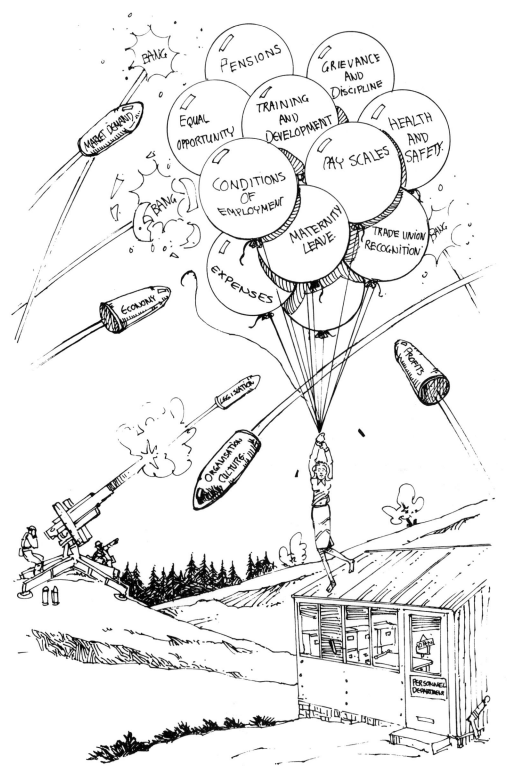

'Personnel policies are affected by a complex variety of environmental, economic, social and organisational factors.'

3.4 KEY PERSONNEL POLICIES

Employment policies are statements which set out in broad principle an employer's intentions and objectives related to its management of people and could include some or all of the following:

- manpower planning
- recruitment and selection
- induction and training
- pay, rewards and benefits
- Health and Safety
- contracts and conditions of employment
- grievance and discipline
- equal opportunities
- employee health and welfare
- negotiation and bargaining agreements
- communication and participation

A considerable number of these are covered by current employment legislation, which requires employers to develop and communicate a policy to its employees. However, it must be recognised that the effectiveness of policies is linked to aspects of management implementation and control. Put more simply, this means that however effective or positive the policy, its effect on employee behaviour may fail if management operate ineffectively.

Such policies create a framework on which to build positive employee relationships; therefore, it is not only important to have policies, but to ensure they are appropriate, acceptable, manageable and achievable. Recent challenges to existing policies have proven that whilst acceptable when first designed, they have become inappropriate in today's climate. The Armed Forces have experienced this recently in relation to the employment status of pregnant women; cases have also been brought in respect of catering personnel changing employer upon privatisation in respect of the protection of their existing employment conditions.

Before moving on to look at common policies in more detail, it is necessary to provide definitions of the words used to describe such activities and explain the use of the most common manner of communicating these – the employee handbook.

Policies, procedures, practices and systems

- *Policy:* a clear and definitive description of a particular company's approach to an aspect of its operation, e.g. Health and Safety policy (see Figure 15), equal opportunities
- *Procedure:* a description or outline of the manner in which a particular activity should be carried out, e.g. application for training and development; grievance; fire and evacuation procedure (see Figure 16)

Le Manoir aux Quat'Saisons

HEALTH AND SAFETY POLICY STATEMENT

The Health and Safety at Work etc., Act 1974 imposes a statutory duty on employers to ensure in so far as is reasonably practicable the health and safety of their employees whilst at work. This duty also extends to others who may be affected by that work.

Employees also have a statutory duty to take care of themselves and others who may be affected by their acts or omissions.

To enable these duties to be carried out, it is our intent to ensure that responsibilities for health and safety matters are effectively assigned, accepted and fulfilled at all levels within our organisational structure.

1. We will, so far as is reasonably practicable, ensure that:

    ● adequate resources are provided to ensure that proper provision can be made for health and safety

    ● risk assessments are carried out and periodically reviewed

    ● systems of work are provided and maintained that are safe and without risks to health

    ● arrangements for use, handling, storage, and transport of articles and substances for use at work are safe and without risks to health

    ● all employees are provided with such information, instruction, training and supervision as is necessary to secure their safety and health at work and the safety of others who may be affected by their actions

    ● the provision and maintenance of all plant, machinery and equipment is safe and without risk to health

    ● the working environment of all employees is safe and without risks to health and that adequate provision is made with regard to the facilities and arrangements for their welfare at work

    ● the place of work is safe and that there is safe access to and egress from the work place

    ● monitoring activities are undertaken to maintain agreed standards.

2. It is the duty of all employees at work:

    ● to take reasonable care for the health and safety of themselves and of other persons who may be affected by their acts or omissions at work and co-operate with us in fulfilling our statutory duties

    ● not to interfere with or misuse anything provided in the interest of health and safety.

3. General:

    ● this Health and Safety Policy will be reviewed at least annually, amended and updated as and when necessary. Communication of any such changes will be made to all employees

    ● there are established and maintained effective procedures for consultation and communication between all levels of management and employees on all matters relating to health, safety and welfare

    ● detailed reference information for employees can be found in the Employee Information Manual which is kept in the Staff Room.

Signed   ....

Position   ....**CHAIRMAN**................ Date......**19 AUGUST 1993**.............

1.1A

FIGURE 15 *Example of a Health and Safety policy.*

Fire Procedures

O *WHAT TO DO IN THE EVENT OF A FIRE.*

If you discover a fire, raise the alarm immediately.

Your departmental fire instructions detail what your specific action is to be in the event of a fire. *But –*

- *Always help evacuate the building as soon as the general fire alarms sounds.*

- *Use the nearest safe exit route.*

- *Do not use lifts.*

- *Do not run, shout or panic.*

- *Do not stop to collect personal belongings.*

- *Always wait at the assembly point for roll call and further instructions.*

- *If you "Live In" ensure you know the fire instructions for your accommodation area.*

O *FIRE TRAINING*

You will have been trained in the fire procedures for your work area. Make sure that you know them. If you are moved to a different work area, make sure that you know where the fire extinguishers are, and familiarise yourself with the exit procedure.

FIGURE 16 *Fire procedures.*

- *Practice*: the usual or common way in which an activity is carried out, e.g. codes of practice in relation to general personnel practice (see box below)
- *Systems*: the way in which a company's personnel policies, procedures and practices are monitored, managed and controlled

The People Policy Statement below is from Travellers' Fare, who employ over 3000 people across 258 operations based at railway stations throughout the country. Their brands include Casey Jones, Station Taverns, Gingham's Coffee Shops, Quicksnack, Upper Crust and Café Select.

PEOPLE IN THE COMPANY

POLICY

- To be a good employer

STRATEGIES INCLUDE:

- Recognising the importance of individuals and undertaking our obligations to employees positively
- Ensuring that pay and conditions reflect the value of any post fairly and are competitive with similar businesses, also linking rewards to performance
- Fostering constructive communications with employees and their appointed representatives and encouraging an open style of management
- Conducting all recruitment in line with carefully developed procedures to ensure that the right quality of entrant is employed
- Providing the necessary training to all entrants to enable them to do their jobs in a professional manner
- Providing development training opportunities to help people realise their full potential and to progress within the Company. Also ensuring that the best use is made of people's abilities by recognising their aspirations, encouraging and assisting them to develop themselves and their careers
- Seeking to fill vacancies by promoting from within the Company
- Providing support for those employees who wish to play an approved role in the community, their Trade Union or the organisation of social events for their colleagues
- Promoting ourselves as highly desirable, equal opportunity employers

TRAVELLERS FARE

You will have identified that all organisations require employment policies, regardless of which industrial sector they operate in. The hospitality industry has particular pressures related to its 24-hour, 365-day per year operation. Irregular working hours and the demands of customers can often put considerable strain on both employers and employees. The development of both effective and fair policies can reduce the degree to which such conditions affect positive employee relations.

Health, safety and welfare

Within this area there exists a considerable amount of legislation and quite rightly so. Employers have a legal responsibility of care towards their employees in respect of working conditions, precautionary measures, training, handling of hazardous substances, protective clothing, guarding and maintenance of dangerous machinery, in addition to the provision of appropriate fire precautions and first aid procedures, facilities and systems.

The main piece of legislation relating to health and safety is the Health and Safety at Work Act 1974 (HASAWA), which has been supported by various other Acts and regulations, including:

- Fire Precautions Act 1971
- The Control of Substances Hazardous to Health Regulations (COSHH) 1988
- First Aid Regulations 1981
- Health and Safety Information for Employers Regulations 1989

Employers have recently had to carry out risk assessments on their premises and practices, whilst additional EEC regulations are emerging which require further actions with regard to Health and Safety.

For the personnel manager, company director or owner the emphasis is quite rightly centred on ensuring adherence to the Health and Safety legislation, an aspect which the majority of textbooks or guides cover in some detail. However, as indicated in the previous chapter, there exist a number of other considerations related to general health and welfare issues which are receiving attention. These include:

- provision of health and medical schemes
- employee health screening
- issues related to smoking
- aids
- provision of employee counselling
- alcohol and diet
- provision of employee relaxation facilities

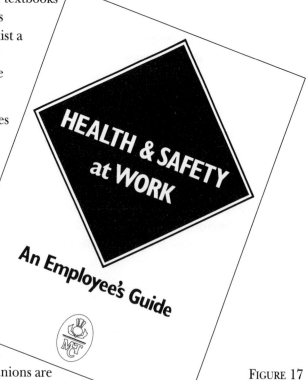

Accepting the pressurised nature of the industry, such considerations have particular relevance and they are ones the hospitality industry is starting to tackle in some depth. Employers, professional bodies and trade unions are taking a much broader view of health, welfare and safety at work.

FIGURE 17
Health and safety handbook for staff.

As indicated later in this chapter, the employee handbook is the most common vehicle for informing employees of regulations and conditions of employment related to the HASAWA and welfare. Employers with over 20 employees must, by law, provide a written statement on the HASAWA and there is a trend to use such information as a training aid, either at induction or as part of ongoing training. Increasingly a booklet covering HASAWA issues, regulations and responsibilities is issued separately (Figure 17).

Legal aspects affecting recruitment and selection

Whilst there exists the need for employers to select employees who best fit the business requirements, there also exists legislation which limits employers' policies.

RACE DISCRIMINATION

Employers must not discriminate against employees or job applicants on racial grounds, i.e. grounds of colour, race, nationality, ethnic or national background. Several codes of practice exist including one on the elimination of racial discrimination and the promotion of equality of opportunity, which came into effect in April 1984.

Several government agencies provide information and guidance on equal opportunities; you will find their addresses in Appendix B, and examples of such material on page 124.

The Race Relations Act 1975 also includes requirements related to discrimination in respect of:

- *job advertising* – advertisements which indicate an intention to discriminate on racial grounds are unlawful.
- *employment applications* – the arrangements for selection or terms of employment should not be discriminating.
- *conditions during employment* – relating to ensuring existing employees are not discriminated with regard to opportunities, training or other benefits.
- *victimisation* – which relates to the victimisation of an individual or group who has raised complaints under the Act.
- *segregation* – where employees are segregated on racial grounds, especially where the segregated group receives less favourable treatment.

SEX DISCRIMINATION

As with the Race Relations Act, the Sex Discrimination Act covers both direct and indirect discrimination and outlaws discrimination on the grounds of sex. Again there are specific clauses in relation to job advertising, job applications and victimisation.

Hospitality employers, similar to employers in other sectors, will now possess a variety of policies related to the two Acts above, normally produced in a written statement on equal opportunities. The aspects of discrimination and equal opportunities will be detailed in the next section.

Final points – personnel policies and procedures

You will see that personnel policies and procedures are complex issues which require careful consideration, planning and implementation. For well established companies such issues remain important, but in reality cause only minor difficulty. For small or newly formed companies the development of personnel policy is obviously more problematic. The following case study provides an example of this:

CASE STUDY. MERCURY TAVERNS: SETTING UP A PERSONNEL SYSTEM

Mercury Taverns is a relatively new company, formed when the Company purchased 115 licensed houses from Bass in October 1993. Prior to this acquisition, the Company (operating as Mercury Leisure Ltd) had concentrated on providing specialist licensing management services. The acquisition of the Bass houses saw personnel numbers rise from 50 to over 500 in a time span of under two months. Currently, Mercury Taverns has over 380 staff directly involved in the management and operation of its licensed premises. As can be imagined, the challenges related to personnel and training were considerable.

Josie Herring, the Personnel Manager who joined shortly after Mercury was formed, describes the situation as follows: 'The opportunity for the acquisition left no real time for prior planning and, whilst Bass provided considerable amounts of information, we basically had to start from scratch. The emphasis had to be to maintain profitable operations, building the functional aspects of personnel as we went along. Added to this was the complication of transferring employees from one organisation to another.'

The other tasks facing the personnel manager were quite basic ones, including payroll set up and systems, and the commencement of basic personnel records. Josie Herring comments: 'Above all else we had to ensure staff were on payroll and would receive correct payment – something which superseded other personnel issues. Within the first two to three weeks, I was constantly reading the transferral information, drawing up basic personnel forms, such as individual records, starter and leaver forms, job descriptions and contracts.'

Another aspect the Company had to consider was the change for employees – transferring from a large national company with agreed systems, conditions and collective agreements, to a new company with none of these. The management team responsible for the Taverns all arrived within a two to three week period and, whilst they possessed operational experience, they were without the backup of a well defined effective personnel system. The emphasis was on 'fire-fighting', due to the speed of acquisition which had not allowed for the development of strategies, systems and procedures.

With over 17 years of direct experience in personnel, the appointed Personnel Manager still faced a challenging task. Working with an assistant, Josie Herring concentrated on the setting up of the basic systems (which many of the larger standing companies take for granted). Since October 1993, the basic systems have been put in place with the direct people management, including recruitment and selection, being dealt with by the operational managers. Additionally, some of the licensed premises have been changed from managed to tenancy arrangements, which has meant additional recording of agreements and contracts.

The Company joined an Employers Federation, which has provided support, advice and assistance. Josie identified the benefit of this and of membership to a local group of personnel managers: 'Such meetings allow personnel members to network ideas and problems, suggestions and solutions.'

Seven months on from October 1993, the Company possesses a functional base of personnel systems, alongside the development of training programmes, concentrating on business priorities, no minor undertaking considering the situation when they started. Having formed the base, the Company was ready to commence longer term strategic planning, especially related to human resource issues. (Note: I am grateful to Josie Herring and Mercury Taverns for the provision of the above material.)

Study Points for Consideration

Whilst newly formed companies would ideally like a period of preparation this is not always possible and therefore leaves a major task for even the most experienced personnel manager:

- the increasing complexity of employment legislation makes the formulation of effective base personnel systems a vital first step for new and expanding companies
- whilst the development of the functional side of personnel and training is important, the business has to be profitable and therefore managers and directors will quite rightly concentrate on this element

However well developed are the policies and procedures, they require communicating to all employees. The next section looks in detail at this aspect.

3.5 EMPLOYEE COMMUNICATION

All organisations need some form of workplace communications about operational matters and contractual employment details. In many successful companies the principles of good management ensure that systematic two-way communication takes place on a much wider range of subjects. These companies benefit from better decision making, greater employee understanding and commitment and improved industrial relations.

Advisory, Conciliation and Arbitration Service (ACAS) *Workplace Communications*

Background to employee communications

As identified in previous sections within this chapter, the manner in which employment policies are communicated to employees is of vital importance. Policies which are badly formed, based upon a minimum of consultation and issued to employees as pieces of information may facilitate the receipt of guidelines or regulations, but have little to do with effective communication.

~SPECIAL~
HARVEST

FOR NEW TEAM MEMBERS STARTING **HARVESTER RESTAURANTS** WORK IN HARVESTER RESTAURANTS

IN THIS ISSUE	COVER STORY	PAGES TWO & THREE	BACK PAGE
	Being a Winner	*Our Business is Hospitality Personally Speaking*	*Notice Board*

Winning Teams mean Business

Winning teams mean business .... you'll hear this a lot at Harvester. If you like, this says everything about our business philosophy.

Although everyone whether based in the pub, restaurant, kitchen or accommodation is aware of his or her own responsibilities, everything is achieved through teamwork. Nobody at Harvester says 'it's not my job'. Everyone works and pulls together to maximise enjoyment for our guests and, through that, make the business as profitable as possible. Teamwork gets results!

There's no magic formula and, as has often been said, to aspire you

have to perspire. But there are plenty of incentives for each team to aspire to be a winning team. We have our much coveted Harvester Team of the Year award. This is awarded to the team which stands out from the winners of 20 individual categories covering high achievers in Sales, Quality, Profit and People. Many of these categories are sponsored by our suppliers and partners.

The latest recipient of this award is the Rising Sun at Dartford. Inside, you'll meet some of the team and have the chance to read what they have to say about working for Harvester.

As for the future, we'll be looking to you to play a part in a winning team!

You've joined the team!

Dear

A warm welcome to Harvester Restaurants. Whatever your job, you are an important team member who, through your enthusiasm, will contribute to your Harvester's success.

We endeavour to provide you with pleasant surroundings in which you work and, if you wish, allow you to develop a career in line with your abilities and aspirations. We also continually review performance, pay and conditions of work so that your efforts are well rewarded.

As a new member of our team, we will give you a thorough training so you soon pick up Harvester standards and understand what is expected of you. To compliment your training, this special edition of Harvest has been produced to tell you more about the company and give you an idea of what you will be doing to contribute to our success.

You are now a key player in helping us deliver our challenging mission. It's great to have you in our team and we wish you a long, happy and successful time with Harvester Restaurants!

TEAM MANAGER

Behind the make-up and studio lights...

Your impressions of Harvester will probably have been gained from our television advertising, particularly those of you in the South and the Midlands. We have run a series of commercials over the years, the latest being based around the title "There's more to Harvester then meets the mouth".

It's important to make it clear exactly why we advertise. The purpose of each commercial is not to tell people what it's like to work at Harvester, but to act as a sales tool aimed at making our restaurants appear welcoming to guests and enticing them

to visit us. Two completely different things.

So just for a minute the cameras aren't rolling. What's it really like to work for Harvester?

Well, for a start it's hard work. Whether you're working in the restaurant, pub or kitchen or, if appropriate, seeing to accommodation, you've got an end product to put before our guests. And that doesn't come without making an effort, thinking about what you're

doing and aiming to achieve, and always looking to improve on your own personal performance. It's not just about

a succulent meal; it's about the preparation and the clearing up as well.

Each of our restaurants has its own financial targets to meet. After all, at the end of the day Harvester is a business and like any other business, particularly in this day and age, has to be profitable. This translates into a series of challenges for each and every one of us as team members which can be broken down into **sales, profit, quality and brand growth**. The common denominator for all these is HOSPITALITY!

FIGURE 18 *Increasingly, companies use employee newsletters to assist communication and create team spirit.*

This section will concentrate on employee communication which refers to a two-way process for the interchange of information, news, tasks and instructions. As a two-way process it requires systems for a two-way flow of information, views and suggestions. The reason for concentrating on such forms of communication is related to the following trends:

1 increasing employer responsibility for communicating with employees due to changes in legislation;
2 recognition amongst employers that effective HRM is based on effective two-way communication;
3 outcome of research on communication related to employee motivation;
4 increased involvement and participation of employees in the decision-making process.

Such trends have been reinforced by various codes of practice and initiatives. Whilst the European Union has produced directives which support a prescriptive approach to employee participation (e.g. Social Charter), the United Kingdom, with support from various professional bodies, has preferred a more voluntary approach.

The Investors in People scheme sets out specific criteria for the communication of information to employees and during assessment seeks to assess the degree to which employees have been consulted on certain matters and understand them.

For hospitality operators, the need to communicate more effectively with their employees is also based upon the:

- results of restructuring the organisation due to economic recession and development of revised systems of management
- effects of increasing competition
- move towards such systems as Quality Management, Quality Assurance and Total Quality Management, which puts increased emphasis on employee communication and involvement

This is particularly true of larger companies and businesses. However, whilst smaller operators may not be involved in TQM, they still need to ensure the positive communication of information. Communication is undoubtedly a complex area and includes the appreciation of how the methods of communication affect the degree of acceptance by groups and individuals.

Methods of employee communication

To be effective, workplace communications must be:

- clear, concise and easily understood
- presented objectively
- in a manageable form to avoid rejection

- regular and systematic
- as relevant, local and timely as possible
- open to questions being asked and answered

A variety of methods will be needed, both spoken and written, direct and indirect. These need not be sophisticated or expensive. The mix of methods will depend mainly on the size and structure of the company.

ACAS, *Workplace Communications*

For smaller independent hospitality businesses, communication will be primarily on an informal one-to-one basis with a minimum amount of formalised processes. As the size of the business or company grows, so too does its need to widen the range of communication methods. A hospitality company comprising of 6–10 units in close geographical proximity will require a specialised personnel system that will assist unit managers and unit employees. Whatever the size, style or structure of the operation, the methods chosen must be appropriate and relevant.

For the purposes of this text, the areas of communication covered will be:

1   the range of information an employer has legal responsibility to communicate (to employees);
2   the range of information communicated (by a two-way process) that will benefit both the individual and the organisation.

The disclosure of information to employees, employee communication, consultation and involvement are covered by various acts and codes of practice, including:

- *Industrial Relations Codes of Practice (Communication & Consultation)*: covers the aspect of change to working practices and requires prior discussion between employer and employees (or their representative)
- *Health & Safety at Work Act 1974*: legislates for the duty of the employer to ensure the communication of statements and arrangements for health and safety policy and issues via a written statement
- written statement of main terms and conditions of employment *(Employment Protection (Consolidated) Act 1978)*: employers must provide a written statement to each employee
- Others include disclosure of information to trade unions; redundancy; contracting out of state related pension schemes; transfers of undertakings and the Companies Act

KEY POINT

Employers and personnel specialists require knowledge and understanding of the information they are legally required to communicate to their employees.

The main method for communicating such information is through the employee handbook (dealt with later in this section). However, a variety of other methods are used and the choice of these is dependent upon the specific legislation.

The communication of information, news and tasks related to the business which is not covered by legislation includes such things as:

- organisational and administration matters
- processing of business data between departments and units
- training, development and promotion opportunities
- employee benefits
- social news
- business development and company expansion

Additionally, there is the whole range of information related to individual jobs, tasks and responsibilities. These will include a mass of information in respect of specific procedures, guidelines on particular tasks, standard working procedures, operating and service standards and job descriptions.

─────────────────────── **KEY POINT** ───────────────────────

A primary function of personnel and line managers is the communication of such information to appropriate employees, in a manner that both satisfies the organisation's need to ensure information is passed down and facilitates employee understanding and commitment to policies, procedures and practices.

It is important to understand that employee communication is not just concerned with the processing of information, but also with the manner in which employees are involved within the organisation.

The benefits of effective employee communication

If you can recognise this shift in communication towards employee involvement and participation, then it is important to identify the specific benefits to both the employee and the organisation. The benefits include:

- assisting the development of improved employee commitment to the success of the organisation
- improving the level of satisfaction employees obtain from their work
- reducing the risk of prosecution (employer and employee) in respect of legislation
- assisting the development of improved standards and customer care
- reducing the risk of industrial disputes
- creating greater trust between employer and employee (management and staff; supervisor and operative)
- assisting the return flow of ideas and problem solutions to management

The basis to all this is the general recognition that the more you involve individuals in the processes of the business, the greater the degree of commitment. However, such involvement does not come easily and requires commitment from top management; systems which facilitate a two-way process and an understanding that as the organisation changes and develops, so too will the manner in which employee communication is handled. Additionally, the role of employees themselves in the communication process should not be underestimated.

─────────────── K E Y   P O I N T ───────────────

For large national companies with a geographical spread of units, the personnel and HRM specialist will be providing a regional and centrally based service. In such situations, unit managers, heads of department and supervisors will play a crucial role in any communication system. The personnel specialist will need to ensure such managers have received the training to deal effectively with such responsibility.

Methods of communication include:

- formalised meetings (at all levels)
- informal meetings (at all levels)
- one-to-one briefings
- team meetings
- conferences and seminars
- bulletin or notice boards
- electronic mail
- cascade networks
- employee handbooks
- newsletters, company or house journals
- annual reports
- employee reports and appraisals

Whilst some of the above are passive, i.e. they concentrate on the passing down of information, the majority include (or should) the facility for discussion, questioning and feedback. For the new employee, the main vehicles for this type of information are the induction process and the employee handbook. Induction is described in detail in Chapter 4, 'Recruitment and selection'. The following section deals with the employee handbook.

Employee handbooks

For newly appointed employees, a considerable amount of the information on a company's policies is usually provided at employment, during the induction period. In researching material for this text over 130 catering companies were contacted and over 70 provided copies of their employee handbook. Whilst there existed a variation in design and approach, all contained written statements of particular policies or practices. This is quite understandable as employers with five or more employees are legally obliged to provide written details of particular policies, with the most obvious being a Health and Safety Policy.

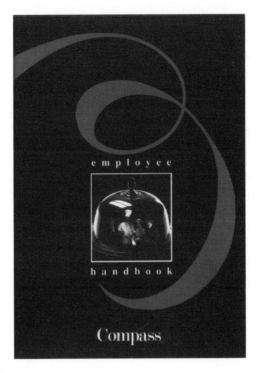

FIGURE 19 *Employee handbook.*

Whatever the size or style of a company, the employee handbook (see Figure 19) is an important document, used as:

- a source of reference to both employee, managers and employers
- a means of communicating information about the company and its policies
- an aid to the effective induction of employees
- most importantly, a means of fulfilling statutory requirements related to employment aspects

Additionally, alongside other effective induction activities, the handbook forms part of the professional relationship between an employer and employee. It may, in addition to stating policy, provide background information on the company or business, its history, facilities, organisational structure, products and services.

Whilst many hospitality operators issue fairly standard handbooks concentrating on the statutory requirements, others use the document to extend training and to act as an ongoing communication tool. Others include humorous cartoons, questionnaires and checklists to maximise the utilisation of the document (Figure 20).

When producing a handbook, the basic guidelines are:

- keep it simple, written in a direct and clear manner, appropriate to the nature of the employees
- ensure that contents comply with legal requirements, but are not too legalistic

- before general issue, the handbook is checked by persons responsible for policies and statements within it and, if possible, a small cross-section of those that will receive it
- ensure information flows in both a logical and prioritised order
- allow for periodic contents review, especially in respect of legislation

Obviously a balance has to be struck between ensuring all necessary information is provided and allowing the document to become too heavy or dull.

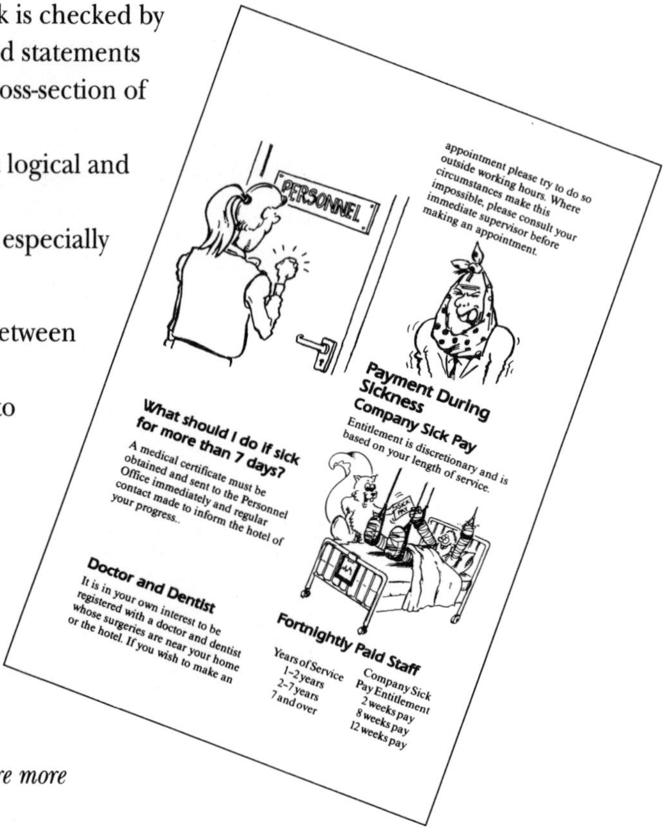

FIGURE 20 *Stakis Hotel absence policies are more memorable due to the use of cartoons.*

--- **KEY POINT** ---

For many within the industry, the employee handbook forms an important functional role related to the satisfaction of statutory requirements and the communication of relevant company information.

Hospitality operators employing small numbers of personnel may often 'buy in' their policies for inclusion into a handbook from a number of professional associations or private companies. Whatever the situation, the handbook or manual remains the most common means of informing employees of key policies and, whilst many such documents remain fairly formal, they do ensure the satisfaction of certain statutory requirements.

EMPLOYEE HANDBOOK CONTENTS

The contents of an employee handbook could, as stated above, cover the key policies or include as much information as is practicable about the company or unit.

"I know our induction handbook emphasises being informed, but do you think we've really communicated what we mean?"

OUTLINE OF EMPLOYEE HANDBOOK CONTENTS

INDEX

Section One   Background information on organisation
a) Welcome by Chairman, Director or Owner
b) Description of business and history
c) Description of Company's procedures, services or activities
d) Organisational chart
NB: The breadth of this section will depend upon the size of the Company.

Section Two   Employment matters and conditions
a) Written statement and main terms of employment
b) Wages/salaries, payment method, deductions
c) Hours of work
d) Notice periods
e) Holiday and holiday entitlements
f) Pension arrangements
g) Unpaid leave, jury service, trade union activities
h) Sickness and accident benefits
i) Termination of employment
NB: Some companies will cover a number of above items within a general contract of employment

Section Three   Policies and procedures
a) Health and Safety at Work Policy and rights and duties of both employer and employee
b) Equal opportunities policy
c) Training and development
d) Review and appraisal
e) Sickness reporting
f) Discipline and grievance policy and procedure
g) Fire precautions and food hygiene procedures
h) Accident reporting
i) Retirement policy
NB: Some of the above items may be also stated as rules

Section Four   Rules and regulations
a) Fire and safety
b) General security
c) Hygiene and dress
d) Personal conduct
e) Employee loyalty – notes on other employment
f) Receipt of personal gifts
g) Use of company facilities and vehicles
h) Personal belongings

i) Right of search

j) Attendance and absence

NB: For some companies this section may be quite detailed, whilst others prefer general statements

Section Five   Employee benefits and amenities

a) Special leave arrangements

b) Personal loan facilities

c) Bonuses and discount schemes

d) Awards

e) Share options

f) Meals on duty and accommodation

g) Use of company facilities

h) Medical, welfare and sports facilities and schemes

i) Map or plan of unit

NB: This section is increasingly becoming the first section within the handbook

OBSERVATIONS ON POSSIBLE EMPLOYEE HANDBOOK CONTENTS

The outline provided in the box identifies a fairly comprehensive list which is not exhaustive. For example, Raymond Blanc's handbook for Le Manoir aux Quat' Saisons also includes a list of well deserved awards, whilst also providing brief information about UK laws and customs for the number of overseas staff he attracts. Other companies may include translations of the handbook for employees for whom English is not their first language. Whilst a number may use the handbook as part of induction training.

———— K E Y P O I N T ————

Whatever the approach, all hospitality operators have a legal responsibility to provide written statements related to employment methods and to demonstrate that they have communicated such statements, policies and procedures to their employees.

Whilst certain of the policies are related to clarifying for employees and managers terms of reference, and not specifically required by employment legislation, their inclusion assists the reduction of conflict.

With respect to employment law, employees have rights under the following acts:

- Employment Protection (Consolidation) Act 1978
- Equal Pay Act 1970
- Health and Safety at Work Act 1974
- Sex Discrimination Act 1975
- Race Relations Act 1976
- Transfer of Undertakings (Protection of Employment) Regulations 1987
- Industrial Training Act 1982

- Wages Act 1986
- Trade Union and Labour Relations (Consolidation) Act 1992
- Trade Union Reform and Employment Rights Act 1993

In addition, there are a number of clauses to the above which focus specifically on certain aspects, including such areas as maternity leave, written contracts of employment, pay structures and time off for trade union activities.

For the purposes of this introductory text, the important factor to recognise is that there exist a number of laws governing employment aspects and that operators and managers must operate within these regulations. The effective communication of such aspects, via various means of communication including the company handbook, is an important element of HRM.

The following sections provide additional information related to equal opportunities, pay and benefits and discipline and grievance.

Summary – employee communication

Effective employee communication, then, is based upon:

- sound personnel policies, procedures and practices
- commitment from management
- involvement of all employees
- systems which facilitate two-way communication
- positive monitoring and review

With the move towards customer-focused businesses, effective employee communication forms a vital base to improved business performance.

The next section outlines the importance of equal opportunities in relation to personnel practice.

3.6 EQUAL OPPORTUNITIES AND DISCRIMINATION

The subject of equal opportunities and discrimination is often considered a difficult and contentious issue, fraught with danger for the inexperienced operator. Yet comprehensive legislation, guidelines and codes of practice exist to which effective organisations can refer. Increasingly the majority of operators recognise the value of positive equal opportunities policies and the contribution they make to sound human resource management. The three main Acts concerned with discrimination in Great Britain are:

- Equal Pay Act 1970 (as amended)
- The Sex Discrimination Act 1975 (as amended)
- The Race Relations Act 1976

Background to equal opportunities

The quality of a business's workforce is the key to the competitive edge which companies require if they are to prosper in the global market of the 1990s. A top quality workforce can only be achieved by organisations taking action to remove all barriers to employment and advancement.

SIR BRIAN COLBY, PRESIDENT, CONFEDERATION OF BRITISH INDUSTRY, EXTRACT FROM CBI PUBLICATION *DISCRIMINATE ON ABILITY 1991*

Despite the array of legislation and codes of practice which exist, the hospitality industry has, historically, had a poor reputation in connection with equal opportunities. The Commission for Racial Equality conducted a major survey in 1990–91 into the hotel industry and stated:

In spite of wide publicity given to the code of practice when it came into force in 1984, we found when we started the investigation that very little had been done by the industry to implement its recommendations ... The hotel industry has a reputation for giving low priority to personnel issues, but the almost universal disregard of the code's recommendations which we found cannot be justified, either on the grounds of inadequate personnel resources or the inappropriateness of the code for use in the industry.

The action points in the boxes below give the 'dos' and 'don'ts' for management. These come from a survey which covered investigations of 20 of the largest hotel groups, with the results from detailed questionnaires analysed; additionally 106 hotels responded to a mailed questionnaire and 98 of these requested further monitoring to evaluate their equal opportunities policies.

ACTION POINTS FOR SENIOR MANAGEMENT AT GROUP LEVEL

DO

- adopt a clear policy on equal opportunities, agreed first with the trades unions or staff associations.
- inform all staff and job applicants about the policy.
- nominate a senior member of management to take overall responsibility for policy implementation.
- issue guidelines on the action needed to implement the policy in each area of the hotel group's activities, and set clear targets for achievement.
- provide adequate resources (both staff and money
- reconsider the hotel group's corporate image in the light of its declared commitment to equality of opportunity.

DON'T

- assume that an equal opportunity policy statement will change anything.
- let the opinion of individual members of staff or groups of workers influence company policy on equal opportunity.
- leave all responsibility for implementing the equal opportunity policy to the local hotel management.

ACTION POINTS FOR PERSONNEL AND GENERAL MANAGERS IN HOTELS

DO

- find out about the ethnic minority populations in your area.
- build links with local schools, ethnic minority groups and the local Racial Equality Council.
- consider placing job advertisements in the ethnic minority press.
- make sure that colleges, Jobcentres and careers services know that you are actively encouraging ethnic minority people to apply for jobs.
- train all staff responsible for recruitment and selection.
- review job descriptions and person specifications regularly to see that they do not include criteria that are not job related.
- monitor the ethnic origins of applicants at each stage of the recruitment process, and analyse the data regularly to check that there are no barriers and to measure performance.
- if there are no ethnic minority applicants for jobs or promotion, ask why, and take action to deal with the problem.

DON'T

- use informal methods of recruitment, for example by word of mouth, if your workforce is predominantly from one racial or ethnic group.
- let a single member of staff have sole responsibility for hiring staff. Decisions should be taken by two people at least or be checked to avoid any possibility of racial bias.
- make judgements about applicants or candidates for promotion which are not based on the job requirements.
- expect change overnight.

The CRE also carried out investigation on college courses in respect of ethnic minorities representation. The survey commenced in 1988 and reported in 1991 identifying positive action points for senior management, personnel and general managers and educational establishments.

Certainly things have improved since 1988 and increasing numbers of employers are developing positive equal opportunities policies. Again it is often the larger companies who have led the way.

The three main Acts of equal pay, sex and race discrimination merge together to form the basis of a developing equal opportunities culture. Other areas are being studied closely, including religious belief, age, disability and sexual orientation. In respect of disability, the hospitality industry lags behind other industries. However there remain, of course, certain problems with particular jobs and tasks.

The Disabled Persons (Employment) Act places a duty on employers with 20 or more workers to ensure that at least 3% of their employees are registered disabled people. This is known as the Quota scheme. It is not an offence to be below quota, but where this is the case the employer has a legal duty to recruit a suitably registered disabled person.

Small numbers of hospitality operators have been very positive in this regard, including special schemes for the employment of individuals with special needs. Charitable organisations such as Mencap and Barnardo's have also assisted, including the setting up of specialist training establishments.

Other minority or underrepresented groups have also been assisted and schemes such as Project 2000, which aims to increase the number of women in managerial posts, are making positive inroads into inequality.

The hospitality industry has always possessed a diverse workforce with a rich mix of nationalities and ages. Nevertheless there remains a predominance of part-time female workers concentrated in lower paid jobs or positions. The work of the professional bodies, the CRE and Equal Opportunities Commission can only assist the industry in tackling this issue positively. However, in the end the responsibility for generating positive practice lies within the organisation itself.

Positive action is one of the many possible components of a good equal opportunities policy.

Race Relations Employment Advisory Service, *Positive Action*

Whilst many operators have developed equal opportunities policies, the pressure is for positive actions which actively promote opportunities for minority groups within the organisation.

Discrimination on the grounds of sex, race or colour is unlawful. However, it is not unlawful to encourage people who are under represented. This is known as positive action.

ACAS, *Recruitment Policies for the 1990s*

The development of equal opportunities policy and practices

A policy statement alone or statements such as 'we are an equal opportunity employer' will achieve little or nothing. They must be supported by action, by training and by publicity. Above all, the working of the programme must be audited – by monitoring.

IPM code on Equal Opportunities

When designing and implementing an equal opportunities policy, an operator needs to ensure that:

- discussions at all levels of the organisation take place encouraging the involvement of all employees in the formulation of the policy
- commitment to the policy is obtained at all levels of the organisation
- responsibility for the policy is allocated to a senior manager
- an analysis of the workforce is undertaken to establish a base line against which progress in equal opportunities can be monitored
- the policy is communicated to all employees
- regular monitoring takes place and corrective actions are identified

The Employment Department issued a Ten Point Plan for employers based upon the concept of positive actions (see below).

The final consideration is the role of the personnel and human resource specialist. They play a key role in developing and monitoring an organisation's equal opportunities policy.

However, certain problems exist for small or independent operators who lack the support of centralised personnel or human resource departments. Hopefully, the industry will move increasingly to a situation based upon discrimination on ability, backed up by positive steps to assist and encourage minority groups.

We need to make the most of the talents of all our people. The UK in the 1990s is a multi-racial society. It is also a society in which women account for nearly half of the working population. Increasingly it is being recognised that those with disabilities can make a full contribution to working life. Yet people from these groups frequently suffer unfair discrimination in employment ... Employers need actively to encourage, recruit and develop them for the skills and responsibilities which they are capable of achieving.

Employment Department, *Ten Point Plan for Employers*

Pizzaland's Equal Opportunity Statement clearly identifies its commitment to non-discriminatory practices. Within the Company's manual the policy is described in more detail in respect of responsibility, the law, recruitment, training, procedures for dealing with allegations and monitoring.

EQUAL OPPORTUNITY STATEMENT: PIZZALAND INTERNATIONAL LIMITED

1   Pizzaland International Ltd is committed to the development of policies to promote equal opportunities in employment, regardless of employees' sex, marital status, creed, colour, age, race, religion, disability, nationality or ethnic origin. The Company will adopt employment policies which provide fair and equal access for all individuals with regard to recruitment, selection, training, development and promotion opportunities.

2   Our principal objective is to recruit or promote the most suitable person for the job based on that person's performance. The recruitment selection process is designed to reach eligible candidates from all groups of people. This process will be regularly reviewed to ensure it is non-discriminatory.

3   All employees will receive induction training to ensure they have a clear understanding of the Company's policy and the consequences if found to be discriminating. A detailed policy can be found in the Management Manual. The effectiveness of this policy will be reviewed at intervals to ensure it is non-discriminatory.

Mike Ludbrook, Managing Director (January 1994)

EQUAL OPPORTUNITIES POLICY: McDONALD'S RESTAURANT

McDonald's is an equal opportunity employer, ensuring employees and job applicants are selected, trained, promoted and treated on the basis of their relevant skills, talents and performance and without reference to race, colour, nationality, ethnic origin, sex, marital status or disability. In support of this policy, McDonald's also has a policy on sexual and racial harassment.

McDonald's deplores all forms of sexual and racial harassment and seeks to ensure that the working environment is comfortable and secure for all of its employees.

The person responsible for these policies is the Company Human Resources Manager, but it is the responsibility of all employees, particularly managers and supervisors, to ensure its day-to-day practical application.

The Human Resources Department monitors the effectiveness of the Policy at regular intervals and takes such corrective action as may from time to time be necessary to ensure it is being complied with.

Employees who feel that they have been unfairly treated in any way regarding these policies are encouraged to use the remedies outlined in the Company's Crew and Employee Handbooks.

EQUAL OPPORTUNITIES GROUP

An Equal Opportunities Group was set up at the beginning of 1992 to evaluate and, where necessary, amend existing policies and procedures and to develop and monitor the implementation of positive action programmes. A report summarising the Group's progress is submitted to the Board of Directors on a regular basis.

WOMEN

- Opportunity 2000 is a campaign set up by Business in the Community and chaired by Lady Howe to increase the quality and quantity of women's participation in the workforce.
- As a company committed to equality of opportunity for all, McDonald's became an active member of the Opportunity 2000 campaign in 1992. The company's goal is to increase the percentage of women holding middle and senior management positions throughout the company by 50%.
- 30% of McDonald's junior management positions are held by women.
- In 1991, McDonald's introduced a Company Maternity Pay Policy giving employees with qualifying service an additional eight weeks full pay while on maternity leave and a Paternity Leave Policy to give men with qualifying service, five days paid paternity leave.

- A Part-Time Management Programme was introduced in 1989 to assist employees where the care of dependent children necessitates a move to part-time employment.
- A Sexual and Racial Harassment Policy will be introduced in 1993 to support the existing Equal Opportunities Policy.

DISABILITY

- McDonald's is a member of the Employers' Forum on Disability which exists to help companies to recognise, recruit and develop the careers of people with disabilities. McDonald's is committed to the Employers' Agenda on Disability and the Ten Points for Action as drawn up by the Employers' Forum on Disability.
- McDonald's restaurants, head and regional offices are all designed to allow ease of access for employees and visitors with disabilities.
- McDonald's in the Midlands has worked with the Birmingham Hotel and Catering Training Academy and The Employers' Network on Disability to provide pre-recruitment training for people with special needs. 14 of the people who have received this training have been given full-time employment with McDonald's. All of the trainees complete the Institute of Environmental Health Officers' Basic Food Hygiene Certificate.
- McDonald's approached the Greater Nottingham TEC and the Nottingham Task Force to run Special Needs Pre-Recruitment Training Courses in the East Midlands, which will commence during 1993.
- McDonald's is one of the companies to pilot the 'Disability Leave Guide' launched by Gillian Shephard in March 1993. The concept was the result of a study undertaken by the RNIB in 1990. Disability Leave is a period of time off work for a newly disabled person, or a disabled person whose condition has deteriorated, during which time their job is protected.

SEXUAL HARASSMENT

- A Sexual and Racial Harassment Policy will be introduced in 1993 to support the existing Equal Opportunities Policy statement.

DEPARTMENT OF EMPLOYMENT

Ten Point Plan for employers: equal opportunities
 1 Develop an equal opportunities policy
 2 Set an action plan including targets
 3 Provide training for all
 4 Monitor the present position and monitor progress in achieving objectives
 5 Review recruitment, selection, promotion and training procedures regularly
 6 Draw up clear and justifiable job criteria
 7 Offer pre-employment training and positive action training
 8 Consider your organisation's image
 9 Consider flexible working
10 Develop links with local community groups, organisations and schools

3.7 PAY AND BENEFIT SYSTEMS

One of the most fundamental functions of the personnel department is that of administering and controlling employees' pay. Larger companies may separate this function from personnel and training managers or human resource specialists by providing administration backup, enquiry handling and advice from a centralised function. The larger the company, the more complex the task and it is an area which has become increasingly reliant upon computerised systems. At this level, the system is concerned with data handling and processing, although the service might, as stated, provide managers and individuals with advice and assistance. Smaller companies and independent operators will also require secure systems and procedures to manage the task of paying employees.

FIGURE 21 *Everyone who works has the right to just and favourable remuneration.*

However, the element of pay and benefit is more complex than first imagined and, in respect of current human resource management tasks, includes the following:

- payroll systems, including the employer's liability for taxation and other employee contributions
- payroll costs forecasting
- pay and wage scale setting
- pension systems
- benefit and reward systems

It is the benefit and reward system which has attracted most attention over the past decade, with employers developing quite complex benefit packages. Prior to looking in more detail at this aspect, it is important to identify the basic requirements of pay systems for both employer and employee.

Basic pay and benefit requirements

EMPLOYEE

The employee has a right to receive an itemised pay statement at or before the time of payment. (Section 8–11 of Employment Protection (Consolidation) Act 1978 as amended by Employment Act 1982.) The itemised pay statement must give the following particulars:

- gross amount of wages or salary
- the amounts of any fixed deductions and the purposes for which they are made, e.g. trade union subscription
- the amounts of any variable deductions and the purposes for which they are made, e.g. income tax
- the net amount of any wages or salary payable

Note: With the advent of computerised payroll systems the pay statement will often include additional information, such as gross salary to date, tax paid to date and tax code.

Additionally, the rate of pay or agreed benefits cannot be altered without prior agreement.

EMPLOYER

The employer requires a system which manages payroll in a systematic, cost effective and secure manner. However, the payslip and written pay statement is the end of a process which includes a variety of other considerations for the employer. These include:

- deciding on the scale or basic rate of pay for individual jobs or groups of employees (*Note:* One method of identifying the rate of pay for particular jobs is a process called job evaluation, which is dealt with in Chapter 4. You may wish to read through that section and then return to this section.)
- estimating the cost of labour against forecasted business and customer demand (This is an element of manpower planning described in Chapter 2.)

- negotiating and agreeing on additions to the basic rate of pay, an element often referred to as additional benefits
- setting up procedures and rules for the payment or provision of additional benefits
- designing systems for the accurate recording and reporting of actual employee wage and benefit costs
- researching systems which may enable the employer to reduce staffing costs whilst maintaining productivity and quality
  (*Note:* This latter element has been high on the agenda of most companies for the past few years. The recession in the early 1990s saw most hospitality operators reduce staffing and introduce more flexible employment and pay packages.)

Pay, reward and benefit packages

As was indicated in the previous section on Employee Handbooks, the range of benefits for employees has increased over the last decade. The pay and reward package is increasingly made up of four components:

- basic pay
- pension package
- additional benefits available to all employees
- specific additional benefits for the individual

Pensions have become increasingly important and more companies are developing their own schemes. The Government is encouraging this trend, which the increase in people of pensionable age is pressurising. Additional benefits could include some or all of the following:

- special leave arrangement
- discounts for company or sister company facilities
- company car
- bonus schemes
- share options
- medical schemes
- welfare and sports facilities
- personal loans
- grants for individual training
- awards
- subsidised meals and accommodation

Companies may have varying levels of benefit package which increase in relation to the seniority of the position. The trend is more noticeable amongst the larger companies; however, the forecasted skill shortages of the next few decades will encourage increasing numbers of smaller companies to develop such packages.

Traditionally such additional rewards or incentives were referred to as fringe benefits and, historically, were not taxed significantly. As employers have developed more comprehensive packages, the Government, through the Inland Revenue, has sought methods of clawing back some of these additional rewards. The company car has been a particular target over the past few years.

For employers the questions to ask are:

- What level and range of wage and compensation package will I need to offer to attract and retain staff?
- What level of packages can the company afford?
- Which additional benefits will provide the most incentive to employees?

In my opinion, effective human resource management concerns itself with all aspects that motivate individuals, and incentives are part of this picture. If labour availability does decrease, as predicted, then competition for skilled labour will increase, the outcome being a rise in the basic rates of pay linked to more comprehensive compensation packages. Skilled, mobile labour will be drawn to the companies which possess attractive packages. However, the retention of such staff is linked to more complex issues, such as job satisfaction and personal security.

--- **KEY POINT** ---

Whilst wages remain as the key element in attracting employees, their motivation, productivity and retention is reliant upon a wide range of variables, the majority of which fall within the responsibilities of personnel and human resource managers.

The hospitality industry's image in the area of pay and reward has not been good and, sadly, certain areas still offer low pay, minimal benefits and long working hours. This general image is, of course, not true of the whole industry and many companies both large and small have developed positive pay and reward packages. Additionally, it is important to understand how the nature of the industry with its shift patterns, accommodation and uniform provision and wide range of working patterns creates particular problems in relation to identifying rates of pay and reward packages.

Regular surveys on wages by professional bodies provide evidence of the complexity of reward and benefits. Figures 22–25 show statistics gleaned by Touche Ross for the HCIMA wages and benefits survey.

Whilst such surveys can report on general and specific situations, they can also indirectly affect the approach by companies to wage rates. The fundamental aspect to recognise is that whatever the complexities of pay and benefits, organisations require effective systems.

Pay is one of the key factors affecting relationships at work. The level and distribution of pay and benefits are an integral part of industrial relations and can have a considerable effect, for good or ill, on both the efficient running of an enterprise and management/employee relations. It is therefore important that organisations develop payment systems which are right for them and which reward employees equitably for the work they perform.

ACAS, *Introduction to Payment Systems*

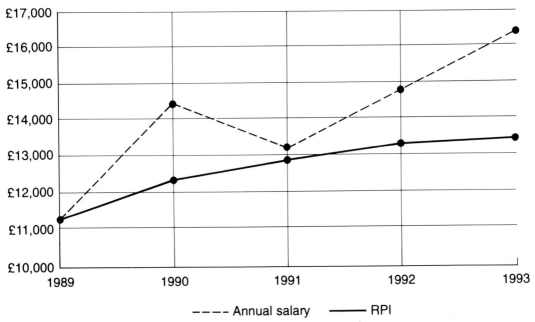

FIGURE 22 *Live-out management salaries, 1989–93, compared to Retail Price Index (Source Touche Ross/HCIMA,* Pay and Benefits in the Hospitality Industry 1993).

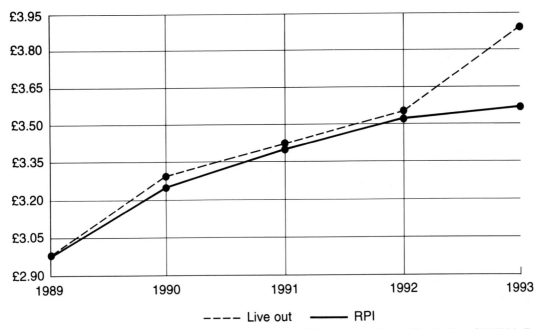

FIGURE 23 *Non-salaried staff, 1989–93, compared to Retail Price Index (Source Touche Ross/HCIMA,* Pay and Benefits in the Hospitality Industry 1993).

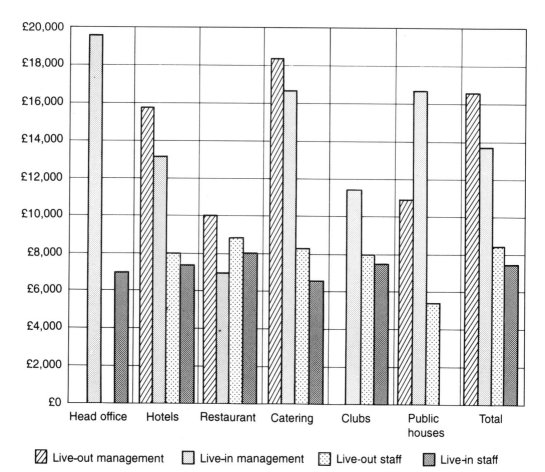

FIGURE 24 *Sector comparison, salaried employees (Source Touche Ross/HCIMA,* Pay and Benefits in the Hospitality Industry 1993).

The company or business will need to consider the internal and external factors which will affect and define a possible system. Legislation sets basic parameters in respect of consultation with employees or employee representatives on such aspects as employees' rights in respect of agreed rates, equality of pay and reward, itemised pay statements, transfer of ownership, pension, sickness and maternity pay.

--- KEY POINT ---

Regardless of the type of pay system, employers have to adhere to the various employment acts and regulations related to pay and rewards.

Alongside these considerations are such factors as the availability of labour and accepted rates of pay. Hospitality operators have traditionally faced competition for skilled labour, and pay and reward packages need to be designed with this in mind. Examples of various companies'

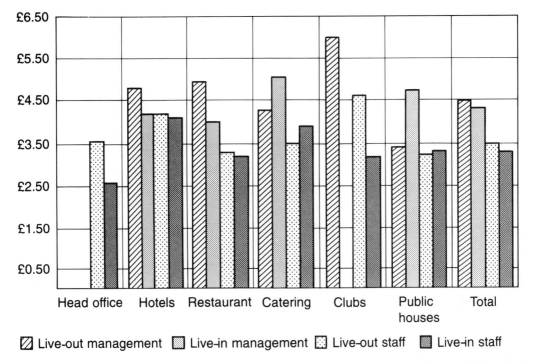

FIGURE 25 *Sector comparison, non-salaried employees (Source Touche Ross/HCIMA,* Pay and Benefits in the Hospitality Industry 1993).

approach to employment packages are provided throughout the text, although a company's ability to pay is, of course, dependent upon its own performance and profitability.

As well as analyses of such policy considerations, there is also the need to involve employees wherever possible in the design of the system. At this stage the employer will want to:

- define and set standard wage rates for specific jobs and positions
- agree the range of other reward and incentive policies

Whether the company is setting up a system from scratch or revising an existing system, it has to ensure that it has the necessary administration systems and resources to allow for effective management and control. Employees involved in handling the system will require training (or retraining) and all employees will require written information on the system and their specific rights within it. Lastly, the system requires constant monitoring and evaluation to ensure that policies and procedures are working appropriately.

As stated, the majority of employers are moving towards elements of incentive pay and reward systems, whilst retaining a base of basic wage rate systems. There exist advantages and disadvantages to both types of system.

BASIC WAGE RATE SYSTEMS

Such systems set a rate for a particular period and the rate is set for certain levels or grades of staff. Such pay is usually set for an hourly rate, weekly wage or annual salary, with minor

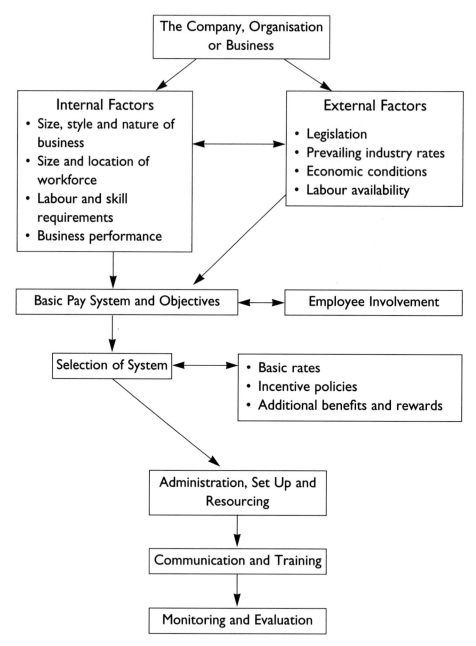

FIGURE 26 *Developing a pay and benefits system.*

differentials in respect of age, qualifications and length of service. Being less complex than incentive systems, they are generally easier to administer, more easily understood by employees and allow for more accurate forecasting of labour costs.

However, due to their standardisation, they do little in themselves to provide additional incentive and do not reward individuals who work above the standard required. The recognition of this factor has led many hospitality operators to implement more flexible incentive-type systems.

INCENTIVE PAY SYSTEMS

There are a wide variety of approaches under such systems, including:

- *payment by results* (PBR) or *performance-related pay* (PRP)
- *merit rating*, where an individual employee's pay is linked to the rating or assessment of personal qualities
- *skill pay*, where individuals are paid set levels in respect of reaching predetermined competence in specific tasks and responsibilities
- *appraisal-related pay*, where an individual's pay is reviewed against predetermined objectives
- *group* or *unit performance-related pay*
- *profit sharing* or *share schemes*
- *flexible pay systems*, where individual employees opt for their own remuneration package made up of a variety of benefits, such as bonus, pension, leave entitlement, car and private health care

Similar to all other personnel policies and procedures, pay and benefit systems require communicating to employees. This communication is central to the whole area of human resource management and was detailed earlier in this chapter.

3.8 EMPLOYMENT RULES, DISCIPLINE, GRIEVANCE AND DISMISSAL

Employment rules

Within the base of personnel procedures and practices, there is the need for rules which set standards of conduct at work and make clear to employees what is expected of them. Such workplace rules and regulations form part of the contract between employer and employee and provide protection for both parties.

This section will provide you with an overview of the necessity for such employment procedures, identify the scope and range of rules, the benefits to the organisation, the employee and the customer and cover the key elements of discipline and grievance.

--- **KEY POINT** ---

Under the Employment Protection Act 1989 employers with over 20 employees are required to provide written details of disciplinary and conduct rules which apply to their company or business.

As was identified in the section on company handbooks, such rules are commonly stated covering the full range of conduct which applies to a particular company. Whatever the type of company or business, rules will exist covering the following:

- time keeping
- absence

- health and safety
- use of company facilities, e.g. accommodation, telephones
- discrimination
- general conduct
- disclosure of company information
- security
- employee loyalty
- right of search
- discipline and grievance
- receipt of personal gifts

As stated the normal practice is for such rules to be included in the employee handbook, with certain aspects being covered in greater detail during induction.

The benefits of rules and regulations

Benefits include:

- setting of standards of conduct at work and clarification of what is expected of employees
- adherence to legislation providing protection for both employer and employee
- allowance for the creation of procedures which deal with misconduct or unfair treatment
- creation of personnel procedures and practices which are not discriminatory

Of course, companies have a certain degree of freedom to set their own rules; however, employment legislation provides protection for employees in situations where unfair treatment could or has occurred. Codes of practice exist which provide guidelines for employers; for example, various Employment Acts have empowered ACAS to issue codes of practice containing guidance on rules and regulations, especially those elements covering disciplinary practice and procedures. Additionally, ACAS oversees an industrial tribunal system, set up to legislate in individual and collective disputes. (This system will be covered later in this section.)

Therefore, there is considerable pressure on employers to set fair rules of employee conduct and provide them in a written form to all employees. Common sense also dictates that all organisations require rules or standards to facilitate the effective and fair treatment of personnel.

Each organisation must decide what procedures and practices best suit its circumstances. It is management's responsibility to ensure that procedures and practices are effective, fair, well understood and consistently applied.

ACAS, *Discipline at Work*

Whilst the range and scope of rules and standards will vary, certain key elements are covered by legislation. These include:

- discipline and grievance
- health and safety at work
- employment of minors
- discrimination, e.g. sex, gender and race
- trade union activities
- industrial actions
- redundancy and transfer of undertakings
- dismissal
- pay

For employers and human resource specialists the key requirement is to ensure that personnel procedures and practices adhere to all aspects of employment legislation. In respect of additional rules, the employer has a duty to ensure that they are fair and appropriate. Employers use two main documents to advise employees of rules – the contract of employment and the company handbook.

THE CONTRACT OF EMPLOYMENT

The Employment Protection (Consolidation) Act of 1978 requires employers to provide employees with a written statement of the main terms and conditions of employment. This contract should contain the following:

- employer's name
- employee's name
- date employment began
- details of any previous employment which counts as part of employee's continuing period of employment
- job title
- amount of pay (or method of calculation) and interval between payments
- hours of work
- holiday pay and entitlement
- sickness and sick pay arrangements
- pension
- notice periods
- notes on disciplinary rules, specifying to whom employees can apply if they are dissatisfied with a disciplinary decision
- notes on grievance procedures
- whether a contracting out certificate is in force

Whilst certain categories of employees are excluded from the legal requirement to receive a written contract, it is good personnel practice to issue all employees with such a document. For casual or part-time workers undertaking under 12 hours per week, such contracts are not required; however, as legislation alters, I would argue that such employees should receive written statements.

—————————————————— KEY POINT ——————————————————

A contract exists as soon as an employee accepts an employer's terms and conditions of employment which may be, in the first instance, verbal.

For larger companies the common practice is to use a standard contract with the specific terms and conditions, e.g. pay, job title, applicable to the employee inserted. Good practice also dictates:

- the completion of contract prior to start of employment at the appointment stage
- the signing of contract by employee, with both the employer and employee retaining a copy
- the storage of signed contract within the individual's personal file

One aspect is that the contract of employment is not a full description of the job, its tasks and responsibilities. This is an area which often creates confusion and conflict. Job descriptions are explained in detail in Chapter 4. The key elements to consider at this stage are:

1   The contract must set out the main terms and conditions, including certain statutory rules and regulations related to the employment.
2   The job description cannot alter the terms and conditions set out in the contract of employment.
3   The contract of employment cannot be altered significantly without discussion between employer and employee, either on an individual or collective basis.
4   A contract of employment may be ended by mutual agreement or by employer or employee giving the required notice of termination.

Note: The dismissal of employees is dealt with later in this section.

Sadly, whilst a considerable amount of legislation and codes of practice exist related to terms and conditions of employment, rules and contracts of employment, significant numbers of employers fail to recognise their importance in maintaining positive personnel management.

Additionally, due to the complexity of legislation, employers may face prosecution due to their lack of understanding or interpretation of employment laws. (The section on The Industrial Tribunal System provides more detail of this later in this chapter.)

—————————————————— KEY POINT ——————————————————

In respect of rules and regulations, the employer commonly relies on two documents, the contract of employment and the company handbook. These provide both employer and employee with guidelines and a framework by which to work.

Discipline, grievance and dismissal

You will find that a considerable amount of legislation, guidelines and codes of practice exist on this subject. Both the Employment Department and ACAS produce detailed booklets on the design, implementation and operation of such procedures.

DISCIPLINARY PROCEDURES

Such procedures assist both employer and employee by:

- setting out the rules and standards which apply
- encouraging employees to achieve and maintain standards of behaviour and competence
- helping to ensure that disciplinary offences are dealt with fairly and consistently

The guidelines available provide sound advice to employers on all aspects of discipline, the main areas being:

- drawing up of rules and procedures (design and compilation)
- communication to employees
- training of those responsible
- handling of disciplinary matters
- employee counselling
- holding a disciplinary interview
- dealing with the outcome of disciplinary cases
- dismissal or suspension
- appeals

Additionally, companies may possess confidential briefing notes on dealing with industrial disputes and individual industrial tribunal cases. This is quite reasonable if it concentrates on providing managers and personnel specialists with more detailed guidelines for dealing with disciplinary, grievance and dismissal matters.

Key aspects of discipline procedures are:

1 They should be written down and clearly communicated.
2 The procedures themselves should be non-discriminatory.
3 The procedures should be regularly checked and reviewed.
4 Managers and supervisors involved in the direct handling of disciplinary matters should be provided with appropriate training.
5 The handling of disciplinary matters must follow the laid-down procedures.
6 Consideration should be given to the provision of counselling for employees with special circumstances.
7 The holding of a disciplinary interview is a stressful time for all concerned; the experienced manager or personnel specialist will seek to minimise the stress and potential conflict by adhering to procedures and conducting the interview in a fair and measured manner.
8 Deciding on the outcome of disciplinary cases is often problematical and many employers build in consideration time, unless the disciplinary case is one of gross misconduct.
9 Excluding cases where summary dismissal is allowable, there exists a variety of outcomes and all should be considered in each case.
10 There is a right of appeal and the procedures should clearly state how the employee undertakes such an appeal.

─────────────── KEY POINT ───────────────

The job of personnel specialists, managers and supervisors with responsibility for staff is to create personnel practices which minimise the need to resort to more formalised systems of discipline.

The accepted practice for discipline handling is to work through a four stage procedure:

- Stage 1: Oral (verbal) warning
  Where conduct or performance does not meet required standards, the employee is given a formal oral warning. Notes should be kept on the individual's personnel file.
- Stage 2: Written warning
  If the offence is a serious one, or if after an oral warning a further offence occurs, a written warning will be given. This will detail complaint, corrective action and timescale required, and employee will be advised on appeal procedure. Again records will be kept on file.
- Stage 3: Final written warning and suspension
  If the offence is serious enough or if employee is still performing unsatisfactorily, then a final written warning is given to the employee. Alternatively, the employee may be suspended for a maximum of five working days.
- Stage 4: Dismissal
  If conduct or performance is still unsatisfactory, dismissal will normally result.

Usually this is dealt with by a senior manager or personnel manager and should, of course, adhere to the legislation governing fair and unfair dismissal.

The one exclusion to the above is where a case of gross misconduct occurs and organisations need to state what constitutes gross misconduct in the written statements on discipline. In such cases the employee can be suspended from duty on full pay for no more than five working days, during which time the company investigates the alleged offence. If the investigation establishes a case of gross misconduct, then the employee can be summarily dismissed without notice or payment in lieu of notice.

CONDUCTING A DISCIPLINARY INTERVIEW

1 *Preparing for interview*
With such interviews, the key aspects are:

- to possess procedures which all are aware of and understand
- for the manager to collect, objectively, the facts related to the case
- to inform the employee of the complaint and the procedure to be followed

2 *The interview*
At the interview:

- the manager should introduce those present and explain why they are there
- an explanation of the purpose of the interview should be given and how the interview will be conducted
- a statement of the complaint should be provided

- the employee should be given the right to reply, ask questions, present evidence and call witnesses
- once information has been collected, a general summary should be given to allow for checking of all details
- the interview should be adjourned for an objective consideration to take place; at this stage the employee should be advised of the procedure and when a decision will be reached

3 *Following the interview*

At this point:

- the decision reached should be noted and the employee advised, either by written letter or at another interview
- the decision will need to be recorded and employee advised on any right of appeal
- a written statement should be sent to employee which should specify:
  - nature of misconduct
  - any period of time for improvement and improvement required
  - the disciplinary penalty
  - likely consequences of further misconduct
  - timescale for lodging an appeal and how it should be made

Again, the personnel specialist's role is to minimise the need to move through formalised disciplinary procedures. However, in certain situations the positive handling of disciplinary matters can provide the employee with the opportunity to re-establish his/her position. Counselling, guidance and training can also assist and dismissal should be a last resort. Experienced managers and personnel specialists will recognise that at times dismissal is the only possible outcome and, whilst difficult, is part of their responsibilities in managing people.

GRIEVANCE

Employers also have to ensure that procedures exist for employees with grievances concerning their employment. Procedures should exist which allow individuals or groups of employees to raise questions related to grievances they may have with their employer. Within the rules and terms and conditions of employment the procedure for grievance handling must be stated or a note provided referring employees to a separate document. For the employer and employee the inclusion of a grievance procedure is just as important as the procedure for discipline. Basically the procedure should state:

- scope and range of procedure
- name and position of individual within the organisation to whom a complaint can be made
- method for making a complaint
- procedure for handling a complaint
- right of appeal

For an example of grievance procedure see the box below. Again the emphasis should be to create and use personnel procedures and practices which minimise the need for grievance complaints and disputes.

GRIEVANCES

The Company recognises that from time to time employees may wish to seek redress from grievances relating to their employment. In this respect the Company's policy is to encourage free communication between employees and their Managers.

The Grievance Procedure exists to protect your interests. Its purpose is to ensure, as far as possible, that any work-related grievance you may have is given a fair hearing.

Any grievances which you have should initially be discussed with your immediate Manager who should resolve the matter as soon as is reasonably practical. Should you be dissatisfied with the decision, you may refer the grievance in writing to your next most senior Manager whose decision shall be final.

You may be accompanied at any stage of the procedure by a fellow employee of your choice, who may act as your representative and speak on your behalf.

TM Group

DISMISSAL OF EMPLOYEES

The last element to describe is that of the dismissal of employees. This aspect is covered by various pieces of legislation and disputes within this area are common. The key aspects to consider are:

- legislation exists which governs the situations and manner in which employees can be dismissed
- whilst dismissal is allowable, the employer must ensure that dismissal has been fair
- employees have the right to challenge a decision of dismissal
- the employee has the right to a minimum period of notice of termination of employment (excluding accepted cases of gross misconduct)

Dismissal occurs when:

- employee's fixed term contract expires and is not renewed
- employer does not allow an employee, who has qualified for reinstatement, to return after pregnancy
- the employer has dismissed the employee for reasons related to conduct or performance
- the employee has reason to resign because of certain actions or conduct of the employer (known as constructive dismissal)

For an employer to dismiss an employee fairly, there must be a valid reason for the employee's dismissal. The employer must also act fairly in treating that reason as sufficient for causing the dismissal of the employee.

Legislation covering dismissal lists five types of reasons which can justify dismissal:

- conduct
- capability
- redundancy

- a statutory requirement
- some other substantial reason

With reference to unfair dismissal there are a number of specific situations where dismissal will be automatically considered unfair, including trade union membership, pregnancy and during the transfer of an undertaking (one company taking over another). Additionally, issues relating to dismissal through discrimination, e.g. on the grounds of sex, race or disability will also be considered unfair.

Employee rights and appeals

For the employee there are a variety of rights to appeal against dismissal, including the use of an industrial tribunal.

INDUSTRIAL TRIBUNAL SYSTEM

This system deals with applications covering a wide range of employment rights. Reported cases across all industry sectors are currently around 70,000 annually. Within the system, the Advisory Conciliation and Arbitration Service (ACAS) operates as a statutory body. Whilst the terms of reference for ACAS have been under consideration, the service continues to provide both arbitration and advisory facilities to industry and individual employees.

Where an individual or group of employees has a dispute or consider themselves unfairly treated, they can make an application to regional industrial tribunal offices. ACAS has a duty to promote a settlement, by conciliation, without the need for a full tribunal. To reach a tribunal hearing an application will be assessed for its likelihood of success. The outcome of any particular case is generally one of the following:

- case withdrawn by applicant
- case settled before a tribunal is held
- case goes to a full tribunal and is dismissed
- case goes to a full tribunal and is upheld

The 1992 Survey of Industrial Tribunal applications conducted by the Social and Community Planning Research and the Employment Department, reported on a sample of applications between April 1990 and March 1991, conducting interviews with 1900 employers and 537 individuals. This comprehensive survey reported on a variety of factors including outcome of cases, the parties' experience at the tribunal hearings and experiences subsequent to the case.

The employer characteristics involved had a median size of 35 employees. In terms of union recognition, around six out of ten did not recognise unions and less than half had a personnel department.

Applicants median age was just over 39 years with two thirds being male and nearly nine out of ten white. Costs in respect of time spent, fees and compensation to the employer was nearly £1500 per case. For the applicant the median cost was £50. Two thirds of employers felt the outcome in their case was fair and over half of the applicants thought the outcome in their case was unfair.

Whilst the statistics offered above are only a summary of the survey, analysis of the full data would indicate messages for business in relation to its personnel and HRM policies and procedures. Catering was identified as one of the industrial sectors with the highest percentage of brought cases. Hospitality operators, therefore, may find themselves involved in such cases and there are a variety of forms of assistance available to them. Larger companies use their legal or personnel department to represent them, or take external legal advice. Smaller companies or operators may often pay an annual fee to a legal advisory service. Additionally, there exists a variety of reference manuals which provide information and advice on employment matters, which are updated regularly to subscribers. Some of these are specifically targeted at the hospitality industry.

ACAS, amongst other bodies, provides a positive advisory and conciliation service. ACAS itself issues an excellent series of 18 advisory leaflets covering such aspects as employing people, personnel records, recruitment and selection, induction, employee appraisals and employment policies. Additionally, via the HMSO, they publish various codes of practice, including disciplinary practices and trade union matters.

For the smaller operator such practical information can be extremely useful. For instance, in cases of dispute the guidelines of employment practices can assist an inexperienced operator to improve personnel and HRM practices.

For both hospitality employer and employee it can be seen that there are available legal and advisory services to assist in cases of dispute and the promotion of positive working practices. The need for such facilities are both recognisable, even though regrettable, yet hospitality operators can benefit from legal systems which:

- provide a baseline on which to set personnel policies and standards
- allow the objective settlement of complex cases
- provide some protection against unfair claims

For the employee the benefits can be identified as:

- providing legal protection against unfair or discriminatory practices
- allowing for various forms of compensation
- reducing the financial cost of bringing an application

There is no doubting the need for employers to have rules and procedures, without which neither employer or employee have guidelines or standards by which to work. The most important element to consider is that effective organisations attempt to create a supportive culture where the emphasis is on team work and conflicts and disputes are kept to a minimum. The nature of the hospitality industry with its often long hours and demanding work creates the need for positive personnel procedures and practices.

3.9 SUMMARY AND KEY POINTS

This chapter has provided you with an outline of the importance of personnel policies in respect of effective and positive human resource management. Organisations possessing sound personnel policies are best placed to deal with the multitude of problems and challenges related to managing the workforce.

Whilst legislation has and will continue to affect personnel policies, so too will the effects of competition, increasing employee involvement and the continuing lack of skilled staff. Hospitality operators are increasingly investing both time and resources in developing policies which seek to retain high quality employees and provide improved flexibility for both employer and employee. However, the industry still has a long way to go if it is to match other industries. Split shifts, poor working conditions and low pay still dominate in certain sectors of the hospitality industry.

To be truly effective, the formulation of policy must be based on a degree of employee participation and policies must be matched by a commitment to positive practice. Such commitment should be clearly demonstrated by the directors, senior management, managers, personnel specialist or owner and is an element of HRM that has to be continuously monitored and evaluated.

Whether the operator uses personnel policies adapted from standardised documents or develops its own, the importance of ensuring such policies and procedures provide protection for both employer and employee cannot be overstated. Such protection forms the base of the contract between both parties and creates the framework for other agreements and practices. Employers will seek to develop personnel practices which are appropriate to their particular situation and the trend is towards ones which provide for increased employee participation. Such participation has been strengthened by the slight improvement in additional employee benefits.

KEY POINTS

- All organisations require a base of sound, appropriate and effective personnel policies
- The primary function of personnel policies is to provide protection for both employer and employee
- The secondary function of personnel policies is to provide a base on which to develop employment practices appropriate to the organisation, its style and culture
- The development of policies, procedures and practices is becoming increasingly centred on employee involvement and participation
- Whilst overall policies may be set by the organisation, the practice is dependent upon the knowledge and skills of supervisors, heads of department and managers
- The growth and change of legislation has and will continue to have a considerable effect on employment policy formulation

QUESTIONS

1   Explain the importance of basic personnel policies and procedures in respect of managing the workforce.
2   Explain the function of the employee handbook in relation to creating a partnership between the employer and employee.
3   List and explain the stages for designing, implementing and monitoring a personnel policy.
4   What assistance is available for an independent hospitality operator in setting up basic personnel policies and procedures?
5   With the growth of employment legislation and the move towards harmonisation of policies throughout the EEC, identify what type of personnel policies and practices hospitality operators will require in the future.
6   Consider and discuss the degree to which employees can be involved in the design of policies and procedures.
7   Identify the methods by which large multi-site companies can ensure personnel policies and practices are both communicated and followed.
8   Using reference to other sources of information (including ACAS), identify the importance and benefits to a company of possessing a well documented grievance and discipline system.

CHAPTER 4

RECRUITMENT AND SELECTION

———

We had a total of 49 applicants for the post of Personnel Manager, eight were invited for interview and two shortlisted. We advertised in a national newspaper and a trade journal. The cost of this exercise was in the region of £1150.

CALEDONIAN HOTEL, EDINBURGH

The enjoyment and enthusiasm of our employees rubs off on our guests to create the unique 'Friday's' atmosphere. But it is not easy being genuinely friendly and spontaneous when you are working at full tilt and have 101 things to remember. So we recruit our people for their attitude and approach to teamwork, not for traditional restaurant skills.

TGI FRIDAY'S EMPLOYMENT BROCHURE

Recruiting the right people is vital to the success of our business. Good recruitment and selection is the first step towards achieving our overall objectives and we need, therefore, to be consistent and professional in our approach.

ALAN REID, PERSONNEL & TRAINING EXECUTIVE, HAVEN WARNER

4.1 AIMS AND OBJECTIVES

By studying this section, reviewing key points, completing the questions, exercises and the assignment, you will be able to:

1 have an understanding of the key stages which form the recruitment and selection process;
2 understand the use of job evaluation;
3 describe the use and benefits of job specifications, job descriptions and person specifications;
4 list the various methods of advertising job vacancies;
5 list the various methods for shortlisting and interviewing job applicants;
6 compare various approaches to the appointment, induction and review of personnel.

4.2 INTRODUCTION

For any hospitality operator a critical success factor is to recruit and select staff appropriate to the present and future needs of the organisation. The process itself contains a variety of stages which are common to all businesses. Following job evaluation and specification, the position needs to be advertised and applicants shortlisted for interview. Interviewing techniques are important in order to appoint the best person for the job. Following appointment, the employee will need induction.

4.3 KEY ELEMENTS OF RECRUITMENT AND SELECTION

This is a process on which a considerable amount of research has been completed and a large number of books written. For the purposes of this text it will be useful to separate the process into what I see as its four key stages:

- *Stage 1: Planning the manpower needs*
  This element is covered in Chapter 2.
- *Stage 2: Identifying specific needs*
  This stage is concerned with identifying the purpose, characteristics, tasks and responsibilities of specific jobs or work roles. The operator uses job evaluation, task analysis methods and possibly develops more detailed job descriptions, job specifications and person specifications.
- *Stage 3: Selection and appointment*
  This stage is concerned with elements covering advertising, shortlisting, interviewing, selection and appointment of personnel.
- *Stage 4: Induction and review*
  This stage is concerned with fitting an employee into a vacancy or new position and covers the elements of organisational and job induction, probation and review.

Separating the recruitment and selection process into these four key stages, makes it possible to identify clearly the specific aims of each stage.

Naturally organisations will differ in their approach to these four key stages and the time they invest will relate to the size, nature and style of the business, in addition to the nature of the vacancy.

ELEMENTS OF THE RECRUITMENT AND SELECTION PROCESS

- manpower planning and strategy
- job/task evaluation and analysis
- determination of requirements
- job specification
- job description
- person specification

- advertising
- receipt of applications
- initial shortlisting
- interview
- selection
- offer of employment
- appointment
- induction
- probationary period and review
- consolidation and progression

As you can see in the box there are specific elements of the recruitment and selection process, all of which require particular skills and knowledge on behalf of the individual or organisation.

The IPM recruitment code

Similar to other IPM codes of practice, the code on recruitment and selection is detailed and logical, representing not only a common sense business approach, but one that emphasises equality of opportunity and professionalism. The code covers the areas of the role of recruitment, equality of opportunity, job and person specifications, application forms and processes, advertising, selection techniques, interviewing, procedures prior to and during interviews, use of references, medical examinations and documentation. It also identifies the business and professional courtesies which should be shown to the applicants.

In explaining the role of recruitment, the IPM states the following:

Recruitment plays a fundamental and crucial role in the functioning and development of an organisation. Successful recruitment is an important factor in contributing to the organisation's ability to retain its employees.

IPM Codes of Practice

For the employer, personnel officer, owner or manager there exist several basic considerations relating to the methods and processes they adopt. The critical success factor of recruitment and selection has already been identified: 'to recruit, select and appoint staff appropriate to the present and future needs of the organisation'. Other key considerations are:

- selection and use of methods appropriate to the organisation or business
- ensuring that procedures and priorities are fair and legal
- ensuring that staff involved in the selection process possess the necessary skills and knowledge
- the cost in terms of finance, time and other resources

In today's competitive market, no hospitality operator can afford to appoint inappropriate staff. The possible effects of poor recruitment and selection for the organisation are:

- prosecution under employment legislation, e.g. equal opportunities or race discrimination
- wrong individual selected who lacks the skills and knowledge to undertake the job
- dissatisfied customers receiving poor service from inappropriate staff
- demoralised staff who, working either under or alongside an ineffective employee, face increased problems and workload
- loss of finances due to incorrect handling or management by the individual appointed
- damage to property or equipment through incorrect handling by employee
- increased costs due to replacement of appointed individual

Whilst incorrect appointments at the operative or junior level may only result in minor problems, consider the risks involved when recruiting and selecting senior personnel who may control large budgets or expensive premises.

Additionally, there exists a risk to the applicant in poor selection. The selection process should attempt to match an individual to a position or work role. Appointed or promoted to a job over and above their skills and knowledge, an individual will struggle, possibly perform badly and be unable to meet the tasks of the particular position. Demotivated and unsure such an individual is unlikely to assist the organisation. There are organisations and businesses which approach recruitment and selection in an ad hoc way, due either to inexperience or time constraints. If lucky, such organisations can appoint successfully.

You have studied the various stages of initial manpower planning; following this the employer should seek to further define the requirements of specific positions – a process known as job evaluation.

RECRUITMENT AND SELECTION INTERVIEWING SKILLS AND PERSONNEL PRACTICE

OBJECTIVES

- To identify the key stages in the recruitment process.
- To be able to write a job description and a person specification.
- To practice the skills of recruitment interviewing.
- To learn how to assess the evidence collected during the interview.
- To understand the Acts affecting employment.
- To identify the key stages in discipline, grievance and appeals procedures.
- To examine the differences between and implications of fair, unfair and wrongful dismissals.
- To conduct a disciplinary interview.
- To develop personal action plans for development of recruitment techniques.

DURATION

$3\frac{1}{2}$ days, and a follow-up interview.

Haven Leisure

4.4 JOB EVALUATION

The second main element identified in the recruitment and selection process focuses on the need to identify characteristics and demands of specific jobs or work roles. This element is often confused with the process of identifying person specifications or job descriptions. Whilst the system commonly referred to as job evaluation is not without its critics and its use has declined over the past decade, it still holds relevance for a high percentage of hospitality operators.

Basically job evaluation is concerned with assessing similar or individual jobs or work roles in respect of their relative contribution to an organisation. There exist several definitions of this process; for the HRM specialist the importance of definitions becomes overshadowed by the need to understand and use effective personnel practices.

Consider the explanation in the box below.

The aim of job evaluation is to provide a systematic and consistent approach to defining the relative worth of jobs within a workplace, single plant or multiple site organisation. It is a process whereby jobs are placed in a rank order according to the demands placed upon the job holder. It, therefore, provides a basis for a fair and orderly grading structure.

ACAS Advisory Booklet

To summarise, job evaluation is concerned with establishing the relative worth of a job and assisting the setting of pay scales within an organisation for either specific jobs or particular grades of staff. Naturally other factors have to be considered when setting pay scales and for organisations who have developed manpower plans and strategies the actual cost of labour forms a major part of the planning cycle.

Job evaluation needs to be considered alongside the other factors which affect the setting of pay scales. The operator will have to consider, amongst other factors, the following:

- availability of and competition for skilled labour
- prevailing economic climate and demand for its services
- economic performance of the organisation and ability to pay at appropriate levels
- the relative demands and responsibilities of particular jobs or work roles
- legislation which affects the equality of pay between groups, individuals or sexes
- the scale or range of benefits associated with particular jobs
- the scale of hardship or risk associated with particular jobs
- regional variances in accepted pay scales

For hospitality operators with small numbers of employees the task of setting appropriate scales is minimal; for large national multi-site companies with thousands of employees undertaking a variety of similar tasks the problem becomes more complex.

Job evaluation systems can thus assist employers in overcoming some of these challenges and their main benefits exist in assisting organisations to set reasonable and comparable pay scales which decrease the possibility of disputes and grievances related to pay.

Types of job evaluation schemes

Whilst opinions differ on the various schemes they are usually separated into two ranges: non-analytical and analytical.

NON-ANALYTICAL SCHEMES

These schemes tend to concentrate on the perceived worth or merits of particular jobs and place them in a form of ranking or hierarchical order. They are more simple to undertake and are more appropriate to organisations with either small numbers of employees or limited types of jobs.

- *Job ranking*: each job is identified by its basic title or perceived worth and then placed in a ranked order; pay and benefits are then awarded to jobs or individuals in respect of where they are placed in the hierarchy
- *Job classification*: overall grades of jobs are identified and specific definitions of the grades produced; key jobs are then evaluated to both validate the definitions and to provide benchmarks for other jobs to be judged against

ANALYTICAL SCHEMES

Here more complex analyses are undertaken with a variety of methods used. The organisation may look at a number of variables which make up the specific characteristics of a particular job.

- *Points rating*: this scheme attempts to break down jobs into a number of factors, such as skills and responsibilities, and with more complex schemes other factors, such as dexterity, decision making, time demands and necessary attributes are included; points are awarded for each factor according to pre-set scales and the total points decide a job's place in the ranking order

Obviously the more complex the scheme the more the need for accurate assessment and ranking and such schemes can be both time consuming and costly to implement.

For organisations with strong employee representative committees, the process can be more effective when undertaken as a participatory exercise; however, the hospitality industry consists predominately of small to medium businesses where such bodies do not exist in significant numbers.

──────────────────────── **KEY POINT** ────────────────────────

Where such employee organisations do exist or where organisations possess large numbers of employees undertaking similar jobs, any alteration to pay scales without either consultation or use of an effective system will possibly lead to major disputes and significant reduction in staff morale.

Accepting that there exist many problems with job evaluation schemes, there are some clearly identifiable benefits which include aspects unrelated to the actual rates of pay or grading of jobs.

Additional benefits of job evaluation schemes

The use of such schemes can provide the operator with the opportunity to:

- review the particular demands of jobs and roles in respect of skills and training required
- review existing personnel policies and procedures in light of changing work practices and personnel requirements
- identify potential problems related to the recruitment and selection of personnel in respect of pay and benefits
- ensure that pay and benefits are offered on an equal basis thereby reducing the possibility of legal cases in respect of legislation
- prevent disputes between staff related to pay and benefits
- assist the identification of appropriate and accurate job descriptions and person specifications

Whilst different methods do exist, job evaluation tends to be used within the larger companies such as contract caterers, public health caterers, hotel and restaurant chains. With the much debated abolition of the Wages Council in 1993, the industry faced several problems concerning wage scales, including the effects of the recession in the late 1980s and early 1990s, increased competition and lack of skilled labour. The introduction of multi-skilling worker flexibility, team working and technological change all affected pay scales and will for some time in the future.

The restructuring of many of the larger hospitality operators in the late 1980s and early 1990s saw reductions in pay scales as jobs were de-skilled. Companies such as Forte rebranded their hotel division and particular units required either higher or lower skill levels. Job evaluation could be used in such circumstances to re-establish comparable pay rates linked to alterations in the demands of specific jobs.

The hospitality industry has had a reputation for generally low rates of pay when compared to other industries, especially in respect of the so-called antisocial hours. However, this type of generalisation is often not supported by investigation. General pay rates rose over inflation in the years 1992 and 1993.

The hospitality industry has often been criticised for its rate of pay related to the nature of the job and related hours and conditions. Certainly it can be recognised that in general pay scales have been low in relation to other industries. However, many studies have identified that the actual rate of pay as a source of motivation is often secondary to factors such as job satisfaction. Whilst pay scales generally remained static in the late 1980s and early 1990s, they increased in 1991 and 1992 (see Figures 22 and 23, page 135).

Job evaluation schemes can and do assist the hospitality operator in a variety of ways. With the ending of the Wages Council in 1993 and with the effects of the recession and growth in competition, the industry faces some interesting challenges in respect of setting pay scales. The tendency during the 1980s was to move towards competitive market rates. The next decade may see a slight reversal in this trend and other types of job evaluation schemes may appear, which will assist both small and large hospitality businesses in attracting and retaining appropriate levels of staff. There is also a specific role in identifying the necessary skills, demands and responsibilities of a job, a factor which assists the next stage in the recruitment and selection process.

4.5 JOB SPECIFICATIONS AND DESCRIPTIONS

One aspect that has exercised personnel managers and operators for a considerable period is that of identifying ways of specifying the skills and attributes required for a particular position and how to compile a list of activities which accurately describe the job. Nothing, you would imagine, could be simpler: surely a manager manages, a chef prepares food, a waitress serves food, etc.

Campanile has a formula for success. Are you the vital ingredients?

Campanile Hotels is a large and successful chain operating on a European basis. With around 350 hotels, the company is presently expanding at a rate of 30–40 hotels a year. The chain is fast becoming a preferable choice in customer accommodation. And who could blame them? With exceptional cuisine in our Bistro Restaurants, plus excellent value for money, the chain offers a unique and thoroughly enjoyable homely and friendly atmosphere. Campanile offer fantastic opportunities for committed and hardworking professionals, and presently seek to recruit

ASSISTANT MANAGEMENT COUPLES

You may be a qualified chef searching for career advancement with your partner, and with your background in the hotel industry this could be the perfect opportunity. You will be professionally qualified, and preferably aged 23–35 years, with a sound and demonstrable career within the industry. Hard working and self motivated, you will be able to contribute to the Campanile atmosphere of friendliness and comfort. In addition, if you prove yourselves to be successful achievers, ambitious and dedicated to providing the utmost in excellence of service and standards, you will be presented with the opportunity to manage a Campanile hotel in the UK or in Europe. Only those who have clearly demonstrated their solidity and their ability to expand beyond their own frontiers will make the grade.

In return we offer a salary that will reflect your achievements, a comprehensive management training programme, all the benefits of a live-in position, leading to a management position with a profit related bonus.

FIGURE 27 *Example of an advertisement which clearly identifies types of skills required.*

However, this element of the recruitment and selection process has, and does cause, considerable difficulties for some hospitality businesses, and often they are the elements which are rushed or ignored.

EXAMPLE PERSON SPECIFICATION

Job Title: Club Manager

Department: Club

Location: XYZ Holiday Village

Date Prepared: April 1992

CHARACTERISTICS	ESSENTIAL	DESIRABLE
Education Qualifications Training	'O' Level/GCSE standard – Maths and English.	Hotel and Catering – Diploma/Degree. B.I.I. Leisure Certificate. Cellar Management Course.
Work Experience	Considerable bar experience and at least 1 year with management/supervisory responsibility.	2 years club management experience in holiday industry, controlling at least 5 staff.
Skills and Knowledge	Good people skills, good administrative ability. Knowledge of company policy and legal requirements affecting club management.	Staff-training skills.
Age/Physical Attributes	Good health. Well-groomed, smart and clean. No visible tattoos. Age open.	25–45 years of age. Tee-total. Physically strong.
Personality/Disposition	Bright and friendly. Shows enthusiasm for the position. Team-player. Enjoys crowds and pressure. Good team-builder and motivator of staff.	Outgoing, smiles a lot. Career motivated.
Communication Skills	Proven verbal/written communication ability.	Confident and open in approach.
Personal Circumstances	Own transport, lives near work. No domestic pressures. Willing to work long and unsociable hours, flexible.	Single. Lives-in.

FIGURE 28 *Accurate job specifications assist in effective recruitment and selection.*

A survey of supervisors and managers conducted in 1993 identified that 60% did not possess *accurate* or *up-to-date* job descriptions.

J. Roberts (1993) *Personnel and Training Survey – Hospitality Supervisors,* Rotherham College of Arts and Technology

The lack of a clear definition of what skills are required and what a specific job or position entails will create problems for both the employer and employee. It is an area which, as stated, has created considerable study and debate.

Job definition debate

KEY POINT

The current trend amongst hospitality operators is to define their objectives and personnel policies in a way which emphasises the sharing of goals and the recognition of the value of individual contributions.

The hospitality industry faces an interesting dilemma in the formulation of job roles and descriptions. On the one hand it is a creative industry where the individual skill and involvement of employees is crucial to the demand for higher levels of customer care. On the other hand there is the need to ensure tasks and responsibilities are carried out in a fairly standardised way, assisting the maintenance of quality.

Certainly amongst other industries, especially those where individual creativity is of major importance to the company, rigid job descriptions are becoming less common. Some of the newer hospitality operators have taken this aspect to a reasonable degree with the blurring of roles and the emphasis on teamwork rather than individual role descriptions.

It is, I believe, a debate which will continue for some time. What is important for organisations is the recognition that, generally, employees work more productively when they possess clear definitions, statements or explanations of the requirements of their job.

The enhancement of a job, of course, relies on a large number of variables. However, when defining job descriptions and developing job specifications, considerations should be given to the nature of the position or positions.

Definitions

- *Job description:* a written statement which attempts to provide a relevant description of the nature, scope, purpose, duties and responsibilities of a particular job, position or role
- *Job specification:* a written statement which describes in more detail the specific tasks a position entails
- *Person specification:* a written statement which describes the essential and desirable skills, experience and qualifications required to undertake a specific position or job role; additionally, the person specification will identify personal attributes which the employer has identified as being necessary for the employee to perform effectively

Benefits of job descriptions and specifications are listed below.

- *For the employer,* they
  - allow the employer to evaluate the need for a particular job, role or vacancy

- assist in the definition of the grade, status and associated pay and benefits attributable to a position
- assist the employer in setting measurable criteria on which to judge applicants
- set the terms and conditions on which employees' performance in the job can be judged
- provide a benchmark or standard in the case of dispute, discipline or grievance
- *For the employee,* they
  - provide a reasonably accurate description of the job or role, allowing the employee to assess the job in terms of suitability
  - define benchmarks on which the evaluation of performance can be judged
  - provide an agreement in respect of tasks and responsibilities which can reduce possible conflict

Allowing that the job has been correctly evaluated and the resulting job description and person specification is appropriate, such a formal process provides protection for both employee and employer.

It is unfortunate that many employers do not use such simple and effective documentation. The risks for the employer who does not complete this process are increasing, relating not only to aspects of employment legislation, such as equal opportunities, but also to the costs involved in recruiting inappropriate personnel.

A guide to contents

JOB DESCRIPTION

Regardless of the position, this should provide an accurate and reasonable description of all aspects of the job and include:

- job title
- nature of job (brief sentences describing the main task or tasks)
- scope (identifying where the job fits into the organisational structure; who the individual reports to and for whom the individual is responsible)
- duties and responsibilities (clear, easy to understand, unambiguous statements concerning specific duties; these may include reference to certain standards or targets, e.g. to increase sales by 10%)
- additions (often a job description will end with a general statement on the lines of 'and any other duties which reasonably fall into the scope of this job'. I often doubt the inclusion of such a statement, as how do you define what is reasonable?)

───────────────── **KEY POINT** ─────────────────

It is important to recognise that, whilst the job description is not a formal contract in itself, it does and should form a part of the general and specific terms and conditions of employment and is an addition to the written contract of employment.

JOB SPECIFICATION

This is a more detailed written statement and is generally used for operative level jobs. Many employers and employees combine this statement with the job description, which can create further problems in disciplinary or grievance situations.

JOB DESCRIPTION EXAMPLE

Job Title: Back of House Manager
Responsible To: Catering Manager
Responsible For: All Back of House Staff

GENERAL PURPOSE AND SCOPE OF POSITION

To provide a quality cleaning service for all Catering and Kitchen areas and equipment.

DUTIES AND RESPONSIBILITIES

1 Ensures the efficient and hygienic operation of the plateroom, basement areas, Floor Service and restaurant service areas, carrying out regular inspections for cleanliness and hygiene.
2 Ensures all back of house areas, i.e. corridors, changing rooms, cloakrooms, stairs and voids, are cleaned on a regular basis.
3 Organises any special cleaning requests made by the Catering Manager.
4 Ensures the correct and efficient use of all detergents and chemicals used in the department.
5 Carries out monthly inventories of all operating equipment and reserve stock and produces consumption figures to set against actual covers forecast and for re-imbursing the operating stock with the breakage figure.
6 Liaises with Personnel for the recruitment and selection of staff.
7 Ensures that all staff are trained to established standards in all aspects of their job.
8 Completes all staff related paperwork, e.g. time sheets, holiday requests etc., accurately and promptly.
9 Appraises all staff within the established time limits.
10 Reviews and updates Back of House standards of performance and job descriptions on a regular basis.
11 Maintains discipline in a fair and consistent manner, liaising with the Personnel department when necessary.
12 In liaison with the Catering Manager, controls all staff costs, particularly overtime and casual payments
13 Maintains effective communication with staff and ensures all information required to carry out their duties is conveyed to them on a timely basis.
14 Reports problems and complaints, where appropriate, to the Catering Manager and generally keeps him informed and ensures that staff report similarly to him/her.
15 Attends and actively participates in the monthly Catering meeting and any other meetings as required.

16 Ensures that all Back of House staff, including himself/herself, are familiar with and work within the Hotel and Departmental Health, Safety and Hygiene policy.

17 Ensures that all Back of House staff, including himself/herself, are familiar with and adhere to the Hotel and Departmental Fire and Bomb procedures.

18 Reports and ensures staff report, any defects in equipment immediately to the Catering Manager.

19 Co-operates with the Security department and Duty Manager to maintain security and prevent theft.

20 Advises the Maintenance Manager of routine maintenance requirements and ensures that these are carried out.

21 Carries out other duties and projects as assigned by the Catering Manager or Assistant.

Park Lane Hotel

PERSON SPECIFICATION

This is possibly the most contentious of this set of documents. What the employer is seeking to do is identify the specific skills, experience and attributes required by and for the job. There are several approaches to this, the standard areas being:

- essential attributes/qualifications, etc.
- desirable attributes/qualifications, etc.

For the employer the importance is to identify objectively what skills/qualifications and attributes are vital and without which the job could not be completed to the standard required. In certain cases this may include the possession of specific qualifications, lack of police record or physical ability.

It is within this area that the majority of problems exist and employers who identify essential elements which ignore such aspects as equal opportunities, race or sex discrimination could face prosecution. This, of course, is just as important in interviewing for promotion as for new employees. Additionally, if the employer has identified a set of personal attributes including ability to work in a team, stamina, objectivity or sense of humour as essential requirements, the question arises as to how such attributes will be objectively assessed.

KEY POINT

The more senior or complex the position, the more complex and detailed the job description and person specification become. Coupled with this is the need to conduct more objective and detailed assessment of applicants.

Over the past four to five years some employers have increasingly used job descriptions and applications which allow the interested applicant to assess themselves against stated criteria. Whilst obvious weaknesses exist with such an approach, at least it allows potential employees to obtain more information about specific jobs and commence the joint assessment of suitability.

"Yes, I appreciate the advertisement did specify the need for experience in catering at sea, but . . ."

This development, although minor, does focus on the fact that the employment contract is or should be a two-way process.

In conclusion, job descriptions and person specifications form a vital and often undervalued part of the recruitment and selection process. Because they provide benchmarks and standards for the protection of both parties, they need to be compiled with care, as mistakes and omissions can prove costly to both employer and employee.

KEY POINT

Descriptions of the job or role, specifications related to the skills and tasks, accurate and reasonable descriptions of the essential skills, experience, qualifications and personal attributes form a vital element of the recruitment and selection process.

The next brief section describes the methods of advertising vacancies.

4.6 ADVERTISING

Recruitment advertising

When the nature of the job qualifications, experience and attributes have been identified, the operator needs to ensure that sufficient applicants emerge to enable effective selection. This section describes the various methods operators use to attract applicants to advertised or potential vacancies. The most common methods include advertising:

- in national and local newspapers and trade journals
- in job centres
- in in-house company newsletters, bulletins or job vacancy boards
- at national and regional career fairs
- in company-produced career and opportunities leaflets
- through recruitment or personnel companies
- through informal networks within the organisation

Before identifying the relative advantages and disadvantages of these methods, it is important to recognise that companies undertake recruitment advertising for several reasons (Figure 29).

- to advertise a single vacancy, which they seek to fill almost immediately
- to advertise a set of vacancies, e.g. advertising to attract applicants to a management scheme
- to raise general awareness of career opportunities within an organisation for certain levels of staff
- to raise general awareness of career opportunities within an organisation for all levels of staff

The selection of the medium for the recruitment is, therefore, dependent upon the specific aim of the advertisement or publicity. With the high turnover of staff within the industry, such

SUCCESSFUL MANAGEMENT COUPLES COME IN ALL SHAPES AND SIZES

(It's what's inside that matters)

Train in pub management London Area

*S*ome brewers only seem to look for pub management teams who fit a blueprint. In other words, **qualified** and **experienced**. As London's fastest-growing pub chain, Wetherspoons believes that other qualities can be far more valuable, and we're now on the lookout for new management talent.

Of course, we're still very particular, but let's face it, there's more to running a pub than pulling pints. We're expanding throughout the UK, having built our success on a return to traditional pub values: good beer, good food, friendly service, reasonable prices and absolutely no juke boxes or pool tables.

Good organisational skills, the ability to bring out the best in other people and hard work are all essential. But if the two of you have got what it takes and are mobile and commitment-free, our 9–12 month training programme will teach you everything you need to know about how to make a success of running a pub.

The rewards? We offer free accommodation, exciting incentive schemes and the chance to earn around £20,000 plus, on promotion to management.

So if you believe that your intelligence, enthusiasm and commitment will influence us more than your CV, please come to one of our selection evenings in Victoria for an initial interview.

Welcome to Jarvis Hotels

(we're sure you'll enjoy your stay)

RECEPTIONISTS – nationwide

A great receptionist is the making of a great hotel. It's not surprising, then, that at Jarvis Hotels we employ the very best behind our front desk. First impressions count, and as the first point of contact, the Front Office is perhaps the most important part of any of our hotels.

As you'd expect, to be the public face of one of the UK's top 5 hotel companies you need a rare blend of personal qualities. What we're looking for is enthusiasm, personality and commitment to excellence – someone whose standards are every bit as high as our own.

In fact, your natural instinct for customer care will be far more valuable than having a long CV. If you've already worked in a front office, you may be able to join us in a more senior position, but don't worry – experience isn't necessary. We'll train you the Jarvis way to provide the best possible service. You'll start with an intensive "off the job" training course, covering all the important skills that you'll need from the

moment guests check in to the moment they check out. And this level of support doesn't stop when you join a team at one of our hotels.

From there, who knows? With the best training behind you, you could make rapid career progress, especially if you're prepared to move. We're ideally looking for people who can work anywhere throughout the UK, but please let us know if you have a preferred location.

FIGURE 29 *Job advertising takes many forms, from advertising single vacancies to raising awareness of general career prospects.*

activities will continue to be both costly and time consuming. Additionally, with the growing demand for skilled staff, the effectiveness of recruitment policies and activities is becoming increasingly important (Table 9). Companies may also advertise via computer networks, a method which is attracting considerable interest in the larger companies.

Table 9 Analysis of recruitment methods

METHOD	ADVANTAGES	DISADVANTAGES
National advertising and trade journals	• Wide coverage resulting in potentially increased numbers of applicants • Additionally, awareness raising of company and job opportunities	• High cost of national advertising • Associated costs of shortlisted applicants attending for interview • Possible negative effect of regular advertising
Job Centres	• Local targeting with facility for advertising vacancy at low cost throughout job centre network • Initial screening of applicants by job centre staff • Possibility for large scale recruitment, e.g. seasonal vacancies or for a new unit	• Vacancies normally of operative or junior supervisory level • Perceived poor image of job centre applicants (not true, of course!)
In-house bulletins or job vacancy boards	• Low cost • Internal marketing of progression or promotional opportunities • Promotes idea of 'grown your own' successful employees	• Restricting to internal applications will reduce number of external applicants • Lack of 'new blood' coming into organisation
College/University presentations	• Targeting of potential 'high flyers' – graduates • Raises awareness of company	• Need for specialist recruitment team • Possible high cost of attendance • Raising expectations amongst college graduates which company cannot satisfy • Suitable for larger national companies who can release staff and produce necessary documentation

Table 9 *Continued*

METHOD	ADVANTAGES	DISADVANTAGES
National, regional or local careers fairs	• Focused event with cost of advertising often undertaken by organisers • Opportunity to promote general and specific job and career opportunities • Opportunity to raise image of industry	• Need for specialist recruitment team • Requirement for quality stand and presentation material • More suitable for larger companies
Company career and job opportunities leaflets	• Opportunity to promote general and specific career opportunities within the organisation • Production of material suitable for sending to postal enquiries • Reduces cost of individual units producing career information • Promotes (possibly) positive image of company	• Expensive to produce and keep up to date, especially for small companies
Recruitment or Personnel Agencies	• Screening service • Confidentiality • Reduction of time and resources	• Cost, especially for more senior posts
Informal networks (in company or between organisations)	• Little or no cost in respect of advertising • Recommendation by colleagues; tried and tested employees	• Restricting companies' ability to attract wide range of applicants • Potential for favourites

With international computer links we are able to advertise specific vacancies at any of our units throughout the company. Interested individuals can enter their interest in a position via the computer and the personnel manager or general manager can gain access to the individual's personnel file, enabling an initial evaluation to take place.

Human Resource Director, international hotel chain

Hilton seeks middle-aged staff

THE Glasgow Hilton has announced plans to recruit more staff aged in their 40s and 50s in a bid to match more accurately the age grouping of guests.

Bill Paisley, manager at the 319-room hotel, said that the older staff did not necessarily need to come from a catering background.

"Half our guests are aged 40 or more, but most of our staff are younger. It seems right to redress the balance a little," he said.

In an effort to instill more enthusiasm in its younger staff, the hotel is also looking for "old retainers" to visit the hotel and pass on their experience by talking to current staff.

"We are looking for the sort of people who worked in country houses from the 1930s to the 1950s. In those days there was tremendous pride in that type of work and we hope to demonstrate that to our younger staff," said Mr Paisley.

"Some of them prefer not to work the so-called anti-social shifts, the late nights and early mornings which are typical of a 24-hour hotel."

Any former domestics who come to the Hilton's aid will be rewarded with hospitality at the hotel.

CATERER & HOTELKEEPER 13 OCTOBER 1994

FIGURE 30 *Advertising for the neglected end of the market!*

For larger companies who possess such technology, this approach would appear quite cost effective and recent developments within job centres on computer link-ups appear to suggest that such methods may increase in the future. Certainly the larger recruitment and personnel agencies possess impressive databases to which employers can gain access. However, the development of any form of national job vacancy computer database with the facility for individuals to register interest appears at present to be impracticable.

The nature of recruitment advertising

As stated, recruitment advertising can serve a variety of purposes ranging from attracting applicants to a specific vacancy to raising general awareness of career opportunities within the organisation. Whilst companies exercise reasonable freedom in their promotional material, advertising in local and national media is governed by certain codes of practice and legal guidelines. Such guidelines cover the content and nature of advertisements and relate to legislation covering race, sex discrimination and equal opportunities. When this legislation first appeared, operators and advertising agencies had all sorts of difficulties in respect of posts which previously were described or titled in certain ways. Job titles such as 'barman', 'waiter', 'housemaid' and even 'manager' were challenged in respect of equal opportunities, resulting in a rash of revised job titles.

Currently, the advertising of jobs has become more positive, although many are beginning to argue against the existence of age barriers within advertisements (see Figure 30). Such adverts are banned in other countries, including the USA where discrimination in respect of age in recruitment advertising has become an offence.

The situation within UK recruitment advertising has certainly improved over the past few years, with advertisements generally providing more relevant information about the job or position. When advertising the organisation seeks to:

- provide relevant information about the job to interested individuals, e.g. title, brief description of duties, wages and benefits, location, company name and details of qualifications and experience required and how to apply
- raise interest in the company by projecting a positive image

Increasingly advertisements attempt to paint a picture of the organisation, especially in connection with the culture of the organisation and other career and training possibilities. (You might wish to run through examples of advertisements in the national trade journals and identify which attract you and why.)

As with many other aspects, the small operator faces particular problems in respect of advertising for personnel. Lacking the finance to fund large advertisements in the national press, they need to seek cost-effective alternatives. One method could be to create a consortium-type approach, joining with similar independent operators allowing for the distribution of costs and the creation of wider opportunities.

Alternatively, in certain of the larger cities, the use of the job centre or specialist job agency would allow for improvement in targeting. London for some time possessed several agencies like this and Springboard, a specialist agency part funded by Government and Industry, has developed some positive initiatives in this area.

Recruitment advertising, then, comes in a variety of forms and operators have recognised that they need to include a number of these methods if they are to attract the required calibre of applicants. Costly in operation, recruitment advertising will remain a significant and important part of the personnel and human resource function into the foreseeable future. Whilst hospitality companies will strive to promote from within, the turnover of staff within the industry will encourage operators to seek more cost-effective methods.

The next section describes the various methods used to shortlist applications for such advertised vacancies.

4.7 SHORTLISTING

Setting up for interviewing

The problem facing many organisations is how to identify appropriate candidates for interview when faced with considerable numbers of applications. The main aim of shortlisting is to identify a small number of applicants who appear on paper, or by initial interviews, to possess the required skills, knowledge and personal attributes.

An operator needs to reduce the number of applications to manageable numbers. The actual numbers for final interviews or assessment will obviously depend on the nature of the vacancy and the size and style of the operation. A realistic number for final interview is two to four.

However, it must be realised that organisations take differing approaches to this element. The key aim is to appoint the most appropriate person in the most cost-effective manner.

Shortlisting is not an easy task, especially when there are a considerable number of applicants. The personnel manager or owner requires some form of measure by which to judge applicants' potential suitability quickly. The measurements most operators use are the description of the key skills, knowledge and personal attributes identified for the particular vacancy. That is the job specification, job description and person specification (those elements were dealt with earlier in this chapter). If these characteristics have been correctly identified then initially any applicant not possessing these aspects can be justifiably rejected. This aspect raises the importance of correctly and clearly identifying the attributes required in any job advertisement.

Many operators use a standard application form, which provides a common document for individuals to complete (Figure 31). Obviously these forms will differ from one organisation to another; whatever the style the main benefits can be identified as:

- a standard form which obtains standard information from all applicants
- applications which overall are easier and quicker to read and appraise
- overall equality of treatment for all applicants
- provision of documents which can be used as initial employee records
- a method by which the organisation can ensure legal aspects have been dealt with
- a document which can be used during interview as a guide to questioning and for checking an applicant's statements

Whilst such forms do provide considerable benefits, they are not without their faults and cannot be relied upon as the only or final method of selection. Common faults are:

- badly designed forms, allowing the candidate insufficient space to insert all the appropriate information
- request for inappropriate information
- assumption that applicants have necessary literary skills to complete the application

If the key factor is to select the most appropriate candidate, then serious consideration has to be given to any document used in the process. Additionally, as already stated, they should not be used as the main element for selection.

Operators may also require candidates to provide additional or alternative documentary evidence of their suitability. This could include a curriculum vitae (a written history of the individual), a personal portfolio, records of achievement, copies of certificates, references or job-related testimonials, photographs of work completed or replies to particular questions in the form of reports or case studies. It is important to use the most appropriate and effective method for initial shortlisting.

───────────────── KEY POINT ─────────────────

When shortlisting, the individual has to match written or other documentary evidence against the criteria set for the particular vacancy.

Ref. No.

THISTLE HOTELS
AND
MOUNT CHARLOTTE HOTELS

APPLICATION FOR EMPLOYMENT

Personal Information

LAST NAME (Mr., Mrs., Miss, M/s) ....

FIRST NAMES ....

ADDRESS: Present ....

....

Home ....

TELEPHONE: Home.. work ....

BIRTHDATE .... BIRTHPLACE .... NATIONALITY ....

NATIONAL INSURANCE No. | | | | | | | DISABLED REGISTRATION No ....

MARITAL STATUS   Single ☐   Married ☐   Divorced ☐   Separated ☐   Widowed ☐
(please tick the appropriate box)

CHILDREN (if any) Number .... AGES ....

ETHNIC ORIGIN:
Please tick the appropriate box)   White ☐   Black African ☐   Black Caribbean ☐   Black Other ☐   Asian ☐   Oriental ☐

Other ☐ (Please specify) ....

Are you required by law to have a work permit?   Yes/No

If yes: State its number, capacity and date of expiry ....

....

Education and Qualifications

Secondary and Further Education

Name, type and location of establishment	From	To	Certificates gained (Please give subjects and grades)

Other Qualifications (e.g. languages, skills etc., please give full details)

Job Information

● What position are you applying for? ....

....

● When would you be able to start work? ....

● Geographical areas. Use numbers 1-5 on adjacent map to show your

  order of preference ....

● Salary range ....

FIGURE 31 *An example of a job application form which can assist shortlisting.*

Finally, in respect of written applications, the personnel individual has to recognise that such evidence is only a statement and requires testing further to ensure validity.

Other forms of shortlisting

Depending on the nature of the vacancy, there do exist other forms of shortlisting and the complexity of these usually relate to the type of vacancy. They include:

- psychometric testing
- assessment centres
- skill or trade testing
- peer group assessment
- head hunting

Some of the above can be used after initial shortlisting, especially for very specialist roles or more senior posts, and further explanations will be provided in the section on interview methods and selection.

Whatever the method used for initial shortlisting the aim is the same, to reduce the number of applications to a number which can be effectively dealt with and provide for the organisation the best possible chance for selecting the right candidate.

Within the shortlisting process, there is a growing tendency to retain written notes on each candidate. Such a process is made easier if the shortlisting is conducted against objective selection criteria. Whilst time consuming, such an approach assists when decisions are later challenged, e.g. in cases of equal opportunities.

Final considerations on shortlisting

The selection of personnel to be involved in the shortlisting process is of vital importance and is best undertaken by more than one individual. By using a team approach to shortlisting, who apply common criteria to the process, the organisation will have an improved method for selecting the right candidate. This team could consist of senior managers, heads of department, the personnel team or worker peer groups. Some organisations will also use subordinates in this process; however, their inclusion in my experience is often best left to the stage of final selection. A team approach, whilst beneficial, is time consuming and for many hospitality operators this would be impracticable.

Therefore, the key aspects of this element are:

- use of appropriate methods to identify suitable candidates for further or final assessment or interview
- the personnel individual or team will require some form of criteria against which to measure or judge applications, e.g. job description or person specification
- shortlisting is best completed by a team
- shortlisting against basic written applications has certain weaknesses and the use of other documentary evidence is advisable

Consideration should be given to ensuring that employment codes of practice and legislation are adhered to.

Following shortlisting, individuals concerned with recruitment and selection have to identify the most appropriate method(s) for final selection, the tenth element in the recruitment and selection process.

4.8 INTERVIEW AND SELECTION METHODS

The criteria which affect job descriptions, applications and shortlisting equally apply to final selection and the employer should seek to ensure this final selection is fair, allowing all candidates the opportunity to demonstrate their skills and adhere to all relevant employment legislation.

Methods of selection

As the employer seeks to match applicants objectively against the criteria for the job, the method or methods chosen must be appropriate. However, employers are increasingly using recruitment and selection practices which decrease the significance of the final selection. This may sound contradictory but in reality it is becoming the norm, especially in the larger catering organisations.

KEY POINT

If the employer has used comprehensive job evaluation and description processes, objectively assessed written applications, effectively shortlisted and possibly used other forms of assessment, the final selection will often be focused on confirming assessment and clarifying points related to the individual's position and willingness to undertake the role.

Of course, this is often not the situation as many employers either do not undertake effective shortlisting or continue to rely on one-to-one interviews as the preferred method. Before we identify the other methods of selection, it is appropriate to describe the process currently referred to as the 'job interview'.

Job interview

Traditionally this was conducted on a one-to-one basis with the manager, supervisor or personnel manager interviewing the applicant against some form of pre-subscribed criteria. Accepting that, by itself, it is possibly the worst method of selection, the interviewer will need to ensure that the weaknesses and risks are minimal. These weaknesses include:

- inherent pressure on the applicant to perform in an unrealistic situation
- possible lack of objectivity on behalf of the interviewer
- the absence of others in the interview process, thereby selection is reliant on the skills of one individual

- the possibility of non-adherence to employment legislation related to the fair selection of individuals
- lack of opportunity for applicant to demonstrate true ability or potential
- possibility that applicant can claim ability or attributes which, in fact, they either do not possess or in which they are weak

For many organisations the job interview remains the main method of selection, based on minimum of resources and time required. If the interview is used either as the sole method of selection or as part of other selection methods then the aim should be to minimise the risks involved.

GUIDELINES FOR EFFECTIVE INTERVIEWING

1 The interviewer should have access to all necessary information, including job description, application form and references (if used).
2 The interview should be structured in that both interviewer and interviewee understand the process and what form the interview will take.
3 The interview should be conducted in a suitable location, free from interruption.
4 The purpose of the interview is to solicit views, comments, questions and answers from the applicant and it is not the time to explain conditions of employment or for the interviewer to express views.
5 Whenever possible, a final decision should be deferred until the interviewer has had time to reflect objectively on the interview.

Guides to interview and selection often describe forms of interview plans, e.g. the 5-point or 7-point plans which progressively take both interviewer and interviewee through the key aspects of the job and which assist the applicant in demonstrating his/her suitability or potential.

Hospitality companies increasingly use a written form on which to record an interviewer's comments and views on applicants. Such forms do assist the interview in acting as a schedule and checklist. Additionally, they can act as a record in cases of possible disputes relating to final decisions. However, such forms possess certain weaknesses, especially when the interview is on a one to one basis. Firstly, the interviewer will need to take notes which reduces time for detailed discussion and is distracting for both parties. Secondly, there exist potential weaknesses in such forms relating to the objectivity and appropriateness of the questions.

Whilst not dismissing the job interview as a method of selection, the trend is for operators to conduct interviews as part of the selection process.

Other methods of selection

PSYCHOMETRIC TESTING

Such tests seek to assess an individual against job or role criteria by means of questionnaire-based forms. Whilst such testing has been in use for some considerable time, it is becoming increasingly popular.

The acceptance of the effectiveness of such a form of assessment is based upon research and studies into personality and behaviour. There is no doubt that such testing can be useful in assisting the selection of candidates and does provide an alternative objective assessment of potential.

These tests exist in a variety of forms, often concentrating on identifying a profile of personality type, e.g. good team leader, innovator, able to deal with conflict. The design of such forms and tests often relies on particular theories of behaviour and personality and a number of companies concentrate on the supply and analysis of the tests. Such testing has received poor press in the past, mainly due to their use by inexperienced and unqualified interviewers, poor construction and inappropriate use by the company.

Often such tests were used as the main form of selection and candidates received little feedback on the results. Analysis was completed by inexperienced managers against a provided checklist with little real understanding of the process. Over the past decade this situation has improved and these tests have been recognised as a useful element in selecting employees, especially for more senior positions.

The Institute of Personnel Management's code of practice on the use of psychometric testing states:

The use of such testing is becoming increasingly common, to which I have no argument as long as its use:

- is appropriate to the position
- is part of other selection methods
- includes positive feedback to the applicant
- is kept confidential
- adheres to both general aspects of fairness and legislation on equal opportunities

There is no doubt that such tests are being increasingly used in both selection and promotional interviews; hopefully, more scientific work will be completed to ascertain their real value to both organisations and employees.

ASSESSMENT CENTRES

The common picture of such centres is an 'Outward Bound' type organisation which puts candidates through team and individual tests and exercises. Their use gained popularity in the 1960s and 1970s often for the selection of senior personnel. Following a decline in their use they are now regaining popularity.

In selecting for a senior management position, we invited the ten shortlisted candidates to an assessment centre. On arrival they were placed in two teams and given a variety of individual and team tasks to complete. The candidates worked from their arrival on Friday night until their departure after lunch on the Sunday. Other senior managers from the company and assessment centre staff observed and assessed the candidates against a series of set criteria. Candidates also completed a number of psychometric tests. The aim of the weekend was to make a final selection from applicants who all possessed the qualifications and experience to undertake the position.

Regional Personnel Manager, national catering company

In assessing the effectiveness of the exercise described above, the organisation identified the following:

- six candidates proved less suitable
- the final selection remained problematic and required further interviewing
- the cost of the exercise was prohibitive

On questioning, certain other problems were identified, including – lack of briefing of candidates, little or no feedback to candidates and demotivation of several of the candidates. The company concerned have now revised their approach to the use of assessment centres.

Overall, the use of assessment centres is appropriate only for certain levels of staff. Whilst external companies exist, several of the larger catering organisations now combine elements of assessment in their national or regional training and development centres.

SKILLS OR TRADE TESTING

As the interest in competencies increases, due in part to the development of NVQs, so does the ability to assess an individual's ability in relation to specific skills. One famous chef of a 5-star London hotel used to ask potential commis chefs to fry an egg, claiming that he could ascertain suitability via the completion of this simple task. Certainly if the main focus or purpose of the job is the completion of certain skills to a pre-subscribed level, then this approach holds some merit.

With jobs that are predominantly skill based, it makes sense to test that skill in a reasonable way. However, as jobs become more flexible and demarcations between positions become increasingly blurred, the skills element should be only part of the selection process.

PEER GROUP ASSESSMENT

With the increasing emphasis on teamwork, certain employers are using selection methods which involve other employees, normally those who will work directly with the new employee. It is part of the wider development of increased employee involvement or empowerment and has much to recommend it.

Similarly to other methods it requires careful handling, with appropriate briefings to staff involved and sensitivity to the need for objectivity. For organisations who have developed a strong team culture, for instance Harvester and TGI, then such an approach can reinforce the team emphasis.

HEAD HUNTING

This method has always attracted a degree of bad press as for many it appears to indicate something underhand. Yet it is a method often used for senior and executive positions and one

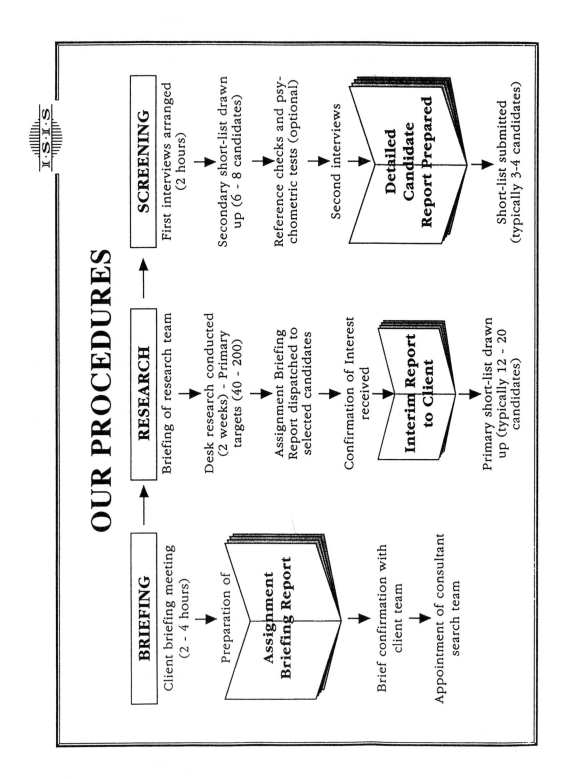

FIGURE 32 *Executive procedure – International Service Industry Search, Berkeley Scott Group.*

Berkeley Scott Personnel Consultants has a database of over 25,000 individuals, who are grouped under a number of specific job functions. For any particular executive position up to 200 candidates may initially be identified. Following further screening a recommended list will be sent to the client.

Berkeley Scott Personnel Consultants

Whilst senior or executive positions are primarily dealt with by the large personnel consultants, agencies, such as the Government's Job Centres, are widely used for the junior or operative positions. Over the past few decades the services offered by job centres have expanded and, as offices are linked, job vacancies can be advertised throughout the UK at minimal or no cost to the operator.

We regularly use the services of the Job Centres for the large number of seasonal staff we require. In addition to national and local advertising we find this to be a particularly cost-effective way of attracting the range of qualified staff needed.

Trevor Norgett, Personnel & Training Manager, Haven Leisure

For the busy owner, operator or company seeking specific types of personnel, or larger companies attempting to fill senior and executive positions, recruitment agencies and personnel consultants do provide a useful service, a service that has increased in popularity over the last two decades (see Figure 33).

The next section will cover the process of appointing staff with particular reference to the present legislation.

4.9 APPOINTMENT AND INDUCTION

One result of good recruitment and selection is reduced labour turnover. If you recruit the right people, they are likely to stay with you. If the wrong people are recruited they will either leave voluntarily when they decide to find more congenial employment, or leave involuntarily when you decide they are not suitable for the job.

ACAS Guide, *Recruitment and Selection*

Appointment

Having conducted the interview and selected the candidate for the position, the organisation will wish to appoint the individual. Whilst this sounds a simple task, there are certain procedures and

LINKING WORK TRIALS WITH DIRECT RECRUITMENT

During the Work Trial you may identify a specific immediate training need, for example:

FORK LIFT TRUCK TRAINING
WELDING
COMPUTER TRAINING

So why not link a Work Trial with Employed Status Direct Recruitment?

This will allow your new recruit to receive certain identified training at no expense to yourself and, in addition, a cash bonus will be paid to your company shortly after you employ the participant.

For further details, contact either the Training and Enterprise Council or your local Employment Service Jobcentre.

"Linking Direct Recruitment with Work Trials has worked extremely well for us. It gives us the flexibility to find out if someone is really suited to working with us without committing ourselves"
IAN FURNISS,
Furniss & White.

HELP IS JUST A PHONE CALL AWAY

DIRECT RECRUITMENT

Q Are you looking to recruit an unemployed, semi - skilled person?

Q Do you only need a short time to train them into the job?

Q Do you feel that you can handle their training needs without requiring an external training provider?

THEN DIRECT RECRUITMENT MAY WELL BE THE ANSWER

● A great saving on the time and expense of recruiting - if you don't already have someone in mind, the TEC and Employment Service will advertise and select them for you.

● Time to assess the applicant's suitability without the commitment of immediate employment.

● No - cost recruitment! You can increase outputs during the short training period before incurring wage costs and then qualify for a bonus of £400 - £600 when you employ the trainee.

● All the training is conducted by you on site, so you don't lose them from the work place and the trainee knows exactly what you expect of an employee.

● An element of specific training to recognised standards may also be funded under Direct Recruitment.

"We've found Direct Recruitment to be a very cost-effective way of training employees"
KEVIN SMITH, Partner,
All Dogs Grooming Parlour.

FIGURE 33 *An idea to encourage employees to recruit on the basis of a subsidised work trial.*

practices which assist the positive appointment of an individual and ensure all the necessary legal aspects are covered.

For operators working with small numbers of staff on a casual or part-time basis, appointment is often restricted to a verbal offer and instructions for commencement. Obviously for more permanent positions with larger companies, procedures are more complex. Whatever the situation the personnel manager or owner has to undertake certain tasks to ensure a successful appointment. These include:

- obtaining verbal acceptance from the candidate
- obtaining confirmation in writing
- setting up personnel records for the individual
- making arrangements for wages and accommodation
- processing necessary tax and national insurance documentation
- arranging commencement date

Additionally, prior to appointment, the individual may be requested to undertake certain medical checks or substantiate qualifications, status or experience. For specific types of jobs, appointment may be subject to police checks, as in the case where appointed individuals may be working with young children or responsible for licensed premises.

Appointment of personnel, then, creates major functional tasks for the employer which all add to the cost of employing staff. For large companies operating nationally this means creating a comprehensive personnel system with either centralised or regional offices. Smaller companies and independent operators will also require such backup, whilst companies operating on a seasonal basis will require personnel systems which allow for a large influx of staff over a concentrated period (see the Case Study of Haven Leisure on page 69 for an example of this).

For the appointment of staff to be effective, the employer requires:

- documented procedures to allow for the efficient processing of new personnel
- standardised forms which ensure that all relevant employment legislation and conditions have been adhered to
- experienced staff who understand the complexities of pay and taxation
- systems which allow for the recording and storage of confidential personnel records

Without such systems and procedures the employer faces possible:

- confusion or potential dispute with terms and conditions of employment
- additional work created by ineffective systems
- prosecution related to non-adherence to employment legislation

There are a wide range of systems which employers can use and, increasingly, personnel systems are being computerised. Whilst such systems do reduce overall workload, they remain relatively expensive and, of course, require specially trained operators. Whether the system is paper based or computerised, its importance is ensuring that all necessary documentation has been completed and the employee is successfully appointed. The employee then requires an introduction to the specific job or position. The process commonly referred to as induction.

Induction

Induction is concerned with the effective introduction of an employee into the organisation, department and job. It is not a process only occurring on the employee's first day, but one which continues over a period. The following example, from a luxury hotel, demonstrates a positive example of this phased approach and also identifies the need to link induction with training, development and performance review.

CASE STUDY. DOWN HALL HOTEL: INDUCTION

Every new employee is given a copy of our induction handbook on their first day at work (both full and part-time employees). Welcoming them at 9.00 am I cover all the subjects in the handbook in some detail. The necessary employment forms are completed and a tour of the whole hotel is provided. The employee then moves into the department and receives specific induction and training related to the job.

I will see them individually after their first fortnight at work, to check on their progress, whether the department training has been carried out correctly and to sort out any queries, problems or further training requirements.

Following the completion of the three-month probationary period, another interview is carried out, where I check on progress, obtain comments from the employee or his/her time with us and plan any further training and development.

The departmental induction is very thorough and heads of department have produced lists of skills obtained from the performance standards required. Accompanying these is statutory training such as First Aid, HASAWA and Fire Precautions.

Accompanying this induction programme is a number of training activities, including monthly departmental training sessions and an in-house evening school open to all employees. All employees participate in regular training development reviews in addition to a more formal annual appraisal.

Pauline Purves, Personnel & Training Officer, Down Hall Hotel

QUESTIONS AND CONSIDERATIONS ON THE CASE STUDY

- If you were a newly appointed employee at the above hotel, what benefits would you gain from such an approach?
- Considering the investment the hotel is making in its induction system, what benefits exist for it in terms of employee motivation, team building and staff retention?

Obviously not all operators undertake such comprehensive induction as the example provided; many new employees commence work with little or no introduction to the job, responsibilities and the organisation. High labour turnover is one obvious outcome of such short-sighted approaches.

However, hospitality companies are improving the manner in which they induct new employees, which is evidenced by the significant number of induction programmes in operation, especially in the larger companies (see Figure 34). This process is an important element of the personnel function and one in which many companies invest considerable time and resources. Consider that the employer has:

- invested management time in manpower planning
- expended financial resources in terms of advertising, interviewing and selection

INDUCTION TRAINING PROGRAMME

AIM
THROUGH INDUCTION, TO AID DELEGATES IN THE PERFORMANCE OF THEIR DUTIES AND RESPONSIBILITIES

COURSE OBJECTIVES
BY THE END OF THIS SESSION YOU WILL BE ABLE TO :-
* STATE THE COMPANY VISION STATEMENT AND WHAT IT MEANS IN YOUR PARTICULAR JOB.
* STATE THE FIRST STAGE OF THE COMPANY GRIEVANCE PROCEDURE.
* EXPLAIN WHAT YOU SHOULD DO, IN THE FIRST INSTANCE, IF ABSENT FROM WORK.
* STATE THE COMPANY GRIEVANCE PROCEDURE.
* EXPLAIN WHO IS ENTITLED TO HOLIDAY CREDITS.
* STATE THE LOCATION OF THE ACCIDENT BOOK AND WHEN IT SHOULD BE USED.
* STATE WHAT YOU SHOULD DO IN THE EVENT OF DISCOVERING A FIRE.
* EXPLAIN HOW YOU CAN CONTRIBUTE TO THE IMAGE OF THE COMPANY.
* EXPLAIN WHAT GOOD CUSTOMER CARE IS.

ALL OBJECTIVES ARE TO THE STANDARD REQUIRED BY CALA HOTELS

FIGURE 34 *Example of Induction Training Programme.*

The employer is also expecting that the new employee will be of positive benefit to the organisation in respect of work completed and customers satisfied. For such investment to be rewarded, the next stage in positive human resource management is to ensure the employee receives and understands information related to the responsibilities he/she will undertake.

Before looking in more detail at the process, it is important to clarify what effective induction attempts to achieve. Effective induction is concerned with:

- introducing the new employee to the company or organisation in which he/she will be working
- ensuring that all the necessary administration has been completed in respect of wages and conditions
- describing in detail the specific responsibilities and duties of the position
- describing the specific working conditions, company rules and working practices to the employee and obtaining their agreement to adhere to them
- providing introductory training, where required, to ensure the employees can carry out the tasks required

In other words, induction is concerned with the smooth transition of an employee into a company and position. The process is another part of the investment a company makes in respect of its human resource management activity.

It is also important to recognise that the process is two-way and is the real commencement of an employer/employee partnership which, if undertaken correctly, provides benefits for both parties.

Table 10 Benefits of effective induction

TO THE EMPLOYER	TO THE EMPLOYEE
• Creates the commencement of a partnership • Ensures necessary legal and employment aspects have been covered • Ensures that tasks will be undertaken appropriately • Allows time for further observation of a new employee's capabilities • Assists positive team building • Provides a framework for corrective or disciplinary actions if required	• Provides them with a friendly and positive start to their employment • Provides key information relating to responsibilities and tasks • Assists confidence building • Details working and employment conditions • Allows time for the obtaining of new skills or systems • Sets a legal framework to their employment

Organisations that do not undertake this process effectively could face a variety of problems which will affect both the individual's performance and the profitability of the unit. Employers may find that tasks are completed incorrectly, procedures not followed and staff are not motivated to perform correctly. Not covering the legal aspects correctly, such as conditions of employment, may result in major problems if disciplinary actions are undertaken. Employees faced with tasks of which they are unsure and procedures they do not understand will find their performance will suffer and their confidence weakened. At worst, the lack of a positive induction process will result in a demotivated employee working to poorly set standards, resulting in potential profit loss for the organisation.

THE APPROACH TO INDUCTION

The majority of companies and organisations which undertake induction will cover these aspects:

1   A general introduction to the organisation, its position, business and philosophy. This may be achieved by a presentation, one-to-one conversation, distribution of company booklet, video or a sampling day. For some organisations this first element may take a few minutes, whilst others will plan a programme of events over a period.
2   The necessary administration has to take place covering all the legal and employment aspects. This functional stage is of vital importance to both parties ensuring all involved understand the contract they are undertaking.
3   There is a need to ensure the individual is introduced to the team he/she will be working with. If the team has been involved in some way in the selection process then this process has already commenced.

4   There is the need to ensure that the individual can undertake the task and responsibilities set. This element is often the one most neglected. New employees require a careful induction into the actual job. This is just as important for existing employees undertaking new responsibilities as it is for new employees. The job induction may consist of supervised training or working alongside a colleague.

5   Some organisations will build into the induction process the opportunity for joint review, the supervisor or manager discussing progress with the employee after a given period, identifying any problem areas and solutions.

This approach, then, has five particular components, all related, and which together provide a positive and effective process.

Naturally, there are variations on approach. Some operators will have a very formal process spread over a period, whilst at the other extreme smaller organisations may cover all their particular aspects in one short session.

A recognisable trend towards longer term induction periods has emerged over the past two to three years where operators plan and operate a series of training activities. In such approaches the employee works to an agreed programme, possibly lasting a few months. The stretching of induction into longer term training programmes creates a continuity which benefits both employer and employee. When companies operate such schemes it is sometimes difficult to separate induction from training. In reality induction should be a part of the working partnership between employer and employee.

Induction provides the legal and cultural framework on which organisations can develop their employees through systematic and ongoing training.

4.10 SUMMARY AND KEY POINTS

This chapter has concentrated on the key elements of the recruitment and selection process. Businesses cannot afford to employ inappropriate personnel and, whilst the process can involve considerable costs, it is not a process to be ignored, hurried or conducted ineffectively.

The four key stages identified provide a useful framework for any operator and the identification of the fourteen key elements focused on the specific aspects related to their use.

Whilst employment legislation has in some ways made it easier to dismiss ineffective or inappropriate personnel, especially in the early part of their employment, the cost of so doing can be quite high.

For some hospitality operators the process of recruitment and selection may be conducted over a fairly short period; others may find that their actual staff turnover is minimal, making the investment in complex processes unnecessary.

Particular skills, knowledge and experience are required of individuals involved in the process, backed up wherever possible by standardised, effective systems and procedures.

The recruitment and selection process provides for applicants their first possible contact with an organisation and, if effective, should result in the commencement of a positive relationship between employer and employee.

―――――――――――――KEY POINTS―――――――――――――

- The effective recruitment and selection of staff is a critical success factor for all hospitality operators
- The process of recruitment and selection contains a number of stages which are common to all businesses
- The recruitment and selection process can be separated into four key stages:
  1 Manpower planning
  2 Identifying specific needs
  3 Selection and appointment
  4 Induction and review
- The recruitment and selection process does not end with appointment, but contains elements conducted when in post
- The process needs to adhere to legal guidelines
- Ineffective recruitment and selection can give rise to considerable problems
- Effective shortlisting for advertised vacancies can only occur if positive and appropriate use has been made of correct job/person specifications and job descriptions
- Research has indicated that selection based on a one-to-one interview is one of the most ineffective methods
- The use of psychometric tests should only be carried out by trained, qualified and experienced personnel

QUESTIONS

1 List the key stages and elements of the recruitment and selection process and provide for each stage a brief explanation of its purpose.
2 Explain the purpose of job evaluation.
3 Explain the importance of compiling job/person specifications and job descriptions in relation to the effective recruitment and selection of personnel.
4 Identify the range of legal constraints which relate to the recruitment and selection process.
5 Identify a range of methods for the assessment, interview and selection of personnel, explaining the advantages and disadvantages of each method.
6 Describe the specific problems which face event caterers in ensuring casual staff are correctly inducted and trained and provide appropriate suggestions as to how such problems can be minimised.
7 List the elements required for the effective induction of newly appointed personnel to a company, in respect of the organisation, the unit, the department and the individual.
8 Explain the main benefits to the organisation and to the individual of conducting a review with a new member of staff in the first six months of employment.

CHAPTER 5

TRAINING AND DEVELOPMENT

—

The better the skills of our staff, the better the quality of service we can offer our customers and clients. The more successful our training, the more productive our service. The better the motivation of our staff, the longer they stay with us.
We invest a great deal of money, time, expertise and energy in creating an environment in which staff will want to develop their skills and take pride in their progress within our business.

EXTRACT FROM COMPANY TRAINING POLICY, COMPASS CATERING 1994

Continual improvement of the skills of the existing labour force will be vital throughout the 1990s and beyond. Fewer young people are entering the labour market at a time when skill levels are changing and increasing.

LABOUR MARKET AND SKILL TRENDS 1994/5
DEPARTMENT OF EMPLOYMENT

There is now an increasing awareness that all managers will need a better understanding of how to manage and lead people so as to get the best from them. However, as yet, the implications in terms of the training and development required are not yet fully appreciated.

IPM CONSULTATIVE DOCUMENT, 'MANAGING PEOPLE – THE CHANGING FRONTIERS',
PERSONNEL MANAGEMENT, NOVEMBER 1993

5.1 AIMS AND OBJECTIVES

By working through this chapter, completing the questions and undertaking identified assignments and tasks provided in Appendix A, you will be able to:

1   explain the role and function of training and development;
2   list, and have an understanding of, the various methods for identifying company, unit, team and individual training and development needs;

3   conduct a brief training audit;

4   compile a basic training plan;

5   understand the importance of reviewing individual competence or performance;

6   design a skills training session;

7   list and appreciate the constraints on delivering training with regard to budgeting, time and manpower limitations;

8   understand the need for organisations to develop an effective training and development culture.

5.2 OVERVIEW OF HOSPITALITY TRAINING AND DEVELOPMENT

Industries based upon high value goals and services can only develop as quickly as the skills and capabilities of their people.

IPM Consultative Document, 'Managing People – The Changing Frontiers', *Personnel Management*, November 1993

The hospitality industry has not been slow to recognise the importance of effective staff training and development. Observers of the industry over the last decade will have identified a significant increase in investment, particularly in the larger companies and businesses. Whilst this investment has been partly due to increased competition and legislation, many companies have now considerably increased such activity.

However, it is important to provide a realistic overview and even the industry's strongest supporters would agree that overall investment is lower than many other industries. The industry is still dominated by small independent operators who spend little or no money on training and development. This, in one respect, is understandable, considering the financial and staffing pressures such businesses face; however they, like all businesses, rely on their staff to maintain a profitable business.

Alongside this aspect, there exists the effect of economic performance on training and development activities. During the recession of the late 1980s and early 1990s investment in such activity reduced considerably, with many companies and businesses laying off staff and halting recruiting with knock-on effects on training.

During the recession we had to concentrate our activities and energies on sustaining levels of business and, similar to many other operators, were not recruiting or replacing staff. The direct result of this was a reduction in training and development activity.

Alison Meldrum, Personnel & Training Manager, Park Lane Hotel

The challenges faced by the industry in recessionary periods are considerable and the majority of companies will have difficulty in sustaining high levels of training when demand and profits are reducing. The main characteristics of training and development in the hospitality industry are listed below.

- Investment in training and development has been and is lower than many other industries
- The majority of businesses being small and independently owned, investment is hampered by lack of capital
- With the large amount of part-time and casual employees, training is often difficult to organise
- Owing to the working hours, it is often difficult for companies to release employees for training
- Whilst over 350 colleges provide training for students and employees, the majority of employees remain untrained and without qualifications
- The majority of training occurs in the larger national companies.

The Government, the industry and professional bodies have all commented on these factors for some time and various initiatives have been undertaken to improve levels of training and

FIGURE 35 *NVQs are about learning and demonstrating competence.*

qualifications. One such development has concentrated on the lack of training within the businesses, which is not just a problem for the hospitality industry. National Vocational Qualifications, providing recognition for competence and skills, has been one of the Government's answers to this problem, concentrating on trainers and employees within the workplace by matching skills against nationally agreed standards. This scheme has both its supporters and critics. Again the response from industry has been mixed and to date uptake has been with the larger organisations. The Government, in the early 1990s, set itself targets for these qualifications alongside others related to educational and business performance.

NATIONAL TARGETS FOR EDUCATION AND TRAINING

FOUNDATION LEARNING TARGETS

- By 1997, 80% of young people to reach NVQ II (or equivalent)
- Training and education to NVQ II (or equivalent) available to all young people who can benefit
- By 2000, 50% of young people to reach NVQ III (or equivalent)
- Education and training provision to develop self-reliance, flexibility and breadth

LIFETIME LEARNING TARGETS

- By 1996, all employees should take part in training and development activities
- By 1996, 50% of workforce aiming for NVQs or working towards them
- By 2000, 50% of workforce qualified to at least NVQ III (or equivalent)
- By 1996, 50% of medium to larger organisations to be 'Investors in People'

Whether NVQs, amongst other training initiatives, will deliver a sizeable increase in effective training remains to be seen.

Of over 180 large to medium sized hospitality companies and businesses researched in 1994:

- 18% reported that they were involved in or considering involvement in NVQ
- 60% possessed a training plan
- 10% were involved in or considering the 'Investors in People' initiative

J. Roberts (1994) *Personnel Practices Survey*, Rotherham College of Arts & Technology

Supporting these governmental initiatives have been the various professional bodies, trade associations, research and awarding bodies and they have not been slow in developing training and qualifications.

Stages of employment and associated training and development activities

Before considering the role training and development plays, it is useful to briefly analyse some of the common training needs related to the stages employees go through whilst in employment with an organisation.

When identifying training and development needs a common mistake is to concentrate activity on response to front-of-house requirements, for example, skills training or customer care. However, as many hospitality operators have experienced, there exists a need to identify and plan for all activities from recruitment and selection, to the departure of an employee through retirement or promotion elsewhere. Such a simplistic approach is useful when both setting up personnel and HRM policies and delivering effective procedures and practices. Table 11 provides an outline of the stages of employment and identifies standard training or procedure requirements.

Table 11 Stages of employment: associated training activities and requirements

Recruitment and selection	• Staff skilled in interview and selection
Appointment	• Systems training for administrative staff
Induction	• Induction skills
	• Induction programme and system for new appointees
Role and skill undertaking	• Skills training
	• Systems training
Legislation	• HASAWA, COSHH, Food hygiene
Maintaining and improving standards	• Customer care, systems knowledge
	• Skills retraining
Team development	• Decision making, problem solving
	• Team training
Individual progression	• Reskilling, progression training
	• Appraisal and review training
Promotion	• Reskilling
	• Induction
Dispute and grievance, dismissal	• Systems and counselling training for personnel and staff
Retirement or move to another company	• Outplacement provision
	• Specialist training

─────────── **KEY POINT** ───────────

Training and development is not an activity which just covers the update of skills and acquisition of qualifications, important though these are. Rather, it is an activity which should occur throughout an individual's employment within an organisation.

Examples of training and development activities:

- skill acquisition
- qualification acquisition
- personal skills and attributes
- systems and procedures training
- team building and team management
- developmental activity, where individuals are being prepared for new roles or responsibilities
- general management and supervisory training
- training in industrial relations, grievance and counselling
- retirement and redundancy counselling (a growing activity!)

Such training can be delivered in a variety of ways:

- specifically designed work activities
- education and training courses and seminars
- assignments and projects
- open and distance learning
- secondments
- job rotation and shadowing
- assessment and activity centres programmes
- ongoing appraisal and performance review

Training and development in the past has been delivered in two ways:

1 by attendance at formal external courses and training programmes;
2 by observation (and participation) in the workplace.

Over the past decade, these more traditional approaches have been considerably extended. Currently, hospitality operators are operating a much wider range of training and development methods, which more effectively tackle the growing demand for training.

There has been a clearly identifiable move away from attendance at time-serving training programmes and a large expansion in in-house training and development.

Role of training specialists and departments

The role of the trainer and training departments is facing significant challenges, similar to the one facing personnel managers and departments. In the research for this book I surveyed over 60 training managers and had detailed conversations with training specialists across the industry. What was clearly evident from this research was the move away from the trainer's role in delivering training to one of facilitating training.

Whilst the style, makeup, roles and responsibilities of training departments and the trainers themselves will vary, the common responsibilities can range across the following:

- To identify the specific training and development needs of the company, business and employee

- Design, resource, deliver, monitor and evaluate training and development activities
- Review and report on training outcomes

Dependent upon the size and style of the company, the training specialist or department could be involved at both the strategic level – analysing business needs and plans, and advising senior management of both short- and long-term requirements – and also at an operational level, designing and delivering training.

In larger companies, such activity may be regionalised with individuals or teams being responsible for a number of units. This structure is often supported by a head office function. Additionally, in units themselves, managers and departmental heads may be responsible for specific elements of training. Within smaller operations, responsibility for training may rest with one individual who often will have other responsibilities and tasks.

───────────────── KEY POINT ─────────────────

Whatever the size or style of the company or business, there is a need for individuals to take responsibility for the training and development of all employees.

FIGURE 36 *The training department perform a vital function in assisting the improvement of the business.*

Industry itself is assisted in this activity by Government in the provision of grants and support, and by the many professional bodies and associations which increasingly work in partnership with hospitality operators to maintain and improve the standards of training.

THE TEAM

All hospitality businesses are made up of teams, be they two to three individuals working in a small operation, a department in a large unit (e.g. kitchen or housekeeping) or a mixed team with specialist functions within a large company (e.g. marketing or training team). Within an effective operation such teams will either be delivering or receiving training and development appropriate to the needs of the operation. However, as a team and not as individuals, they have an important part to play in the success of the business.

Training and development can assist teams within the hospitality business by creating a team or united approach to responsibilities, tasks and projects. For a small team within a unit, this could involve providing skill training and standards and procedure training.

It can also assist in the development of a team culture in respect of monitoring and improving levels of efficiency and quality service. For a departmental team, this could involve interpersonal skills training and team building exercises. This is particularly true of multidisciplinary teams involved in regional or national activities on behalf of the larger catering organisations.

An example of this could be the national marketing and sales team of a large hotel chain, with responsibilities for national campaigns, regional sales activities and local advice to unit operators. Training would cover operational functions, strategic planning and management issues, or the training team itself identifying and servicing a large multi-site organisation. Given the correct type of training and development, teams, whatever their size, will operate more effectively, thereby assisting the business in a variety of ways.

KEY POINT

Targeting effective training and development at the team assists the creation of a team approach to problem solving.

THE INDIVIDUAL EMPLOYEE

Staff are an expensive resource and the success of any business in part relies on their individual ability to perform effectively. Training and development assists the employee by:

- ensuring they have the necessary skills and knowledge to undertake their duties, tasks and responsibilities
- providing a set of standards to which the employee can and should perform
- encouraging their on-going development
- providing increased motivation and job satisfaction
- providing opportunities for self-advancement, e.g. promotion
- minimizing personal risk in respect of health and safety and other legislation

Therefore to the catering employee, at whatever level, training and development not only ensures they have the necessary skills and knowledge to carry out duties and responsibilities, but also it provides for the individual opportunities to develop and obtain improved job satisfaction.

THE CUSTOMER

Customers benefit from the training and development that a catering operator undertakes.

- Catering businesses effectively managed can provide services of value and quality, enhancing a customer's experience
- The safety, quality of services and facilities are directly affected by the quality and effectiveness of training
- When problems occur, properly trained staff will be able to deal with these in a positive way
- Customer needs and expectations will be correctly identified and service and facilities amended to meet these needs
- Risk to the customer in respect of unsafe premises and practices is reduced

The majority of catering operators will be concerned with providing profitable quality services and will recognise that ongoing investment in training and development assists the achievement of this aim.

A factor which underlines all of the listed benefits to the economy, the industry, businesses, the team, the individual and the customer, is the contribution effective training makes to the profitability and survival of a catering organisation. This contribution is often difficult to evaluate, a factor which will be dealt with later in this chapter.

It is now important to explain how catering operators identify what training and development activities are required.

5.4 IDENTIFYING TRAINING AND DEVELOPMENT NEEDS

KEY POINT

Whatever the type, style, size or location of the business, there is a requirement to identify correctly training and development activities that match the needs of the business and its customers.

Consider the following:

1 Training is often an expensive activity, taking employees off direct customer service. (For an interesting approach to reducing such costs, see Case Study on page 229.)
2 Increasingly Government and European Union legislation is pressurising employers to provide more training and the complexity of such legislation can cause employers to invest in inappropriate training. (Note: This was certainly the case in the early 1990s when proposed changes to food hygiene legislation saw a rush to train and qualify staff.)

(this is the most common method and often tends to embrace a variety of objectives)

- *Review by performance,* where an individual's performance is judged against set targets
- *Review on objectives,* where an individual's performance over a given period, related to previously set objectives, is reviewed and analysed
- *Peer group appraisal,* where an individual's performance is judged by his/her peers
- *Subordinate appraisal,* an individual's appraisal is undertaken by those in his or her team, especially with regard to the effectiveness of team management and leadership
- *Self-appraisal,* where the individual analyses his or her performance and identifies targets and self-improvement actions for a forthcoming period

The most common method is down-line appraisal, where individuals have responsibility for appraising or reviewing their immediate subordinates. Such schemes are characterised by:

- formal methods, using standardised forms and procedures
- regularity, in that it is an annual activity
- review of past performance against job description, responsibilities and tasks
- inclusion of objective setting and individual action planning for the forthcoming period
- some link with pay, reward or incentive
- inclusion of identification of individual's training and development needs

--- **KEY POINT** ---

Whatever the reason for appraisal or method used, formalised schemes which attempt to cover all aspects in one discussion or interview will often prove ineffective and counterproductive. The best schemes involve a variety of methods conducted throughout the year.

Main roles of appraisal

Companies are increasingly using appraisal, especially forms of performance appraisal for a variety of reasons. These include:

- target setting
- identification of training and development needs
- pay reward and succession planning

Such activities are quite appropriate in their own right and, where appraisal is linked to other forms of involvement, it can be beneficial to both employee and employer. With effective systems the employee will receive formalised feedback on individual performance and development; the opportunity to comment on problems encountered and challenges overcome; a facility for requesting additional training and development and an opportunity to identify promotional possibilities (Figure 41).

For employers and line managers the benefits could include opportunity to formally praise and motivate individual employees; obtain feedback on organisational effectiveness; provide information on business plans; identify potential problems and the opportunity to identify individuals for further development and promotion.

III. PERFORMANCE CHARACTERISTICS

The following managerial performance characteristics have been identified as being particularly relevant to management effectiveness. The manager should write comments against each characteristic on the performance of the job holder. Consider the characteristics against what the job holder does, bearing in mind that not all will necessarily be appropriate in every situation.

PERFORMANCE CHARACTERISTIC	COMMENTS
KNOWLEDGE AND INFORMATION: (a) How extensive is the job holder's technical knowledge and competence in the job. (b) How well does he/she command basic facts of the organisation, its products and services.	
ANALYSIS AND PLANNING: How well does the job holder logically analyse, plan and organise his/her work against the objectives.	
PROBLEM SOLVING & DECISION MAKING: How well does the job holder balance the judgement of facts and use his/her intuition in solving problems and making decisions.	
LEADERSHIP: How effectively does the job holder motivate subordinates and how well does he/she develop their skills.	
DRIVE: How dedicated and committed is the job holder to starting and seeing a job through. How well does he/she initiate and respond to action.	
CREATIVITY: How effectively does the job holder initiate and/or recognise original ideas and responses to situations.	
MANAGING RELATIONSHIPS: (OUTSIDE THE TEAM) How well does the job holder make and maintain effective personal relationships at all levels to achieve commercial success.	
MANAGING RELATIONSHIPS: (WITHIN THE TEAM) How well does the job holder manage relationships within team towards commercial success.	

III A. ACTION REQUIRED

Summarise any personal development or behaviour changes which have been identified in the review of past performance, (Sections II and III) which will assist in the achievement of future objectives.

ACTION PLAN TO IMPROVE PERFORMANCE CHARACTERISTICS	CONTRACT FOR BEHAVIOUR CHANGE ON TEAM RELATIONSHIPS

FIGURE 41 *An example of a staff appraisal form from Harvester Restaurants.*

At its best, appraisal can and does provide considerable benefits to both employers and employees. However, appraisal and performance reviews are also not without their critics. W. Edwards Deming, one of the gurus of total quality, has suggested that performance appraisal is one of the seven deadly diseases of current management practice.

Ineffective appraisal or performance review systems can result in:

- demotivated employees who, faced with criticism (whether justified or not), will react by becoming less effective
- a mismatch between individual employee expectation and business needs – this may relate to promotion, pay or training and development needs
- a personnel driven, bureaucratic system overladen with formality and paperwork which is time-consuming and ineffective
- industrial dispute and grievance, when an employee considers him/herself to have been unfairly treated
- the breakdown of working relationships between appraiser and appraisee
- a feel good factor, where individuals undertake the activity in a ritualistic manner in attempts to satisfy the system and one another – outcomes are then of no real use to either party
- unrealistic target and objective setting

The above will occur if:

- the system is not accepted or understood
- appraisers and appraisees have not been trained or briefed on the system and how to make it effective
- the appraisal is the only method by which pay increases or incentives are identified and awarded

ANNUAL STAFF APPRAISALS: HOTEL PERSONNEL, STAKIS HOTELS

OBJECTIVES

1 To provide a formal mechanism for evaluating the job performance of all hotel employees
2 To provide a vehicle for communicating achievements, strengths and weaknesses
3 To involve the appraisee in a measure of self evaluation
4 To identify individuals suitable for promotion and development
5 To identify training needs and organisational strengths and weaknesses
   - All management and supervisory staff at hotel level will be assessed annually to evaluate job performance, identify training and development needs and assist the company in its manpower planning strategy
   - Each member of staff, below supervisory level, will be assessed annually to evaluate performance, identify training and development needs and identify candidates suitable for promotion
   - Appraisals of supervisors and managers will be conducted according to procedures detailed in

the Corporate Human Resources Manual and in the General Manager's Manual. Heads of Department and subordinate managers will be appraised by the General Manager. The General Manager will be appraised by the Area Executive

- Appraisals of departmental operatives will be conducted by HODs in accordance with the procedure given in the Hotel Personnel and Training Manual
- Where an appraisee is not satisfied that the conclusions of an annual appraisal are fair, provision is made for referral to higher authority for reconsideration of the findings
- The Personnel and Training Department at Corporate Office is responsible for providing documentation and guidelines for the conduct of annual appraisals, consolidating information and making recommendations to the Director of Personnel in respect of manpower planning and development strategies on a yearly basis

NOTES ON CONDUCT OF ANNUAL APPRAISALS FOR MANAGERIAL AND SUPERVISORY STAFF

Between January and March each year, all management and supervisors will undergo a formal performance appraisal to assess achievements and determine their training and/or development needs. Arising from this appraisal, performance objectives will be set and progress monitoring arrangement determined. Hotel managers will be appraised by their Area Executive. Subordinate staff will be appraised by the Hotel Manager.

Before the appraisal interview
a) Interviews will be scheduled in advance.
b) The appraisal form issued by Corporate Office will be used.
c) An appraisal checklist must be issued to the appraisee sufficiently in advance of the event to allow for prior preparation.
d) Prior to the appraisal interview, the appraisee must receive:
   - a job holder's checklist
   - a copy of his/her current job description (for review and revision)
   - the appraisal form to enable them to complete their section (self-appraisal component).
e) Two days before the appraisal, the job description and the completed self-appraisal must be returned to the appraiser to enable their section to be completed prior to the meeting.

At the appraisal interview
a) Meetings will normally last between a half to one hour to enable documentation to be finalised and objectives for the next twelve months agreed.
b) The job description will be revised as appropriate.
c) The completed appraisal form (S) must be signed by both interviewee and interviewer and sent to the appraiser's superior for consideration, approval and signature.
If an appraisee believes that the appraisal does not fairly reflect either their potential or the quality/effectiveness of their performance, they may request reconsideration of the conclusions at higher level. For a Subordinate Manager the request will be dealt with by the Area Executive. For a Hotel Manager the review will be conducted by another Area Executive.

After the interview

a) A copy of the endorsed appraisal form (S) must be sent to the job holder.

b) A copy of the appraisal documentation will be retained in the Personnel file at the Hotel, and a copy sent to the Personnel Department at Corporate Office.

Post appraisal

a) The appraiser will undertake reviews of performance and objectives arising from the annual appraisal to monitor progress, maintain contact and assist with any development.

Stakis Hotels

Courses are run on appraisal skills and handling staff problems.

APPRAISAL SKILLS AND HANDLING STAFF PROBLEMS

OBJECTIVES

- To understand the purpose and benefits of an effective performance appraisal system.
- To practice the key skills of questioning, listening and summarising.
- To know how to prepare, carry out and follow up the appraisal interview.
- To understand the importance of setting measurable performance objectives.
- To discuss methods used to deal with subordinate's problems.
- To establish approaches to help individuals understand and resolve problems.

DURATION

3 days, and a follow-up interview.

Haven Leisure

5.5 DEVELOPING TRAINING AND DEVELOPMENT PLANS

Whatever method or methods are used to identify the training and development needs of a business, there is a need for a mechanism to achieve the desired outcome. This is most commonly satisfied by the design of a training plan, which details the process by which the training will take place.

The industry currently approaches this in a variety of ways, ranging from comprehensive statements matching specific training activities to particular business strategies and objectives, to fairly simple documents which identify training activities in order of completion. Training plans can often include detailed costing and budget figures, responsibilities, target participants, scheduled dates, desired outcomes or statements on purpose and systems for monitoring, review and evaluation. Such plans may be accompanied by separate documents including in-house training programmes and policy statements.

For smaller businesses with minimal amounts of employees, such detailed documentation may be inappropriate and management staff and owners will often lack both the time and expertise to design such plans.

─────────────────────── KEY POINT ───────────────────────

Effective training plans are ones which assist the improvement of the business and the individual employee. The success will not rely on any written plan, however detailed, but more on the business's ability to maximise on the investment it makes in training and development.

───

Training and development plans may cover the following areas:

- annual training plan for a company or business
- regional training plan for a national company, whose size necessitates a segmented approach
- unit training plan for national companies
- sector training plans for particular groups of employees, e.g. unit managers, unit personnel and training managers, company sales staff and food service staff
- unit/business training plan for independent unit
- department training plan for group of employees involved in a particular section of a unit
- individual training and development plans

It is quite common for larger companies to undertake all of the above to some degree, with the general aim that all plans relate to stated company strategies and objectives.

Training plans may also be designed on shorter periods and, with the increasing pace of change, hospitality operators will nowadays often produce quarterly or six-monthly programmes.

Key elements of a training plan

Whatever the reason or scope for the training plan, there is a common set of guidelines for their completion:

1 The plan should be based firmly on clearly identified business objectives.
2 The plan can be produced in a variety of forms; however, all elements must be clear, understandable and, most importantly, achievable.
3 To be successful, any training plan must have the commitment and support of senior management.
4 The responsibilities for the activities must be clearly identified and accepted.
5 The details of the plan should be communicated to all who are affected by it; by involving employees any plan will have an increased 'chance' of both acceptance and success.
6 The resources required in terms of cost, time, people and facilities must be identified and made available.
7 Systems for monitoring, review, evaluation and adaptation should be included.

Without such elements or considerations, the plan may fail for a number of reasons.

- There may be an incorrect match to key business objectives, with the result of investment in inappropriate activities
- Overcomplicated plans written in 'management jargon' will be difficult to communicate to employees
- If training activities are expressed poorly, the real objectives may not be achieved
- If individuals fail to take responsibility for all elements of the plan, activities may not be completed
- Ineffective communication will possibly result in employees not contributing to or supporting planned activity
- Lack of support from senior management, in terms of overall commitment and resources, will communicate itself to the employees, thereby devaluing the plan and activities
- As training and development is a fairly dynamic activity, lack of monitoring and evaluation will possibly result in waste of resources in terms of finances, facilities and people

––––––––––––––––––––––––––– KEY POINT –––––––––––––––––––––––––––

Training plans will differ dependent upon the size and style of the company or business. Additionally, the format and scope will vary dependent upon the number and type of staff involved.

Before providing explanations and examples of training plans, it is important to detail the factors operators will have to consider when developing and designing such plans. The company, business, unit or owner will have to consider all the factors which will affect the plan, similar to the analysis and consideration given to identifying training needs. Presuming that the training needs have been correctly identified, then the operator will need to consider the following:

- the priority of each training activity within an identified list
- the possible costs of the training activities, including staff cover costs, external course costs, accommodation, travel, trainer costs and certification
- the preferred or required delivery mechanism for the training activities, e.g. in-house, off the job, distance learning, seminars or workshops
- the expertise available to deliver the proposed training
- the scheduling and location of activities; many organisations will deliberately target training during quieter periods to minimise effect of staff absence

In a survey of 250 companies' training activities and plans conducted in 1993, all identified preferences in respect of training:

- 70% favoured in-house courses

- 65% identified the months of January and February as the best time for externally provided training
- 72% stated their preferred days for training as Tuesdays and Wednesdays
- 80% favoured short courses in preference to more traditional time-serving certificated courses

J. Roberts (1993) *Training Needs in the Hospitality Industry Survey,*
Rotherham College of Arts and Technology

- the availability or commitment of employees to attend and fulfil training activities
- the expected outcome and benefits of the training for the company, business, unit, department or individual

There must be a recognisable and measurable benefit to the organisation of training activity and if benefits and values cannot be identified then the training should not be undertaken.

TRAINING MANAGER, LONDON 5-STAR HOTEL

For some organisations, such considerations will require detailed analysis and discussion, whilst for others, such elements will receive scant attention as they concentrate on other business practices. However, all involved in the organisation will have a stake or interest in developing and delivering effective training. The training plan should not be the sole responsibility of an individual without reference to other interested parties. In large to medium sized companies, the training plan may have to be discussed and agreed by senior managers or directors, whose role is to evaluate the plan against business plans and objectives.

I conducted a review of specific aspects of our business, identifying weaknesses and priorities in terms of training and development. The training proposal was presented to the Board of Directors who, after detailed discussion, supported the proposals. This was a vital element in the improvement of the business through targeted and focused training activities.

BOB RUSSELL, DIRECTOR, PAYNE AND GUNTHERS (EVENT CATERERS)

For any training plan, in addition to gaining senior management approval and support, it is becoming increasingly important to involve others, including shareholders, the individuals responsible for aspects of the programme and the recipients of the planned training.

For standard training, which is required by legislation, e.g. HASAWA and food hygiene, the reasons for inclusion in the training plan are self-apparent, and the majority of employees will readily accept such training as both necessary and personally beneficial. This is not necessarily the case with all training, especially when the reasons for the employee to attend training have not been effectively communicated. Increasingly, hospitality operators are recognising that the employees themselves need to understand the importance of training, in terms of benefits both to the organisation and to themselves. This aspect is being tackled in a variety of ways, including revised use of appraisal, team activities for identifying training needs and employee involvement in the evaluation of training.

─────────────────── K E Y   P O I N T ───────────────────

By involving all employees in the identification, delivery and evaluation of training and development, increased commitment and ownership of such activity is achieved. The result is an improvement in outcome in terms of business improvement and individual employee satisfaction.

Such involvement in identifying training needs is being supported by various government initiatives. In seeking accreditation under the 'Investors in People' programme, companies have to demonstrate that they have encouraged individual employees to identify their own training needs and that the company has communicated the range of training opportunities to them. Such initiatives help companies to focus in on training and development and recognise the importance of all employees being involved in the process.

When reviewing proposed training and development priorities and strategies against the performance criteria for 'Investors in People', we quickly identified a close correlation between the two. The IIP standards assisted us in pushing forward our plans.

BOB RUSSELL, DIRECTOR, PAYNE AND GUNTHERS

The national Standard

AN *INVESTOR IN PEOPLE* TAKES ACTION TO TRAIN AND DEVELOP INDIVIDUALS ON RECRUITMENT AND THROUGHOUT THEIR EMPLOYMENT.

- Action should focus on the training needs of all new recruits and continually developing and improving the skills of existing employees.

- All employees should be encouraged to contribute to identifying and meeting their own job-related development needs.

© Investors in People UK 1994.

The development of training plans then, is dependent upon the effectiveness of systems for identifying needs and the ability of the organisation, company or business to design, resource, deliver, monitor, evaluate and adapt its plan. Such plans will have greater chances of success when all involved employees participate.

Common types of plan

COMPANY PLAN

Such plans are characterised by broad statements on overall training targets, often accompanied by a match to business objectives. The detail in respect of activities will often be provided separately in a training programme which identifies the range, content and duration, and which targets employees. Individual units may then respond by identifying and facilitating group or individual employee attendance on training courses or activities.

UNIT TRAINING PLAN

Within units of larger companies, plans will be developed to satisfy the criteria and objectives of the company plan, whilst identifying in more detail individual or team training. This may mean that unit plans will differ in relation to the situation they face in terms of staff experience, qualifications and availability.

DEPARTMENT TRAINING PLAN

For larger businesses and units, the number of staff may result in the need for separate departmental plans. Departmental heads, who are increasingly taking over aspects of training, will have responsibility for identifying training needs and the submission of a plan. Such plans will, similar to unit plans, identify specific training, individual employees, forecasted dates, mechanisms for delivery and estimated costs. Departmental heads are also increasingly designing and delivering training programmes themselves, which may include standard elements, such as induction training and regular skills training.

INDIVIDUAL TRAINING AND DEVELOPMENT PLANS

With the increasing involvement of all employees in identifying and evaluating training, the increased use of appraisal and performance review and the growing recognition of the need to develop a training culture, individual training and development plans are becoming more common. This is particularly true in larger more formalised companies, especially for employees at supervisory and middle management level. Additionally, employees in trainee management positions will follow a presubscribed training plan on an individual basis.

The value of such individual programmes is the ability to monitor individual and group development against an agreed set of performance criteria, whilst the employee can readily measure their own development against set targets. Progression via the acquisition of experience and skills provides increased motivation, which some companies reward by relating pay increase to the satisfactory completion of particular stages of the training programme.

Whatever the type of plan, its success relies, in part, on the correct targeting of participants and the degree of involvement these individuals have in identifying needs. However, as previously indicated, plans are at best projections and forecasts of activities and they reflect the needs of the business at a particular time. Hospitality operators are as aware as other industries of the need to be more flexible and adapt to changing markets. The investment they make is quite considerable

FIGURE 42   *Staff training rewards: Bronze, Silver and Gold Awards at Bass Taverns.*

and therefore it is necessary to build into the plans, mechanisms for the analysis of training activities.

Monitoring, review and evaluation of training plans and programmes

As identified in the key elements of training, a mechanism and ability to manage such investment is of vital importance. However, the evaluation of training is a difficult task, due to the complex nature of training itself and the problem in identifying long-term costs and benefits. This is an aspect which has attracted much debate over the last decade and one which continues to cause problems for some operators.

For the personnel manager, training officer or department, owner, senior management or directors, the reason for such activity is recognisable. They will (to varying degrees) wish to know:

- whether the planned training is taking or has taken place
- the success and effectiveness of the training in respect of the outcome related to stated objectives
- that costs have been kept to the designated, estimated budget
- any particular problems associated with planned training and development
- the satisfaction of employees with delivered training
- any external or internal demand which necessitates alteration to the plan, e.g. a change in legislation

The national Standard

AN *INVESTOR IN PEOPLE* REGULARLY REVIEWS THE TRAINING AND DEVELOPMENT
NEEDS OF ALL EMPLOYEES.

- The resources for training and developing employees should be clearly identified in the business plan.

- Managers should be responsible for regularly agreeing training and development needs with each employee in the context of business objectives, setting targets and standards linked, where appropriate to the achievement of National Vocational Qualifications (or relevant units) and, in Scotland, Scottish Vocational Qualifications.

© Investors in People UK 1994.

KEY POINT

Effective training plans are ones which include a degree of flexibility, allowing for adaptation or amendment in the light of changing circumstances.

Hospitality operators use a variety of mechanisms and processes to review and update training plans, including:

- reports from managers and training officers
- in-course and post-course evaluation by participants commenting on aspects, such as personal satisfaction with training and identification of personal benefits
- general performance review of the unit, department or individual to ascertain whether the training has contributed towards business improvement
- customer feedback on quality of service and facilities to ascertain whether training is resulting in improved services
- line manager appraisal of individual employees or groups of employees who have undertaken training
- financial or systems reviews to ascertain whether training has contributed towards increased profits, reduced waste or safer working conditions and practices

The degree to which such review and evaluation is undertaken depends heavily on the operator, and the scale and scope of training.

Companies may also pilot training schemes in specific areas, prior to agreeing to a wider take up in an attempt to ascertain the validity of the training to current and projected business needs. Monitoring, review and evaluation is, therefore, an important and increasingly key element of training and development. Its purpose is wider than managing the cost and delivery and includes the validity, effectiveness and identification of the outcome.

When developing training plans, the organisation has to take into consideration a variety of factors and, whilst training plans will vary, they should contain common elements related to ensuring that investment in training results in significant improvement in both the business and the individual.

Approaches to training and development

Traditionally, the hospitality industry relied on two main methods of training: attendance at college on a full-time or day release programme, or by observation and experience within the workplace. Some hotel companies did provide training, which was often geared around apprenticeships and trainee management training programmes. Critics of such traditional systems pointed to the inappropriate method of time serving and the generally poor standard of training programmes.

Whilst there were some excellent schemes, training was, overall, inadequately planned, under-researched and relied heavily on supervisors and operatives passing on skills and knowledge in unstructured ways. This approach was often referred to as 'sitting beside Nellie', where new or inexperienced employees relied on the willingness and skills of more experienced staff.

As previously indicated, the growth in more formalised training over the past two decades has been significant and currently employers use a wide variety of methods.

There are obviously constraints on the type of training a hospitality operator undertakes and this aspect would normally be dealt with when developing training plans. (See section on training plans, page 212.) What the operator will wish to do is identify the most cost effective method.

─────────────────── **KEY POINT** ───────────────────

Whatever method or methods of training and development are used, they must be appropriate to the organisation and assist a positive outcome.

For independent businesses with relatively small numbers of employees, that do not have the back up of in-house training facilities, the choice will be limited to those methods which possibly provide a low-cost solution. As staff time is limited, long courses or blocks of time away from the unit will cause problems with regard to covering for absence, whilst larger companies with sophisticated training departments will often be able to consider a much wider variety of methods.

The method or methods of training will also rely on the attitude and commitment to such activity, an aspect which is becoming increasingly important as companies and businesses reduce overall numbers of staff and increase the emphasis of ongoing training.

The common methods and approaches to training and development

There are two basic approaches to training:

1   On the job training, where the activity is undertaken within the workplace
2   Off the job training, where the activity is undertaken outside the workplace

THISTLE HOTELS

AND
MOUNT CHARLOTTE HOTELS

MANAGEMENT TRAINING

WHAT kind of a training scheme are you looking for?

Is it one which:
- ❏ has commitment from the Company at all levels
- ❏ recognises potential
- ❏ trains technical and management skills to the highest standards
- ❏ offers exciting opportunities and career advancement
- ❏ treats trainees as individuals as well as part of a team
- ❏ produces successful managers?

Mount Charlotte Thistle Hotels Management Training Schemes offer all these features.

Commitment from the Company

This begins at the top. Mr Robert Peel, Chief Executive and former trainee himself, stresses the importance of involving all management in the responsibility for training.
Our Company Training Policy is centred on the principle that trainees will receive thorough training and development. The onus of meeting our high standards, however, rests with you the individual.

Recognising potential

As a trainee you will need to demonstrate you have the potential to become the type of manager we require.
We will ask you to complete monthly progress reports and at the end of each three month period you will be involved in assessment interviews with senior management within the hotel.
You will be encouraged and expected to take an objective view of your own performance.
During assessment by senior management, you will receive constructive advice to help you improve and develop so that your management potential may be realised.

Training technical and management skills to the highest standards

Mount Charlotte Thistle Hotels issues a comprehensive log book to every trainee manager. This is you own personal record of your achievements to date and becomes part of your career portfolio.
The log book contains all the objectives and skills it is necessary to acquire in each department.
In addition you must complete departmental fact sheets and learn to interpret the information from a management perspective.
Departmental performance reports, completed by Heads of Department, assess your technical ability whilst training control records, monitored by Senior Managers and Regional Personnel and Training Managers, are an instant record of your achievements.

Opportunities and career advancement

Flexibility and adaptability are two attributes we look for in all trainee managers.
You could be involved in functions attended by Royalty or you may be required to assist with a one-off specialist Company project.
When your training is complete and you are considered ready and suitable for promotion, you will be given every assistance by your Regional Personnel and Training Manager to find a suitable position within the Company.
To mark your successful completion of a recognised training scheme, you will be presented with a framed certificate by the Chief Executive at the annual Presentation Dinner.

Trainees as individuals and team members

Mount Charlotte Thistle Hotels are 'managed with individuality and flair'. You will be encouraged to develop your own management style and will receive counselling and guidance to enable you to do this.
Whilst your individuality will certainly be nurtured, you will also work in close liaison within the hotel management team.

Successful Managers

Our Management Training Schemes are merely the beginning; resources are available to develop our successful trainees from Junior Assistant level to that of General Manager.
After your first promotion your further training and development will encompass the following areas:

- ❏ Standard setting
- ❏ Planning and forecasting
- ❏ Budgets and control
- ❏ Sales
- ❏ Disciplinary procedures
- ❏ Motivation
- ❏ Training
- ❏ Appraisal
- ❏ Leadership
- ❏ Counselling
- ❏ Negotiating
- ❏ Interviewing

You can be certain that if you choose one of the Mount Charlotte Thistle Management Training Schemes, the training you will receive will be amongst the best on offer.

FIGURE 43 *Mount Charlotte Thistle Hotels Management Training Scheme. Well designed schemes assist both the organisation and the employee.*

Overall the last decade has seen an increase in on the job training with a decrease in off the job training. The main reasons being the increasing costs of off the job training, reduced numbers of staff, improvement in in-house training, developments in open and distance learning and the growing use of job and performance competencies.

Additionally, the approach to training may include:

- individual training
- team training
- one to one training

FIGURE 44 *Torquay Leisure Hotels training and development schemes. A bold way to inform staff of commitment to training and development.*

So, you can see that the industry has moved towards a much more dynamic approach to training and one which includes a variety of strategies. Methods include:

- *External long course,* where the aim is to obtain certification or validation
- *External short course,* normally of one to three day's duration where attendance is aimed at knowledge acquisition or certification
- *Seminar/workshop,* becoming increasingly popular, especially for management level staff; usually of a day's duration and based on a specific element.

- *Distance or open learning*, also increasing in popularity, with courses operated by private training companies, professional associations, colleges and companies themselves; the individual works through a series of tasks/modules and assignments in his/her own time, supported by periodic one-to-one tutorials or short blocks of study

The majority of the methods above relate to individual employees undertaking training to update knowledge and qualifications. The company or business will normally provide support in terms of fee payment, time off for study or attendance and associated costs of travel and accommodation.

The second group of methods include more in-house programmes, where individuals or groups of employees undertake training commonly related to acquisition of skills, knowledge and experience. This could include:

- *Company-organised short courses*, often on specific skills
- *Programme of courses, modules and activities*, usually designed for a group or level of employees such as trainee managers; in such situations the employees will complete a variety of training activities whilst gaining day-to-day experience within the job itself
- *Team activities* where a unit and team approach to training has been developed, enlarging the concept from team participation in training delivered by another, to a situation where the team itself is empowered to identify training needs and create solutions to those needs; Harvester Restaurants is one such organisation and, earlier in the text, examples and explanations were provided of their particular approach to involving employees in such activities (page 33)
- *Skills training* (the design, delivery and evaluation of such training was described in the preceding section); such training may be on a one to one basis, or to a group of individuals; with increasing responsibility being passed down to line managers and heads of departments, such activity is increasing

Other methods of training which are increasing in popularity include:

- *Secondment*, providing individual employees with the opportunity to spend some time in another work environment, the aim being to assist the individual in obtaining new skills and knowledge; companies may do this to prepare a manager for a new role, or to further enhance an individual's skill base

To assist the development of new menus, it was arranged for two of our chefs to spend a short period training with Georges Blanc, a Michelin 3-star chef. The chosen venue for the menus was the Henley Regatta.

BOB RUSSELL, DIRECTOR, PAYNE AND GUNTHERS

- *Project work*, proving popular with companies which have a reasonably sized group of supervisors or managers; specific projects may also be given to an individual with the aim of assisting a particular problem
- *Interactive video and computer programmes*, developed with the advent of the relatively inexpensive desk top computers; these can include knowledge testing or training packages

related to particular types of software, to more complex personal development and problem-solving programmes; the advantage of such programmes is that the individual will work at their own pace without the fear of failure or embarrassment associated with more traditional forms of instruction; however, this method presumes a reasonable level of computer literacy and there remains a considerable amount of work to be done in its development

Summary

The hospitality industry has advanced considerably in its approach to training and currently employs a wide variety of methods. All the methods possess advantages and disadvantages and the company or business will, as stated, need to identify the most cost-effective method suitable for their organisation.

It is also important to recognise that individuals learn at a different pace and will respond differently to specific methods. Experienced, confident employees used to undertaking training will feel comfortable in a variety of situations, whilst less confident individuals will respond better to less formal training methods.

The final sections in this chapter will look at the constraints on operators when designing and delivering training and the growing importance of developing a training and learning culture.

5.6 DESIGN, DELIVERY AND EVALUATION OF TRAINING

The design of training and development is concerned with the identification of:

- required outcome and benefits
- methods and approaches to the training
- the range of employees, target groups and individuals
- the programming or scheduling
- communicating the availability and range of programmes to employees

and the creation of systems which allow such activities to take place, including resourcing, expense accounting and administrating.

Additionally, there is the design of the course or programme itself – the content, method, timing, materials and facilities required, location and duration. For many trainers the design of a course is the most challenging and exciting aspect and experienced trainers will know that, each time they deliver a standard course, differences occur. An aspect which is due to the fact that all groups and individuals react differently in training situations.

────────────── KEY POINT ──────────────

The design of training and development activities is one of the most challenging elements of a personnel or training manager's role. For many it forms the focus on their approach to developing people.

"I'm not sure our training and development manager has got her skills training right!"

The design of training and development can range from company-wide programmes encompassing a range of courses and modules, to the setting up of a five to ten minute skills training session for employees in the work situation.

With the existence of such a wide range, the trainer or personnel specialist will require a variety of skills and experience. This aspect has been recognised for some time, with various training bodies and professional associations developing 'train the trainers'-type programmes. Whilst the merger between the Institute of Training and Development and the Institute of Personnel Management may bring some alterations to such schemes, there is a wide acceptance that those who design and deliver training should be trained themselves to a form of national standard.

During the 1970s and 1980s the then Hotel and Catering Industry Board developed a range of trainer skills courses. These included Trainer Skills I and II, with specific programmes for group and individual training. With the development of National Vocational Qualifications, the Training and Development Lead Body has developed a number of units at Levels III and IV, with specific units on the design, delivery and evaluation of training.

Additionally, NVQs have provided systems for individuals in the workplace to be registered assessors or verifiers of training, related to individual competence. Such schemes certainly assist the general raising of standards. However, they are not suitable for all situations and the cost may be restrictive for smaller operators.

Whilst the involvement of trainers and personnel specialists in the design of in-house programmes is of vital importance, such individuals have a role to play when courses and training material are provided externally, either for use within the workplace or when individual employees attend courses outside the company.

─────────────────── KEY POINT ───────────────────

The design of training and development programmes includes the evaluation of possible external programmes or trainers. The choice of trainer is not so important as the quality and effectiveness of the training itself.

For smaller organisations, training requirements may only be satisfied by employees attending external courses, the cost of the courses themselves being offset by not having to employ someone specifically to undertake this role. Conversely, for a larger company with a predominance of in-house training, the problem is that such activity becomes too 'company' or organisation-based, with employees having no opportunity to obtain learning and experience from other situations.

A debate our Company is currently having relates to the need, on occasions, to expose our managers to external trainers or managers who can provide additional perspectives and viewpoints.

VICTOR ARCINIEGA, SENIOR HUMAN RESOURCE OFFICER, MCDONALD'S RESTAURANTS

The choice of external trainers or courses and their inclusion in training and development programmes is dependent upon a number of factors. During 1992–93 I conducted a major survey into the training and development needs of the industry. One section asked Personnel and Human Resource Managers about their involvement in and use of external training organisations and how they selected particular providers. Of the 300 odd companies canvassed, representing some 180,000 staff, the results were as follows:

IDENTIFICATION AND USE OF EXTERNAL TRAINING PROVIDERS

- 60% used external providers to a reasonable degree
- 85% used on an infrequent basis

The criteria for selection were mainly:

- quality of programme or trainer (usually based on previous experience)
- flexibility and degree to which course reflected the business needs
- responsiveness of the training provider

Note: Cost, interestingly, was not considered to be a significant problem

J. Roberts (1993) *Training Needs of the Hotel, Catering and Leisure Industry,*
Rotherham College of Arts and Technology

The use of external trainers may also be included to provide certain levels of skills not available within the company or on a consultancy basis linked to forms of public relations. Several of the national airlines have undertaken this, working with high profile chefs to create new menus, train staff and act as a focus for promotional activity.

The design of training programmes, then, covers a variety of important tasks, including general programme outline, resourcing, administration, communication and promotion. Ranging from the design of company-wide programmes for considerable numbers of staff (see McDonald's Case Study in Chapter 4 and Threshers Case Study in this chapter for positive examples), to the design of short skill sessions.

KEY POINT

Without effective designs, the effectiveness of training and development programmes will reduce considerably.

TOM COBLEIGH TRAINING PROGRAMME

Tom Cobleigh is a fast-growing, progressive licensed house operator with a Mission Statement: 'To provide real food and beer in unspoilt pubs where total customer satisfaction dominates our actions.' The Company has developed a variety of training approaches. The example provided below is an outline of a specific training programme designed for newly-appointed assistant managers.

OBJECTIVES OF PERSONAL TRAINING PACKAGE

1 To train the Assistant Managers in the most comprehensive manner to prepare for unit management in the most effective time period
2 To identify stages in the training process and training needs of each individual
3 To provide a record of progress within the company
4 To specify tasks and sources of standards within the training process
5 To provide an opportunity for both Trainer and Trainee to review progress

WELCOME TO TOM COBLEIGH'S FAST TRACK TRAINING

Fast-Track Training is designed to proceed at the speed of the individual Assistant Managers and there is no time limit on any given section, but the aim is to equip the Assistant Managers, within a 3–9-month period, with the knowledge and expertise to manage a Tom Cobleigh outlet.

Both partners must complete the *whole package* but it is acceptable that one partner, for example, understands the working of the cellar but the other partner would have to be proficient in cellar management.

No part of the package will be signed off until understanding/proficiency is achieved.
If you have any queries or need further clarification, please contact any member of the Personnel and Training Department.

Our industry is an interesting, exciting, stimulating and social environment in which to work.
It is also fiercely competitive, so we must ensure that our standards in every aspect of the business are consistently of the highest order.

As a growing company we are constantly seeking new people like yourself to join us. You may have some previous experience of our industry, but if not, don't worry. The objective of our training programme is to ensure that you and all other newcomers are able to understand, maintain and indeed improve upon our standards.

The Personal Training Package has been devised to help achieve that objective. Both you and your trainees will be able to record your progress throughout your training; what you have done and where you have been. In fact, the title says it all – it is personal to you, it's about your development within the company and it manages and records your progress.

We don't, however, train commonsense or maturity, nor do we train attitude. These talents should already be in your possession, because if they are not, no matter how proficient you become technically, you will not succeed.

Start on your first day with us as you intend to be seen and measured for the rest of your career with Tom Cobleigh Limited.

If you have any comments about your training programme, please don't hesitate to talk to your House Managers or anyone within our Personnel and Training Department.

Good Luck!

Maggie Pearson, Human Resources Director, Tom Cobleigh plc

CASE STUDY. THRESHER WINE SHOPS AND DRINKS STORES: DELIVERING EFFECTIVE TRAINING

BACKGROUND

Thresher is part of the Restaurants and Leisure Division of Whitbread plc. Thresher is a national business split into five retail brands: Food and Drinks Stores, Drinks Stores, Thresher Wine Shops, Wine Rack and Bottoms Up, with a total of over 1600 retail units employing over 10,000 employees throughout Britain.

Its Mission Statement is 'To be Britain's Favourite Drinks Retailer ... by delivering the highest brand standards and making people count ... every day'.

With such a large number of outlets, spread over a wide geographical area, and with over 48% of staff being part-time, training and development was a major challenge, one which Thresher has tackled in a variety of innovative ways. Recognising the problems which faced food and drink retailing and following the successful incorporation of 650 shops from the Dominic Group in 1991, Thresher undertook a major review of its training and development function.

Training at Thresher is provided by a head office function, based on two sites – Welwyn Garden City and the office in Huyton. The central team's task is to develop, in conjunction with operational management and functional specialists, focused training and development activities to meet business and individual needs.

Thresher's training policy statement is as follows:

- to encourage self-development
- to provide professional qualifications and/or company recognition
- to include appropriate action plans to consolidate learning and encourage further development
- to support the business aims to maximise sales and profitability
- to communicate personal and business benefits
- to fulfil the defined objectives
- to develop confidence and enhance team effectiveness.

Whilst training has always been seen as important, no business plan existed for training activity. The company identified that to achieve the business plan it had to ensure training was delivered to meet needs; increase the productivity of training; increase numbers of branch personnel provided with centrally driven training; increase the emphasis on individual development/education on-job; reduce off-job training; achieve improved value from the training budget and, lastly, ensure training was evaluated in business benefit terms.

RESULTS

Following the development of a series of activities based on achieving the targets the training team were set, the outcomes were considerable. The company researched and analysed the contents in some detail, and the results are identified below:

- increase of over 65% of staff receiving centrally driven training (over 5290 in 1993)
- increase in training days by 51%

- 41% reduction in number of off-job training days
- open learning costs reduced
- 41% reduction in labour costs related to training
- trainer productivity increased by 65%
- 70% increase in employees passing Retail Wine & Spirits Award (1500 candidates in 1993)
- 103% increase in Higher Wine Certificate passes
- overall business performance increase
- increase of 25% in number of new accounts opened following training
- achievement of Investors in People accreditation for Thresher training
- increase in level of employee satisfaction.

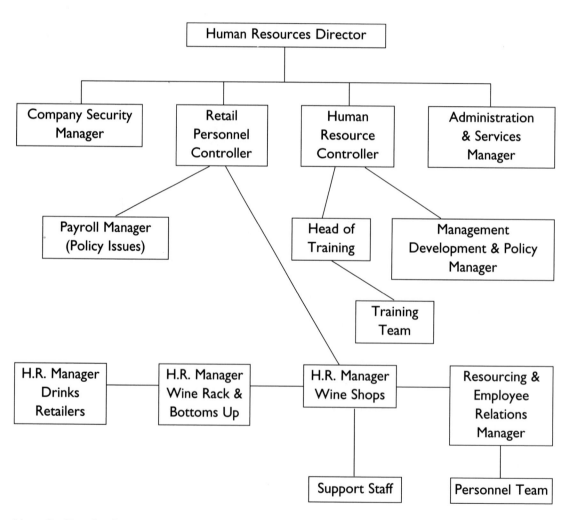

Note: Staffing for Security and Administrative Services not shown.

FIGURE 45 Thresher's human resources structure.

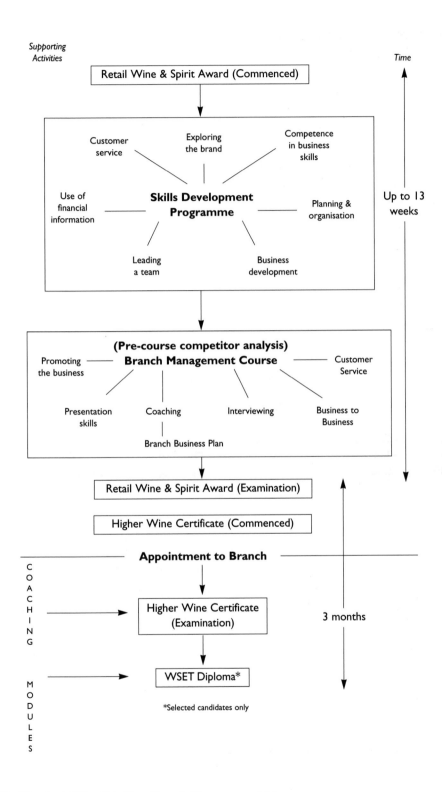

FIGURE 46 *Thresher's Wine Retailing Branch Manager model programme.*

Chris Jeffries, acknowledging the support of colleagues within the Human Resource and training team, also identified other benefits, including:

successful media coverage, individual employee success in achieving advanced qualifications, publication by one trainer of a book on wine, development of a video training package which has generated significant sales. The development we undertook has enabled us to both maintain and improve the level of training and assist in setting even higher targets for 1994–95 and beyond. With distance learning firmly embedded in the work-based culture, a secure foundation exists for NVQ expansion.

HOW WAS THIS ACHIEVED?

In 1992 the company decided to create the Thresher Training Company as a wholly owned part of Thresher. Building on the existing training function it used the 'Investors in People' approach to benchmark performance, identify standards and develop the training team. The training team consists of seven managers and their support staff, whose job it is to focus on the delivery of training and development, working in conjunction with 95 area sales managers and the shop managers.

Training consists of the following:

*   open learning packages in Retail Wines and Spirits Award and Higher Wine Certificate
*   targeted training progress for shop managers and deputy managers
*   series of coaching modules for shop managers
*   off-job training programmes

Backing these training activities are a number of policies and practices which provide for both the support of the employees and the management and evaluation of training.

Performance standards are set for each job, which clearly identifies the competencies required. On appointment at shop level, an employee receives a competency card which identifies the standards, knowledge and training required. Trained shop managers control this process and employees take an average of six months to complete all the competencies. Encompassing knowledge-based tests, employees work towards a silver award, receiving financial and company recognition upon achievement.

With regular performance reviews and annual appraisals, employees are involved in the identification of their own development needs, a process that all employees undertake. Retail shop personnel can work towards a gold award and, wherever possible, promotional ladders are created.

OBSERVATIONS

There is no doubting the success of Thresher's training and development activities, responding effectively to the challenges of geographically spread units and large numbers of employees.

The case study provides some useful pointers to developing effective training and development and, whilst it is a retail company, there are lessons for many hospitality companies facing similar challenges.

Chris Jeffries, Training Manager, Thresher

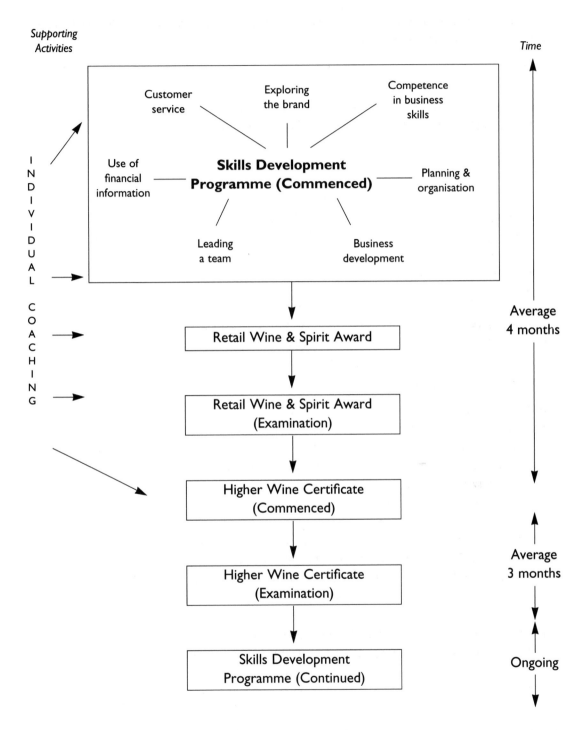

FIGURE 47 *Thresher's Wine Retailing Deputy Manager model programme.*

QUESTIONS

1   Consider the approach that Thresher undertook; what do you think were the problems the Company faced?
2   As the development of open learning material was a key aspect in reducing off-job training costs, how can a company ensure the effectiveness of such material?
3   What other aspects related to effective human resource management would you expect to exist to support such activity?

Note: Figures 5.12–14 provide the organisational structure of Thresher and details of the managers' and deputy managers' training programmes.

Design of a skills training session

With the increase in on-the-job training, supervisors and heads of department will be directly involved in both the design and delivery of training, especially at the skill level. Whilst such individuals have been undertaking this training for some time, approaches have been variable. For many employees their first experience of training will be at this level, during company or department induction, with the majority of activity based on providing the employee with the necessary skills or competencies to do their job satisfactorily.

In Appendix A, Exercise 12, you will identify a particular assignment based on the design, delivery and evaluation of a skills training session. This section will describe some common approaches to such sessions. For existing managers, personnel specialists and Human Resource Managers, the design and delivery of short training activities is often their first step towards their current roles.

To follow an acronym often used in training, WIN, which stands for 'What, Interest and Need', this activity is concerned with:

- *What*   the following section will describe common approaches and methods for the design and delivery of skills training
- *Interest*   delivery and effective training can be immensely satisfying and reduce conflict and problems in the workplace
- *Need*   to progress and develop yourself you need to understand how inexperienced employees learn (additionally, this section will help you with the assignment!)

FIRST STAGE IN DESIGNING TRAINING SESSIONS

Firstly let us look at general considerations. As already mentioned, the design of training must take into consideration a number of factors. These factors will, of course, vary depending upon the situation. For a skills training session, certain basic questions need to be asked. As trainer you will need to identify the parameters in which you will operate, so:

- *Who*   relates to identifying individuals or groups for the projected training

- *Why*   relates to the reason for the training; is it an update of skills, reinforcement, corrective coaching or the provision of new skills for an inexperienced employee?
- *What*   relates to the training itself; will the training be on one specific task or part of a larger task? Is it necessary and relevant to the organisation and employee?
- *When*   relates to the time, duration and location of the training activity; what will be the best time for both trainer and trainee? will you have the time to complete all the training or do you need to separate tasks and skills?
- *How*   relates to the method you, as the trainer, will use to impart the skill or technique; is it a one-to-one situation or a group activity and what facilities and equipment will you need?

KEY POINT

In the design of short skill training sessions, the trainer must consider all the elements which will affect it. He/she will need to identify and set the parameters and framework of the training.

Following other maxims on training here are those of recapping and questioning! Read through the introduction section again and answer the following questions:

1   What are the five main elements to consider when designing short skills training sessions?
2   What do the initials WIN stand for?

SECOND STAGE IN DESIGNING TRAINING SESSIONS: THE TRAINING SCHEDULE

Having identified the basic framework, the trainer should have decided on the following:

- type of training
- method for training
- desired outcome
- target participant(s)
- time, date, duration, location, facilities

The trainer is now ready to plan the detail of the training session, breaking it down to manageable and achievable sections. For sessions to be repeated it is worthwhile creating a written schedule. Obviously there are a variety of ways of writing a training schedule; whatever the method the benefits are:

- trainer has a checklist to assist focusing on the desired outcome
- others can use the schedule as it has been designed and checked
- it creates an additional standards check
- a plan will always assist the trainee

One method to use is to frame the training around the 'ABC' system. This suggests separating the training into three sections:

- *Attention*   when the trainer gets the trainee's attention, explains the task (using WIN) and possibly demonstrates task or skill. *Note:* If it is a complicated skill, it may mean breaking down the skill and task into smaller sections

- *Breakdown* having checked the trainee understands the task, the trainer then breaks down the task, involving the trainee by questioning and explanation; at this point the trainee may be asked to repeat parts of the task
- *Check* having involved the trainee by questioning and participation, the trainer wants to check the trainee can complete the task satisfactorily; this means allowing the trainee to finish the task or skill unaided, with the trainer only interrupting if absolutely necessary; this physical check should be extended by verbal questioning.

On completion of the session, the trainee should be thanked, feedback provided and indications given of follow-on training.

——————————— KEY POINT ———————————

In short training sessions, involving complex skills, it is better to break the activity down into manageable steps, thereby ensuring the trainee can competently carry out each section as well as the whole task.

The above example of the design of a short skills session is, of course, only one approach. However, the general approach is one commonly used and is effective especially in one to one training sessions.

For longer sessions – half, full-day or even longer – then the design and planning has to be more detailed. The key elements to remember for any training session are the:

- desired outcome
- participants
- methods
- resources

Delivery of training sessions

Having designed and delivered countless training sessions in a wide variety of situations involving operative, supervisory and management staff (and attended a considerable number!), I would identify the following guidelines:

1 Any training programme has to be planned and designed in detail.
2 Whilst the 'trainer' is leading and managing the session, the participants should be involved – ineffective training allows the trainee to be passive.
3 Timing is crucial and the trainer is responsible for managing time effectively, ensuring all planned points are covered.
4 The participants should know what both the programme and objectives are.

5   Appropriate time should be built in for questioning.
6   The session should end with feedback from the trainer and the participants.

Additionally, the trainer should ensure the correct material is in place, resources are available, seating is appropriate, HASAWA aspects are adhered to and domestic arrangements for breaks are arranged.

Lastly, training should be enjoyable: a little humour goes a long way, as long as it is not at the expense of the participants or minority group.

Evaluation of training

If training and development is to be successful, evaluation of the outcome is of vital importance. Evaluation will fall into the following categories:

- evaluation by trainee or participant, during or post-training, using a variety of methods
- post-course evaluation by trainer
- external assessment of training and outcome
- post-course evaluation by line manager
- evaluation by the company or training department

The benefits of evaluating training and development are:

- ability to assess the effectiveness of the training in respect of improved individual, team, unit or company performance
- opportunity to ascertain the validity of training and development to both individual and business needs
- the evaluation of cost related to benefits
- opportunity to further develop employee as he/she is encouraged to develop self evaluation techniques and skills
- opportunity to review ongoing training and development in terms of outcome and allow for correction if problems exist

With the increasing development of competence-based training, evaluation and assessment of the outcome can be more readily identified.

Companies may also use annual or periodic employee reviews to evaluate jointly training and development undertaken. Whatever the method or approach, the evaluation of training is a key element of the training and development cycle.

The next section looks at the constraints that exist on training and why it is important for personnel and training specialists to consider these when planning training.

5.7 CONSTRAINTS ON TRAINING AND DEVELOPMENT

You have now seen that there are a considerable number of external and internal factors which affect the design and delivery of training and development; the operator needs to consider these carefully when identifying training requirements and priorities. However, when implementing training plans such factors will also act as possible constraints, reducing the ability to complete all activities and affecting the quality of the outcome.

--- KEY POINT ---

Hospitality operators want their training and development to be successful, with a quality outcome and with minimal disruption to normal operating conditions, otherwise the investment is wasted.

Hospitality companies and businesses operating in today's competitive climate recognise that they will often not achieve all they set out to do. Training and development will be affected by a number of factors, some of which will be out of their control. Experienced human resource managers and trainers will attempt to minimise disruption to planned activity in a variety of ways. Increasingly, developments in training will be conducted on a pilot basis, to iron out teething problems, and companies are building in more comprehensive monitoring and evaluation systems to allow for amendments due to a change in circumstances.

The constraints on training and development usually fall into categories:

1   those which force the operator to change priorities at short notice;
2   operational factors which affect the ability of the company or business to implement all its plans;
3   personnel difficulties which affect the ability to staff and support such activities;
4   personnel difficulties which affect the availability of staff to attend training;
5   the effectiveness of both the training plans and the training activities themselves.

Examples of the above include:

- changes in legislation which place pressure on operators to focus on specific training against other planned priorities
  - the rush for Food Hygiene training was a classic example of this in the early 1990s, where considerable numbers of operators attempted to satisfy proposed regulations on food handling and storage
- operations factors such as:
  - budgeting or financial restrictions – obviously reduction in monies available will result in a reduction or curtailment of training activities
  - structural change, where the company or business undergoes major change, either in ownership, customer profile, increase in staff or units

With the sudden take-over, the majority of training and development activities and procedures were put on hold as the new parent company attempted to integrate all systems.

PERSONNEL AND TRAINING MANAGER, RESTAURANT CORPORATION

The acquisition of over 100 units caused some obvious difficulty; priorities were to set up basic personnel systems and training activity became minimal.

PERSONNEL MANAGER, LICENSED HOUSE GROUP

In addition to external pressures and operational elements, there are the constraints related to the staffing situation. For training and development to be effective it requires the commitment and support from the operator and the individual who has the overall responsibility. The effectiveness of training will be reduced if:

- basic support systems are not in place
- staff with the responsibility for training lack the correct skills, qualifications and experience

Additionally, the receivers of the training and their ability to respond to such development is of vital importance. Again the effectiveness of training will be reduced if:

- staff are not able to attend due to operational demands
- staff are not committed to the training (which may be for a variety of reasons)
- the staff see little value in the training and attend due to direction, rather than agreement; the outcome will often be negative

This aspect also brings into question the quality and effectiveness of the training itself. Poor quality training or training which has been identified incorrectly will often result in the demotivation of staff and their longer term commitment to training will decrease.

We were only informed of the training course at the last minute, which resulted in disruption to schedules and rotas. The training itself was not what we expected and we did not learn anything. The whole weekend session was demotivating and the common feeling was one of embarrassment.

UNIT MANAGER, MEDIUM-SIZED HOTEL AND LEISURE GROUP

Other factors could include:

- *facilities for training*, where organisations do not possess the right facilities for completing the training

The new regulations on pool safety required training of lifeguards in traditional swimming pools. Our problem was that all our pools were fun pools and, therefore, not of sufficient depth. This resulted in us having to bus staff to various other swimming pools.

T. NORGETT, PERSONNEL AND TRAINING OFFICER, HAVEN LEISURE

- *culture within the organisation*: this aspect is one which will be described in the last section of this chapter; the manner in which the organisation approaches training and the degree of importance it places on it will affect the level of effectiveness

In conclusion you can see that factors exist which will act as constraints on an operator, possibly reducing the ability to implement training and reducing the quality and effectiveness of the training itself.

The final section in this chapter will describe how companies are increasingly creating a training culture and how such a culture assists business performance.

5.8 DEVELOPING A TRAINING AND DEVELOPMENT CULTURE

Previous sections in this chapter have concentrated on the methods by which companies and businesses identify, deliver and evaluate training and the constraints facing operators in undertaking such activity effectively.

This last section will look at the increasing need for operators to create an appropriate culture, within which senior management, teams and individuals recognise the value of training and development.

For the personnel manager, trainer, human resource manager or owner, the development of an appropriate culture may at first analysis appear to be of low priority when compared with the more practical day-to-day personnel issues. However, as many organisations and human resource specialists have recognised for some time, training and development contributes towards both continuous quality improvement and business improvement.

We have, for many years, had the simple and deeply held view that in an industry where our employees work every day on clients' premises to provide a service, it is the quality of those people and the people who support them that will determine the future success of the business. We are determined to meet the ongoing challenge of managing our people with the skill they deserve. We will give the highest priority to planning how to motivate our people, on directing them to opportunities in their careers that bring out the best in them, and in giving them the tools they need to do the job to the standard that we promise.

Gary Hawkes, Chief Executive, Gardner Merchant Ltd, *Annual Business Report 1994*

Explained in basic terms, for training and development to be really effective, it needs to be an integral part of a company's day to day activities. Companies and businesses need to develop a culture or way of operation that is participative, involving employees at all levels in problem solving and business improvement. Generally speaking, traditional companies organised their culture with an emphasis on top down control. Such organisations depended (and some still do) on fairly rigid systems which support acceptance of laid down procedures and rules. Human resource issues were considered secondary to strategic business objectives and decisions, with power being centralised in a few top positions. The personnel role including training and development was, in the main, seen as a functional activity responding to the direction the company was undertaking and individual employees were the receivers of training, not the instigators.

In such cultures, job definitions and roles were fairly fixed, with individuals rarely crossing job barriers. Within the most extreme of such examples, individual employees often did not understand, nor were provided with the means to understand, other jobs and demands within the organisation.

Over the past few decades, the hospitality industry has recognised that business development and success is dependent upon a quality team approach which, whilst backed up by sound personnel policies, involves all employees.

Haven Leisure operates leisure parks and centres around the UK. It has developed a systematic and positive approach to training and development with a comprehensive list of company organised courses. Under the statement 'People are our strength', the company identified five key aims for its training and development plan:

- to develop a climate within the company that encourages and supports training activity
- to develop management in line with business needs and career opportunities
- to develop the knowledge, skills and attitudes of our people in line with business needs
- to support the active implementation of key health and safety initiatives
- to provide quality training material for park and centre staff

See the box below for Haven's training programme course outline.

TRAINING PROGRAMME, HAVEN LEISURE

The training and development plan contains three key elements:

1 Management skills programme for park management and BTEC Certificate in Management Studies
   - Introduction to management skills and trainer development
   - Selection interviewing and personnel practice
   - Managing people effectively
   - Appraisal skills
   - Finance and personal management
   - Management of health and safety
   - BTEC CMS
2 Operational skills
   - Basic food hygiene certificate
   - Hygiene instructors certificate
   - Retail catering management
   - First aid at work
   - Emergency first aid
   - Safe use of LPG in caravans and non-permanent dwellings
   - LPG practical installation
   - Pool plant operations
   - Receptionists workshop
   - Caravan sales

3   Training materials for park and centre staff
  • Induction and personal training record
  • 'People Business' customer care programme
  • A guide to professional bar service
  • 'Safety First' health and safety programme
  • Professional standards for food handlers
  • Lifeguard and pool attendant training programme
  • The professional way – entertainments staff

Such recognition has not been based upon philosophical concepts, but business-related factors including:

• the increase in competition, rise in customer expectation and lack of appropriately skilled staff, which has encouraged operators to put more emphasis on ongoing training and development
• the 'flattening' of organisations, especially during the last three years, reducing the numbers of staff within companies, which has placed increasing responsibility for training and development on line managers, heads of departments and supervisors
• the movement of labour, where companies have realised the cost both in financial and customer terms of losing employees to other organisations
• the research and reports on effective organisations: the late 1980s and early 1990s saw an increase in the analysis of 'effective business strategies' with many high profile business writers and 'gurus' identifying the need to change business culture

For the larger organisations, changes in culture to assist team approach have been relatively easy. With well defined personnel and training policies, change has and will continue to be an ongoing activity. Whether the growth in company acquisitions and the generally larger size of companies will restrict such developments remains to be seen.

New small to medium size companies will have some advantage over the larger companies. Their task is to create from scratch a culture which reflects a participative approach. The case study below is an example.

CASE STUDY. VILLAGE LEISURE HOTELS: DEVELOPMENT OF A LEARNING CULTURE

Village Leisure Hotels currently operates six hotels in the North West. Formed in 1987 by the acquisition of three Boddingtons' hotels (Boddingtons is a brewery company which commenced trading in 1778). Up until the late 1970s Boddingtons had concentrated on brewing and licensed house operations. During the late 1970s the Company expanded into retailing whole wines and spirits and introduced the 'Henry's Table' catering brand in 1987.

During the late 1980s, a restructuring took place with the sale of the Brewery Division to Whitbread and the acquisition of Country House Retirement Homes. In 1993 the Company was split into four divisions – Drinks Wholesaling; Public Houses; Health Care, and Hotels and Restaurants, comprising Henry's Table and Village Leisure Hotels. In early 1993 Henry's Table became part of the Pub Division and Village Leisure Hotels became a division in its own right.

With plans to open several sites in 1995, followed by a site each year, the Division has developed an impressive and effective personnel, training and development culture. With a concept which comprises a Leisure Club, Hotel Conference and Banqueting facilities, Pub and Restaurant under one roof, the style is informal with a strategy of developing a lively mix of business and pleasure customers. To support such an approach, the Company has worked hard to develop a culture which is based upon continual quality improvement with the aim of being a customer-driven company.

The Company's senior management spent a considerable time in developing its mission statement and vision (see page 13), which acts as a base for a wide variety of training and development policies and practices. The people charter was based on external and internal research, including an attitudinal survey of its 1300 staff. With the help of an external consultant, the survey asked a number of wide ranging questions related to individuals' perceptions of current company performance and future expectations. Following agreement by the Board, the people charter was launched to senior managers in 1993 and has been followed by two-day workshops in each hotel for heads of department.

Recognising the need to maintain a personnel and training function within each hotel (despite strong leadership support from the Division's personnel and training team), has helped with additional cascading and training. Village Leisure also recognised that all employees should be involved in decision-making processes – a key objective of its people charter.

Managers from the hotels were tasked with the compilation of a unit report in discussion with the staff. This report focused on actions geared towards achievement of the people charter and business objectives.

Training plans were based upon individual training needs – analysis matched against a range of management competencies and then matched to corporate needs. Fairly generous training budgets were allocated, both centrally and to each unit. Such activity is constantly monitored to ensure that its strategy of continuous quality improvement is being met.

To further ensure this strategy, the Company has developed SOPs. SOPs are standards of performance teams which operate in each unit to identify standards required, again clearly focused on customer services. These standards have been further developed to assist induction and training, with each member of staff receiving a personal log book upon employment. Pay increases are partly dependent upon the achievement of both standards and competencies. Whilst obviously favouring in-house training, the Company is piloting NVQ Levels I and II for operatives, but sees the main development in training being based on its own scheme.

Heads of department have been provided with extensive training and the Training Department has instigated a customer focus training programme consisting of a variety of modules. The Company's Training and Development Manager, David Haworth, underwent additional training to deliver the modules to heads of department and the aim is for this training to be cascaded down. The modules run for one to two hours and participants undertake one module per month, identifying individual action plans for personal and departmental improvement. These action plans are followed up by unit managers and the training team.

Currently the Company is looking to develop its skills development programme further and the team of unit personnel and training managers are involved in developing skills assessment documents.

Such programmes have required a considerable investment in sessions on coaching and training, and individual employees and teams are encouraged to resolve problems and improve quality. The Company has recognised that quality comes from a team approach, with employees empowered and involved. With such a unique concept, business performance has been extremely promising, with high occupancy rates and positive customer feedback.

With the continual focus on quality improvement, operating from the base of its people charter, the Company has quickly developed a learning and improvement culture which many larger companies would wish to emulate.

David Haworth, Training Manager, Village Leisure Hotels

The development of such systems and practices requires major commitment and significant financial investment, which can only be based upon sound operational management coupled with profitable business.

Consider the following questions:

- What advantages did the Company possess over other, more established, larger operations with regard to setting up such systems?
- As the Company develops and expands, what alteration to its training and development culture will be required?

KEY POINT

The type of culture which an organisation possesses or develops will directly affect the commitment to and quality of training and development activities.

If you compare different types of organisational culture, or the ways in which operators approach and do things, you can evaluate to a degree the effectiveness potential. This is not a theoretical exercise, but one which human resource specialists increasingly undertake.

In conducting research for this text I received a considerable number of employee handbooks, training policies, company mission statements, values and objectives. One factor was easily identified: clearly expressed statements of how employees were viewed by the organisation and the increasing value placed upon participative development. Whilst such statements can be useful and are positive starting points, real changes in both structure and culture are more difficult to achieve.

The benefits of developing a training and development culture, based upon participation rather than control, are:

- employees will be better motivated if they are involved in decision making
- employees work more effectively if managed in a participative way
- increase in effective teamwork

- increased understanding of and commitment to the company's mission, goals and objectives by employees
- the creation of a customer focus to the business where quality improvement is seen as an integral and natural part of the responsibility of all employees
- the creation of a culture where all employees take responsibility for their personal development
- increase in flexibility and responsiveness in relation to business problems and challenges

Other benefits include easier introduction of new systems; reduction of labour disputes; harmonisation of benefit packages and the development of quality management principles. The underlying philosophy is one in which people are viewed as assets, not as costs (Table 12).

The comparisons made in Table 5.2 are, of course, generalisations and consideration must be given to the size, history, geographical distribution and style of the company or business. Such

Table 12 A comparison between a control or cost culture and one in which a team quality culture is present

CONTROL AND COST CULTURE	TEAM QUALITY CULTURE (TQC)
People seen as costs and potential problems	People seen as assets and problem solvers
Emphasis is on rules and procedures	Emphasis is on joint identification of common goals and values
Human resource issues are secondary in relation to other strategic business objectives	Human resource issues are of primary importance and HRM is an integral part of the decision making process
Power and authority is top down with control via employee acceptance of rules	Power is devolved throughout the organisation, with the views of individuals actively sought and participation in decision making
Systems policies and procedures are rigid and closed, resistant to change	Systems are open and flexible, facilitating improvement and change
Training and development is seen as a cost and response to compliance with external factors	Training and development is seen as an investment both in the business and in the individual
Authority and responsibility rest upon position and status	Authority and responsibility rest upon competence and skills
Employees want to be managed, controlled and supervised	Employees are empowered to participate in decisions and contribute to personal and organisational growth
Employee communication is characterised by reminders of rules and procedures	Communication is characterised by regular two-way meetings, success news, informal events and shared problem solving
Grievance and discrepancy systems emphasise individual inadequacies	Grievance and disciplinary systems emphasise shared responsibilities and protection of employee

factors will affect their ability or willingness to create what is seen by many as a more positive and effective culture.

Key elements of a training and development culture

These include:

- investment in short- and long-term training and development for the business and the individual
- emphasis on communication and participation
- management systems which influence the need to effectively manage and involve all employees
- team approach to problem identification and solution
- equality of opportunity to all employees

Participative systems, be they based on concepts such as total quality management, quality of working life, empowerment or team and quality circles, will become the norm in the future. You should be aware of such approaches, not just as philosophical concepts but as practical and effective strategies for developing both the business and the individual (see Figure 48).

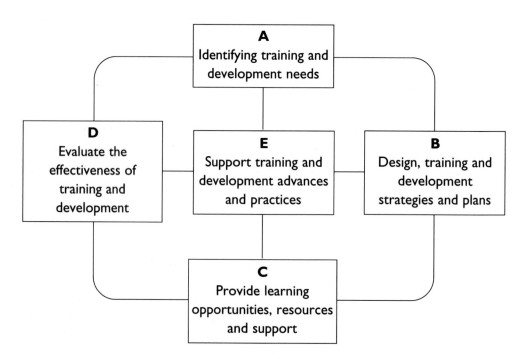

FIGURE 48 *The training cycle.*

INNOVATION IN TRAINING

The twin challenges of Human Resources in the 1990s are the importance of maximising job satisfaction through the development of the best people and ensuring that everyone is an efficient champion of the cause of customer care. This is why training plays a vital part in life across the brands of Travellers Fare. Most staff training takes place in the units and there are training centres in Glasgow, York, Manchester and Bristol for the wide assortment of training courses being run for managers.

A developing and important innovation within the company is the increasing commitment to open and distance learning, enabling new managers to develop their core management skills through monitoring their performance on the job.

Each brand within Travellers Fare has its own training system, which applies brand requirements to the task of defining standards and recording progress in line with the standard Travellers Fare unit training plan.

Travellers Fare Ltd

The key purpose of training and development is to develop human potential to assist organisations and individuals achieve their objectives.

National Council for Vocational Qualifications

5.9 SUMMARY AND KEY POINTS

This chapter has identified the importance of effective training and development to the variety of partners within the industry. Whilst an understanding of the benefits of such activity is important, personnel, training and human resource specialists are concerned with the practical aspects of identifying designing, delivery, monitoring and evaluation of training and development.

Catering businesses operating in an increasingly competitive market face the challenge of balancing expenditure on training against the needs of the business and its ability to fund such activity.

Over the past ten years the pressure from both competition, the customer and legislation, has increased the need for a professional approach to this element of HRM regardless of the size of the business. Therefore, the need to identify training needs effectively has been increasingly important. For the operator or manager, identifying needs is only the start of the story, and there are a considerable number of tasks to be undertaken. These include the design and delivery of training matching the needs of the business, where possible, to the expectations of teams and individual employees.

The industry has certainly progressed significantly since training was predominated by either long apprenticeships or rapid induction by watching another employee. The hospitality operator of the 1990s will often have comprehensive systems, policies and procedures in respect of training, with the emphasis being on developing a culture which supports such activity. Certainly the professional associations have assisted this development, raising the standards of training and the status of catering as a worthwhile industry.

The pattern that has emerged over the past few years is one where training and development managers have involved themselves in partnerships with the whole team, and employees are encouraged to identify, instigate and deliver training.

KEY POINTS

- The main aim of training and development is to establish effective activities which meet the needs and expectations of the business, the employee and the customer
- The more effective the investment in training and development, the greater the chance for business survival and success
- Effective training and development is a carefully planned activity which legislates for the future, in addition to satisfying short term needs
- Many factors exist which affect the need for training and development, and hospitality operators need to understand the relative importance of each factor when prioritising training activity
- Training has to be targeted to the unit, the team and the individual
- Considerable investment is made in training and development and the evaluation of the cost benefit is often difficult to undertake
- There has been a significant increase in interest and commitment to training and development from the industry itself, professional bodies and associations
- Hospitality operators are moving away from the more functional aspects of training and increasing emphasis is being placed on individual and team development

QUESTIONS

1 Explain the role training and development plays in assisting the hospitality industry.
2 Explain the role training and development plays in assisting a hospitality operator maintain and improve standards.
3 Identify and explain the benefits of effective training and development to the team and the individual.
4 Identify and briefly describe the methods for identifying the training and development needs of a catering organisation and business.
5 Describe the steps you would take in preparing a skills training session for an individual employee.
6 Describe the advantages to both employer and employee in undertaking regular performance reviews and identify possible areas of conflict.
7 Taking the role of a unit personnel and training manager, describe the factors you would consider when preparing a unit training plan.
8 Explain the term 'training culture' in respect of a catering company and describe what elements should exist in a company to allow for the development of such a culture.

CHAPTER 6

THE FUTURE OF HUMAN RESOURCE MANAGEMENT IN THE HOSPITALITY INDUSTRY

—

Understanding and practice in managing people is developing radically and altering radically. The capacity to handle such changes will need time and expertise. The abandonment of in-house specialist personnel back up need not be perverse, if a sufficient depth of outside specialists can be established. As the importance of people management is more widely recognised, a new relationship between line managers and personnel specialists will evolve.

INSTITUTE OF PERSONNEL MANAGEMENT, 'MANAGING PEOPLE – THE CHANGING FRONTIERS', *PERSONNEL MANAGEMENT*, NOVEMBER 1993

I see my role in the future as one of facilitating the involvement of employees. The company needs to appreciate just how important effective people management is and the contribution it makes to the business. Yet, due to staffing reductions and other responsibilities, I just cannot commit the time to such activity.

PERSONNEL & TRAINING MANAGER, 3-STAR HOTEL, MIDLANDS

The key aspects for the future are lean, efficient, flat structures with empowered employees who have responsibility and authority to react to customer demands. Well trained employees, well rewarded, sharing the action.

M. WORTHINGTON, DIRECTOR OF HUMAN RESOURCES, FORTE POSTHOUSE

6.1 AIMS AND OBJECTIVES

By reading this chapter, reviewing the key points and completing the questions and assignments in Appendix A, you will be able to:

1   list the main challenges facing HRM practitioners in the future;
2   appreciate the role HRM will play in developing effective hospitality operations in respect of the changing economic and social climate;
3   identify the future potential key HRM functions.

In brief, the main challenges can be identified as follows:

* *demographic trends,* which will affect the availability and type of labour
* *customer demands,* which are set to maintain a continued rise in expectations
* *manpower planning,* including particular approaches to recruitment and selection
* *recruitment and selection*
* *training and development,* recognising that companies, whilst increasing their investment in this activity, will seek greater cost effectiveness
* *quality management:* as industry progressively concentrates on this movement, how will organisations respond to the demands it makes on the organisation and, specifically, the HRM function?
* *legislation:* with the increasing influence of the European Union and tightening governmental control, what will be the effect on the industry?

Underpinning all of the above are questions raised about the role of HRM within hospitality companies and business. With many of the larger operators reducing their personnel departments and decentralising, what future exists for the traditional personnel department and manager?

KEY POINT

The personnel or HRM function has always been a dynamic function, adapting to both the prevailing economic and social climate and the internal demands of the organisation and the industry.

6.2 INTRODUCTION

This final chapter will look at the future role and development of HRM within the hospitality industry.

There are, of course, difficulties in both identifying trends and predicting developments, yet for readers in the early years of their careers, the inclusion of such a chapter is of direct relevance. You will quickly identify a degree of personal prediction within the outlines, and for this I make no apology. As an avid industry watcher for a considerable number of years I hope to match personal views with those from industry. Additionally, reference will be made to research conducted in this area by a number of government agencies and professional bodies.

What is important is to provide an outline of the challenges which face hospitality operators in the next decade and attempt to identify how particular sectors of the industry will manage these challenges.

6.3 DEMOGRAPHIC TRENDS

For personnel managers and HRM specialists the following concerns are apparent for the next decade:

- availability of appropriate labour within an area
- decline in school leavers, which will affect any manpower strategy and personnel aspects, such as recruitment and selection, pay and benefits, working hours and patterns and training and development programmes
- alternatives in customer demand and expectations of both service and staff
- decline in demand from certain areas due to economic factors which will affect the level and number of staff required in units

Hospitality operators and particularly personnel managers will, therefore, need to be more aware of the effect demographic trends will have on employment strategy and policies.

In a survey of over 180 catering organisations I conducted in the Spring of 1994, 85% reported concerns in respect of availability of labour to meet business demand; 95% of these companies also indicated that they were worried about skills available and staff turnover. One organisation reported a concern with low staff cover.

J. Roberts (1994) Personnel Survey on Hospitality Industry

Whilst hospitality operators can do nothing to affect demographic trends, they have to respond to them and, increasingly, this will mean HRM strategies which effectively respond to these challenges.

6.4 EFFECT OF CHANGES IN CUSTOMER DEMAND

There is no doubt that over the past decade customer demands and expectations have risen. Briefly this has been due to the following:

- increase in disposable income despite recessionary periods
- greater awareness of the public in respect of food, drink and service standards
- increased competition for customers
- general rise in customer expectations in respect of value for money and improved levels of service

- improvements in both quality and service for industry itself, thereby generating increased customer expectations
- increased knowledge and concern of the public with regard to health and safety and food hygiene issues

───────────────── KEY POINT ─────────────────

If customer expectations increase in respect of the quality and value of products, services and facilities, so too will their expectations of catering personnel. Hospitality operators will, over the next decade, need to address continually the match of staff skills and effectiveness to both business and customer demand.

───

Increasingly over the next decade, hospitality operators will seek a better match between the customer and personnel profile. This will result in a major shift in respect of human resource strategy, personnel policies and procedures. For personnel managers this will mean developing more effective practices in relation to analysing customer expectations of staff.

Customers are increasingly asked to comment on facilities and service and will, in my estimation, in the future be asked to evaluate staff. This will be above the normal employee of the

FIGURE 49 *Customers are best placed to comment on facilities, food and service.*

month type scheme and be geared towards operators more effectively identifying what they require of personnel.

Consider a traditional 3-star hotel, where guests are invited to comment on cleanliness of the room and facilities. It does not require too much alteration to the comment card to solicit views of expectations of staff rather than response to past service. Hospitality operators will begin to appreciate that they need to ask their customers different questions if they are to match and, more importantly, exceed expectations.

In conclusion, the role of the personnel manager or HRM specialist in respect of customer demands and expectations will be to:

- more closely match the personnel profile to customer profile
- identify more accurately customer expectations of staff
- develop policies and practices which respond to these expectations

Such considerations lead on to the aspect of manpower planning and, in particular, recruitment and selection policies.

6.5 MANPOWER PLANNING AND STRATEGY

The effects of demographic trends and changes in customer demand on manpower strategy and planning are easily recognisable; what is more problematic is the identification of how such practice will alter in the future. You are recommended to review Chapter 2 on Manpower Planning prior to studying this section. It is also worth repeating one definition of manpower planning.

Manpower planning is a strategy for the acquisition, utilisation, improvement and retention of enterprising human resources.

Department of Employment, 1994

As indicated earlier, this definition has certain weaknesses, including the aspect of referring to individuals as units of resource, which can be moulded and trained to perform effectively. However, this is an approach which has gained favour over the past few years and one which has emerged based on the concept that individuals are an asset possessing value to the organisation.

The trend to identify the financial value of an employee or group of employees has been assisted by several factors, including:

- the increase in technology, allowing for more detailed analysis of all aspects of staffing costs
- the increase in competition and the need for organisations to be more cost effective
- the flattening of organisations by the reduction of staff, especially at middle management level

- the recognition that to be effective, companies have to undertake a more detailed, scientific approach to manpower planning

---

A licensed trade company operating in the Midlands has developed a sophisticated manpower planning model, based upon detailed analysis of local market trends and needs, population and historical financial data. The model is used to develop a manpower profile for specific units, including the range of attributes required of unit personnel.

Licensed trade company with 45 units

Hospitality operators are increasingly using manpower models based on versions of, what is referred to as, human asset accounting. In circumstances when demand and profits reduce, such models can be used to identify potential short-term savings by laying off numbers of employees.

Developments in this approach have recognised the importance of measuring the investment the organisation makes in its staff. This could include the costs of recruitment training and replacement, in addition to the standard costs of salaries and benefits. Furthermore, there is the worth of the individual in terms of quality and public recognition. How far such concepts will develop in the future is difficult to ascertain; however, for many operators such approaches are becoming increasingly important.

My role is increasingly being centred on analysing and reporting on all aspects of staffing costs, coupled with a demand for effective strategies to reduce costs whilst maintaining quality.

SENIOR PERSONNEL MANAGER, LARGE HOTEL COMPANY

Other noticeable trends in manpower planning are:

- increase in the use of technology
- development of more flexible working practices
- increase in short term contracts, allowing the organisation to decrease its commitment to full time staffing
- improved analysis of manpower requirements, both short and long term
- improvements in succession planning by developing individual development plans for employees

Succession planning is becoming increasingly sophisticated to the extent of us looking 3–5 years into the future, identifying both specific roles required and the targeting of training and development of individuals to undertake such roles.

PERSONNEL MANAGER, NATIONAL CATERING RETAIL CHAIN

Succession planning has always been problematic due to the acceptance of employees regularly changing jobs and employers. This mobility of staff has both advantages and disadvantages to the employer. Whilst recessionary periods are characterised in part by reduction in labour movement, generally speaking the industry has always had to accept a reasonable shift of labour, which obviously affects its ability to plan effectively.

The breaking down of European barriers is, in my opinion, unlikely in the short term to result in a large increase in labour mobility. However, longer term hospitality employees, especially at the senior level, will move more freely through the European Union. This will be assisted by the growth in European-style hospitality management qualifications.

The hospitality company of the twenty-first century will require strategies and policies to react positively to such developments and, what would be beneficial, is for similar companies operating in different countries to create employment links.

Manpower planning in the future will have to be less reactive and more proactive, especially in respect of analysing staffing costs, movement and needs. This will require sophisticated technology and systems allowing personnel managers and human resource specialists the tools by which to plan more effectively.

6.6 RECRUITMENT AND SELECTION

There has been a noticeable improvement in the effectiveness of such activities over the past decades, with companies and businesses at all levels recognising the importance of developing cost-effective approaches. Certainly within the larger companies, policies and procedures have become more comprehensive, adhering positively to the variety of employment legislation (especially those concerning equal opportunities).

The generally inadequate recruitment and selection systems of the 1960s and 1970s were replaced by almost panic measures in the mid to late 1980s. The early 1990s saw recruitment and selection being affected by a period of recession, and figures provided earlier in this text will have identified for you an underlying trend for growth in recruitment. Detailed analysis of recruitment trends indicate that the key aspects in the next few decades will be:

- *increase in the sophistication of the recruitment process*, with growth in the use of psychometric testing, aptitude tests, personality profiling, assessment centres and computerised personnel systems.
- *decrease in the appointment of full-time staff*, as companies move towards more flexible working patterns, short-term contracts and flatter structures.
- *slow increase in the appointment of women to senior positions*, due to a number of factors (unfortunately, however, not all of them related to equality of opportunity)
- *decrease in the employment of young people*, due in part to the decline in numbers of this cohort of potential employees
- *development of recruitment policies which aid staff retention*, as operators increasingly recognise the cost of replacing staff
- *marginal increase in the use of recruitment or personnel consultants*, with organisations concentrating on core activities and the relative cost effectiveness of such services increasing, especially for middle management positions and for short-term projects

Additionally, recruitment literature will improve in quality with an increased use of benefit selling in job advertisements. Companies facing the increasing competition for skilled employees will have to target such specific groups more effectively. For the larger groups with significant levels of staffing requirements, these may need the re-emergence of job fairs and career conventions, although not aimed solely at the school, college or university graduate.

The various attempts to reintroduce forms of modern apprenticeship will possibly aid operators in attracting younger employees. However, this type of scheme, in addition to the other trends, will encourage the development of new employment policies and practices.

─────────────── **KEY POINT** ───────────────

Operators will require a variety of methods and approaches to recruitment and selection with improvements in levels of pay and working conditions to ensure their staffing profile matches the needs of the business.

───

In seeking to recruit and retain the best people, hospitality operators will additionally have to maintain and improve the level of training.

6.7 TRAINING AND DEVELOPMENT

Within Chapter 5 we discussed the relevance of this activity to the development of the business. The growth in on the job training and continuous quality improvement was identified. Such approaches will, in my opinion, form the base of developments and improvements over the next decade.

To stay ahead of the competition we will have to put increasing emphasis on and investment in effective training and development for all employees throughout their working lives.

GROUP PERSONNEL & TRAINING MANAGER, LUXURY HOTEL CHAIN

However, training is an expensive undertaking and, as the industry is still dominated by small businesses, the main developments and improvements will occur in the medium to large companies. Whatever the political make-up of Government in the future, there is cross-party agreement on the need for improved investment in training and development and, therefore, the skills of the workforce. Government will in the future:

- increase its emphasis on training via a number of accreditation schemes and initiatives
- further develop the Training and Enterprise Councils' (TECs) role in initiating and promoting local and national schemes
- fund additional places in colleges and universities
- possibly provide further tax benefits to both individuals and businesses undertaking training (specifically in respect of national targets)

- adapt legislation to 'force' employers to train employees in specific areas
- fund (with the assistance of the European Union) regional training schemes and specific training initiatives; this will be particularly noticeable for certain minority groups

All these will encourage employers to come into greater partnership with schools, colleges, TECs, universities and other training providers. This aspect has been developing for some time and personnel specialists and human resource managers will have to spend increasing amounts of time on such schemes.

Whilst Government and its policies will directly affect training and development, so too will the industry itself, by joint schemes or via pressure from the growing numbers of professional associations. Groups such as the Hotel Employers Group, the HCIMA and Hotel Catering Training Company all have an interest in promoting training and development. Additionally, industry itself has a vested interest as the improvement of skills within the workforce enable it to have access to better qualified staff.

Whilst groups or associations of catering organisations have joined together for training purposes, such practices are not widespread and in the short term are unlikely to increase. The reluctance of independent operators to become involved is understandable yet, in my opinion, short-sighted. If you compare the UK situation with that of some of our European partners, or Third World countries where the degree of cooperation is much higher, then clear evidence can be provided on the long-term benefits to the whole of the industry. Longer term, more groups of operators or personnel and human resource directors will recognise the advantages of such cooperation, joining together for training and development and, perhaps, recruitment.

Training and development approaches are, as indicated, already changing. I would forecast the following trends over the next decade:

- increase in on the job training
- increase in the concept of continuous training within employment
- growth of computerised training systems, such as interactive software
- improved recording of training again using computer-based systems
- increasing acceptance of the need for individual development as against traditional training
- decline in traditional training departments, with responsibility for skills training being increasingly placed at departmental level
- increasing use of secondment or project work for specific levels of staff
- partial move away from individual training to a team-centred approach
- improved recording by the individual of training and development undertaken, using documents such as competence passbooks, personal portfolios and records of achievement

Hospitality operators seeking to reduce the costs of training, whilst retaining its quality and effectiveness will obviously favour systems which concentrate training within the workplace.

In-house training, especially for the larger companies, will become the norm, which will require different systems and skills. Personnel managers and trainers will, therefore, be increasingly involved in system design and monitoring rather than actual delivery. Matched to this development will be an increased requirement for tailor-made and 'off-the-peg' training systems and firms offering such services will marginally expand.

Qualifications and standards

If on-the-job training continues to expand, questions must be raised about the nature of national standards and qualifications. The move towards forms of national standards – using NVQs and SVQs at the lower to middle skill range and MCI and TDLB at the top of the middle range – has developed over the past three to four years. However, many still question the validity of such standards and query whether on-the-job training linked to a particular operations standard is appropriate. The four (possibly five) levels, although they accept similarities in technical ability for levels of jobs or tasks, are too complex when it comes to actual skills and, therefore, can only generalise. For the personnel manager facing a range of recruits all possessing, for example, an NVQ Level III, the task of selection will become difficult. Therefore, national standards especially related to skill levels have a long way to go and industry will continue to be reluctant in their involvement.

This obviously raises questions about the future role of colleges and universities in training. With continued expansion in the industry and improvement in economic performance, a growth in college/industry partnerships is likely although, again, it will be the larger companies and colleges which will undertake such initiatives. Additionally, types of specialist training establishments may develop, especially ones dealing with higher level skills. The failure of the Culinary Academy in the early 1990s was perhaps a result of the recession at the time; with improved funding and a wider range of programmes it may succeed in the future and prove to be a catalyst for others.

INVESTORS IN PEOPLE ...

... Is a national standard which has just been launched in the UK, across all businesses, to recognise Companies who carry out effective training and development of their employees. 'Investors in People' is about action and excellence, and Torquay Leisure Hotels has become the first hotel in the south west to commit itself to achieving this standard.

It is set to become the national benchmark against which all organisations will be judged in the future. "We are adopting this policy because we recognise that people are of crucial importance for us to achieve business success and we are now taking positive steps to put this into practice", said Managing Director, Laurence Murrell.

FIGURE 50 *News about Investors in People scheme, published in an in-house newsletter (Source:* Connect, *newsletter of Torquay Leisure Hotels).*

Whilst the provision of higher level skills training may improve, the overall trend will be to the deskilling of tasks, especially in the traditional craft-type positions. The deskilling of jobs, through different purchasing and production methods, alterations to menu ranges, the acceptance of less formal service skills and improvements in technology, has been a factor for the last decade. It is a factor that will continue to affect both the need for training and the range and depth of training itself.

The role of personnel and human resource specialists, human resource managers, personnel and training managers and owners will, in the future, need to be aware of all these trends. Increasingly their role in respect of training and development will be to:

- address more cost effectively the ongoing training needs of the business, with increasing focus on the customer
- design and monitor in-house schemes
- assist the development of a training culture within the organisation
- consider the benefit of training and development partnerships
- assist in advising on the deskilling of tasks and jobs

Overall I foresee a radical change in the way in which training and development is identified, approached and delivered within the next decade, with the main emphasis being on continuous training within the workplace. This trend will be assisted by the movement towards continuous quality improvement, an element which will be dealt with in the next section.

6.8 QUALITY MANAGEMENT

This section will provide an overview of initiatives and trends, such as Quality Management and 'Investors in People', and how their development will affect human resource management in the future.

If you study the lists of new publications connected with Quality Management and management principles in general, you will identify the preoccupation with such developments. Alongside various pieces of Government legislation and initiatives have emerged the so-called management gurus. Such individuals as Tom Peters, Professor Hardy and Sir Harvey Jones have become acclaimed as the prophets of business success. Studies and articles on Quality Management are commonplace, as are numerous one-day seminars and conferences. There is no doubting that issues related to quality management will be with us for some time. The trend towards developing quality management approaches and systems has also been helped by the following:

- the effects of European Union harmonisation and legislation
- the effects of the recession in the late 1980s and early 1990s, which forced many organisations to focus its energies on retaining customer loyalty
- the growth in other industrial sectors of quality management systems, such as BS5750 (UK version) and IS9000 (international version)

- UK legislation, such as the Food Safety Act 1990 and various alterations to HASAWA legislation
- the influence of numerous management writers
- initiatives such as 'Investors in People'

During the early part of the 1990s there was a growing recognition of the value and benefits of such approaches, reflected by the move towards customer-focused businesses. (You will have seen this trend by the content of company material within this text.) That is not to say that the concept of Quality Management is one which originated in the last decade. The Second World War provided an impetus to aspects of quality assurance as the Forces depended on equipment that worked 'first time every time'. Teachers and writers, such as Edward Deming, were influential in developing approaches to overall concepts of quality, a term later developed as Total Quality Management.

KEY POINT

Whilst the term Quality Management is not a new one, it has only been in the early part of the 1990s that the hospitality industry has moved towards the large scale implementation of its principles.

Quality management centres on the following aspects:

- systems and methods for assuring the quality of services, facilities and goods
- development of the concept of continuous quality improvement
- increasing focus of quality improvement via the involvement and empowerment of all employees
- recognition that a team approach to maintaining and improving quality is the best strategy for customer-focused businesses
- quality improvement has as much to do with organisational culture change as it has with systems and processes

Of course quality is a term with many definitions; is it what the individual employee, department, unit or company perceive, or is the customer, the professional association or the restaurant the food critic? Certainly the rise in customer expectation over the past few years has altered their perception of quality. However, individual customers will have varying definitions of quality and may relate these to such factors as facilities, value for money, cost, or efficiency level of staff responsiveness and care.

The recent debate amongst hotel operators over grading systems, which attempt to indicate a level of quality or facilities, shows just how difficult the definition of quality really is. With the development of external quality assessment and accreditation systems, the creation of benchmarks or minimum quality standards has become perhaps easier.

DEFINITION OF A QUALITY SYSTEM

The organisational structure, responsibilities, procedures, processes and resources for implementing quality management.

British Standards Institute

Key terms in quality management related to HRM:

- *Quality Assurance:* methods and systems for ensuring that products, services, facilities, policies, procedures and practices reach the same level of requirement
- *Quality Systems:* methods which underpin and provide for the delivery of quality
- *BS5750:* the UK standard for quality assurance systems
- *Investors in People:* Government initiative aimed at improving organisations' investment, training and development of its employees
- *HACCP (Hazard Analysis Critical Control Point):* a system related to the monitoring and management of approaches and methods related to the production of food
- *Total Quality Management (TQM):* an approach to quality management which encompasses a variety of tools centring on the philosophy that the organisation can only develop with the involvement and commitment of all employees

For us BS5750 does not represent what our business is or will be about. The concept of TQM, however, matches more closely our needs and it is something the Company will be continually working towards.

HUMAN RESOURCE DIRECTOR, NATIONAL RESTAURANT AND LEISURE COMPANY

Overall there exists two types of development in Quality Management, both of which will affect the management of people in the future.

1   *Functional Systems and Approaches*
    These concentrate on processes, systems, written documentation and procedures to enforce a quality management approach on the organisation and its employees. Additionally, this area could include 'Investors in People' (IIP) which, whilst a developmental approach, does rely heavily on functional systems, policies and procedures. An example would be BS5750.
2   *Conceptual Approaches*
    These concentrate on the development of organisational culture via people, to maintain and improve quality. Such approaches, whilst in part paper based, rely heavily on the involvement of all employees in quality improvement. TQM is an example of this.

The effect of developments in quality management on HRM

There is no doubting that HRM specialists recognise the need to incorporate Quality Management approaches into their systems; what will be interesting is how far these developments will affect organisations in the future.

For the hospitality industry, with its increasing customer focus and customer orientation, the relevance of such methods can be easily identified. However, as the industry will remain dominated by small independent operations, the uptake of such methods may be concentrated on the medium to large companies. Certainly the cost of creating a BS5750 system of moving towards IIP is prohibitive for smaller employers.

KEY POINT

Regardless of its benefits, the costs of developing and installing Quality Management systems within an organisation will be too high for many hospitality operators. Such businesses will continue to rely on the skills and experience of owners and managers to maintain quality through basic people management approaches.

Obviously, any change to operational strategy and approach will have effects on the management of people within an organisation. The personnel and human resource specialist will rightly be concerned with changes which impinge directly on the HR function. Systems such as BS5750, HACCP and IIP will affect policies and procedures related to:

- recruitment and selection
- employee working conditions and benefits
- employee communication
- training and development

Approaches such as TQM (and in part IIP) will affect the manner in which the organisation communicates to, involves and empowers its employees and, therefore, has more to do with culture and approach than systems and procedures.

Overall, the trend has and will be to identify approaches that concentrate on the involvement and development of people, rather than the more functional based systems. This will result in personnel and human resource specialists increasingly being involved in the following activities:

- assisting the move towards people-based business strategies
- facilitating increased involvement and empowerment of staff
- designing 'systems' which help line managers and supervisors manage, motivate and encourage their staff
- more closely linking people development to business strategy and objectives
- developing improved lines of communication between all staff
- concentrating more on the internal customers of an organisation, i.e. the individuals and teams who make up a company's workforce

Such activities will also involve changes in the future to employment practices and policies including:

- growth of more flexible employment and benefits packages
- improvements in equality of opportunity

- minor increase in alternative payment and reward systems, including:
  - *team based pay*, where small teams of employees are rewarded on the quality of performance and output of the whole team
  - *individual performance related pay*, where an individual's pay (and potential increase or bonus) is based on the individual's achievement in terms of 'quality'
  - *standards achievement pay*, where newly appointed employees' pay levels are set against the individual achievement of laid down standards of competence and quality

---
KEY POINT

Increasing numbers of hospitality companies are developing pay and benefits packages which relate individual pay to the achievement of agreed standards and the demonstration of competence.

- involvement of employee in both personal and organisational development – employers will increasingly recognise that by assisting and encouraging individual employees to improve, the organisation itself will improve. As one director reported 'the quality of the business is dependent upon the quality and involvement of each of its employees'.

Quality management, then, is both a system and an approach and it is an element of HRM that will remain a central focus for hospitality operators over the next decade. Of the total group of developments currently under the quality management title, there are two which require, for such an introductory text, more detailed explanations:

BS5750

This standard provides a national series of guidelines for suppliers and manufacturers on what is required of a quality system. It lays down the requirements for a cost-effective quality management system. First introduced in 1979, and adapted from a variety of sources, it has not been without its critics. This criticism has largely centred around the fact that BS5750 is concerned with processes and only a part of the wider move towards Total Quality Management.

The standard is currently separated into parts and Part 2 is generally accepted as most relevant to the hospitality industry. Whatever the realities of the debate, the improvement in standards and processes required for BS5750 has a link towards the approach to HRM in the future. The benefits to hospitality operators can be identified as:

- external auditing of the operator's quality management system
- developing quality assurance, the operator is more confident of supplying goods and service of an expected standard
- cost savings, due to the system being controlled across all functions of the organisation and reduction of errors
- satisfied customers who can rely on the establishment to meet their expectations

> The Cardiff Copthorne reported that the process of obtaining BS5750 cost in the region of £35,000 and produced nothing tangible in the way of extra sales.
>
> *Hospitality Magazine, February 1994*

BS5750 relies heavily on written procedures, documentation, quality manuals and formalised reporting. For the HRM specialist knowledge of such functional systems are useful and, whilst bureaucratic, they do create, in part, standards on which to manage people.

The second method concentrates more on the development and involvement of people within the organisation and currently has proved more popular with hospitality operators:

INVESTORS IN PEOPLE (IIP)

This initiative was originally launched under another name in the late 1980s. Quickly revised it has gained popularity due to its focus on people rather than processes. The current Government has set itself targets for the number of organisations achieving this kitemark and founded the local Training and Enterprise Councils to spearhead and promote its uptake.

IIP is an approach which links to the achievement of a business's objectives; its method is to assess an organisation against performance criteria in four specific areas, all of which relate to the management of employees.

The national Standard

AN *INVESTOR IN PEOPLE* MAKES A PUBLIC COMMITMENT FROM THE TOP TO DEVELOP ALL EMPLOYEES TO ACHIEVE ITS BUSINESS OBJECTIVES

- Every employer should have a written but flexible plan which sets out business goals and targets, considers how employees will contribute to achieving the plan and specifies how development needs in particular will be assessed and met.

- Management should develop and communicate to all employees a vision of where the organisation is going and the contribution employees will make to its success, involving employee representatives as appropriate.

© Investors in People UK 1994.

The process of obtaining the IIP kitemark currently involves the organisation making a public commitment to IIP, collecting evidence to support its case and being externally assessed by a trained IIP assessor. This individual will visit the organisation, review evidence and conduct private interviews with a cross-section of employees. Companies and businesses achieving IIP status are reinspected every three years.

A considerable amount of research has been conducted on the benefits and outcome of IIP to organisations, with the general consensus being that the initiative assists both employer and employee. For the personnel or HRM specialist IIP assists the development of a more people-based approach.

In a survey conducted on 180 hospitality companies IIP was being developed or undertaken by over 70% of them. Examples of comments on the benefits of IIP included:

'It encourages and recognises effective training and development of employees and improves business performance.'

'Catering is a people business – investing in people is therefore logical.'

'IIP allows us to gain a recognised award for what we are currently achieving.'

'It has helped us streamline training and development to aid business objectives.'

'Provides for more structured training.'

'Enables our workforce to develop and be more aware of the business they work for.'

'Helps us achieve the most out of our employees.'

'Good managers achieve results through people – a better one will develop his people to achieve better results.'

J. Roberts (1993) *Personnel Practices Survey*, Rotherham College of Arts and Technology

---

Conclusion

Investment in quality involves an investment in people and, as such, the personnel specialist will play an increasingly important role in the development of future policies and procedures which directly aid the maintenance and improvement of quality.

The next section in this chapter looks at the aspect of legislation and its growing influence on the role and function of HRM.

6.9 EMPLOYMENT LEGISLATION

Whilst hospitality businesses and companies may be tackling the wide range of issues facing them related to managing people more effectively, they do this against the increase in legislation. Throughout this text the effect such legislation has on all elements of the human resource and personnel function has been stressed. As individuals concerned with human resource become more central to the organisation, their role in advising the organisation on possible legislation change becomes more important.

Overall, hospitality operators will face increases in legislation from two main sources:

- *European Union,* as the move towards harmonisation develops
- *Government,* as pressure from interest groups encourages the development of more protective type legislation

Excluding specialist legislation related to complex financial matters, the main legislation developments will be centred on the areas of:

- *Pension and benefit schemes,* especially when employees transfer from one company to another
- *Protective legislation,* concerned with such aspects as maternity and paternity leave, rights of disabled employees, employment of young people and Health and Safety
- *Rights of older workers:* as demographic trends have their effect, the industry will increase its numbers of older employees, which may be assisted by legislation similar to that of the United States
- *Part-time employees:* recent alterations to European law related to the rights of part-time employees has improved the status of such individuals. With the industry continuing to rely on a large percentage of part-time employees, pressure may increase to further improve both employment benefits and legal rights
- *General employment principles:* alterations to previous employment law has seen the increase in providing employees with more precise information related to their working conditions, benefits and rights; this has been balanced by a reduction (some would say worsening) of individual rights in respect of employment protection and trade union activity; two factors may alter this trend: possibly, a change in government and a move towards acceptance of the European Social Charter

For companies and businesses there has always been a need to amend policies and procedures in the light of changes in legislation and such considerations will continue to play an important part in planning.

Whilst companies have become better at identifying future legislation and adapting policies, this has not been without its problems.

In respect of possible alterations to the food hygiene laws in the early 1990s, we invested a considerable amount of money in altering and upgrading equipment, staff training and qualification, only to find that the laws related to hygiene qualification did not end as forecasted. Whilst everyone can accept the need for improved hygiene, the cost of training was extremely high, money which could have been spent on other things. Perhaps we should have waited until the legislation was finalised.

DIRECTOR, NATIONAL CONTRACT CATERING COMPANY

The ability of a company or business to forecast the effect of possible legislation will rely, in part, on the expertise of the personnel specialist. For the smaller operations, lacking such backing, increasing reliance will be placed onto external specialists. The numbers of legal helplines, personnel specialists, consultants, subscription-type legal protection and advisory services have increased over the past decade. Additionally, consortiums concentrating on groups such as hotels and restaurants offer independent operators legal advice as part of overall fees.

— K E Y P O I N T —

The rise in legislation and its increasing complexity has led to the increased use of external specialists and advisory services. The cost of such services is seen as a necessary investment to offset the risk of prosecution.

How well the hospitality industry responds to the pressures brought about by increased legislation will, as stated, be largely dependent upon the skills and knowledge of internal and external personnel specialists.

Whilst professional associations have had some minor successes in getting certain pieces of legislation altered, overall, major pieces of legislation have passed through Parliament with little opposition. Whether such groups will have greater success in the future will depend in part on their ability to work together to form more powerful lobbying groups.

In addition to these pressure groups, the role of professional associations and Government agencies in advising on employment legislation will increase. During the early part of the 1990s such services as ACAS and the Department of Employment underwent major reviews of structure and practices. Whilst retaining their original roles, their advisory services came under close scrutiny and, in the future, employees may face higher charges for obtaining advice and information.

The Institute of Personnel Management merged with the Institute of Training and Development, forming in mid-1994 the Institute of Personnel and Development. The HCIMA formed a revised structure in late 1993. The personnel specialist who, in the past, may have relied on such organisations will, in the future, need to understand changed structures and a realigned focus.

In conclusion, the possible developments in legislation will continue to have major effects on the manner in which companies manage their human resources. This element, in conjunction with other elements detailed previously in this chapter, will result in fundamental changes to the role and function of the Personnel and Human Resource Manager. The last section in this chapter will describe some of these key changes.

6.10 FUTURE ROLE OF HUMAN RESOURCE MANAGEMENT

Following this review of some of the key developments which will affect the function of HRM in the future, it is appropriate to provide a summary of these and indicate how the role will alter.

HRM encompasses all the elements described throughout this text, ranging from the standard personnel functions of pay and benefits to more complex elements, such as strategic planning and culture change. Obviously the role will change according to the style and size of the company or business. Certain generalisations can be made about the change in the nature of HRM, which will be more relevant to particular sectors of the industry than others. Increasingly accepted as a key element in organisational development and business success, the contribution of HRM towards business planning and performance improvement will be recognised, following more effective systems of analysing the cost and the benefit of investing in staff. Overall the role of HRM in the future will be:

- to forge close links with the strategic planning process, as companies and businesses identify more effectively how to match management to company improvement
- to assist in the development of positive working cultures, where continuous quality improvement is accepted as the norm and where all employees are encouraged to contribute and participate
- to identify improved systems of pay and benefits, which support the retention of staff
- to design systems which devolve certain aspects of personnel management and training down to line managers; such systems will require effective back up and support

Such alterations to the role will result in the development of new skills and competencies required of personnel and human resource specialists. Whilst their role remains crucial to the organisation, they will become advisers and designers of schemes rather than deliverers. This will be particularly noticeable for individuals with medium sized companies. They will be acting as support specialists rather than direct managers.

I see my role as providing a support service for unit managers and area managers, in that central personnel and training will provide the systems, policies and procedures in which such managers can operate on a day to day basis.

GROUP PERSONNEL AND TRAINING MANAGER, LEISURE GROUP

In response to questions related to their future role and challenges in a survey I conducted in 1994, a considerable number of comments were made. Whilst a significant number of the total of 180 responses related to specific objectives, such as obtaining 'Investors in People', improvements in staff retention and meeting business objectives more effectively, a number referred to the specific future role of personnel. Overall the majority of comments related to changes in job role away from more functional aspects to culture development. As one senior human resource manager stated: 'it's a major shift from traditional authoritarianism to a 'player-coach' management and development style.'

Other comments included on the role of human resource managers:

to provide a total human resource service to the organisation involving the development of policies in accordance with the strategic plan.

PERSONNEL MANAGER, CONTRACT CATERING COMPANY

to assist the development of people via the development of a learning organisation.

PERSONNEL MANAGER, LICENSED TRADER

to assist the rationalisation and harmonisation of practices against the background of a completely different structure and culture. HRM is about a professional service to all managers in all aspects of people management.

PERSONNEL DIRECTOR, LEISURE COMPANY

Whilst the responses to questionnaire-based surveys always require considered analysis, the examples provided above were representative of the general acceptance of fairly major alterations to the role of HRM in the future. Against this background was the continued identification of more practical considerations, including retention and motivation of staff, the problem of high staff turnover, lack of craft skills in the future and a need to reduce staffing costs. For many personnel and human resource specialists such challenges will remain and they are elements of the role that should not be underestimated.

The personnel or human resource specialist holds a unique position within the organisation; as their value has become increasingly recognised, so too have the pressures on them to achieve more. Their contribution to the company and the industry will continue to develop and become more central to an operator's overall development and performance.

6.11 SUMMARY AND KEY POINTS

Within this chapter I have attempted to outline some of the key challenges and developments in respect of people management over the next decade for the hospitality industry.

The importance of understanding demographic trends in relation to labour availability and customer demand identified the need for future alterations in manpower planning and recruitment and selection policies. The approach to training and development can be seen as a dynamic activity linking more closely with the factors identified above.

Training and development will, as stated, become more closely linked to organisational change in respect of culture and aspects such as quality management.

The increase in legislation and its effects on all aspects of hospitality operations has been explained especially in relation to the role and responsibilities of personnel specialists.

Underpinning all of the above is the development of and possible changes to the role of both personnel and human resource management. Whilst they will have to respond to all of the above and other issues, they clearly face some challenges not least of which is the trend to reduce the staffing dedicated to the more functional aspects of personnel management. For the larger organisations, this trend has been apparent for the last few years and many companies have taken strategic steps to download personnel responsibilities to line managers, whilst creating a framework of regional or area personnel and training advisory specialists. In management jargon, this delayering could be reversed as organisations realise some of the disadvantages of such strategies.

We reduced the numbers of middle managers and specific areas of head office staff. Whilst this had some short term advantages it led to some significant problems, especially as we had pushed down increased responsibility for personnel and training matters to line managers. This resulted in reductions in quality which we've quickly had to address.

PERSONNEL DIRECTOR, INTERNATIONAL HOTEL CHAIN

The trend towards buying in personnel services when required is increasing and, as the demands and pressures on operators also increase, so too will the demand for external assistance. This is particularly true in respect of smaller or independent operators who, with minimal resources, will concentrate on staff directly in contact with customers.

To be effective, personnel and HRM specialists not only need to respond and react to existing situations, but possess the skills to consider longer term challenges. Observations from personnel professionals on potential challenges have been given which evidence the need for strategic planning, an element of HRM which is increasing.

The Human Resource element is now represented at Board level and considerations related to the management and development of people, whilst not the main focus for strategic planning, have become more central to organisational development.

GROUP PERSONNEL & TRAINING MANAGER, CONTRACT CATERING COMPANY

Employment policies look to become more flexible with the growth of more flexible benefit packages and in certain types of operation team-based pay systems. Some of these may tackle the large amount of absenteeism which costs the UK economy in the region of £9 billion per year. Hospitality operators will increasingly make use of computerised personnel information systems (CPIS) and other activities such as counselling and team standard setting to tackle absenteeism.

Such developments will also demand knowledge of benefits and welfare support for staff, especially in larger organisations, when the hospitality industry, similar to others, recognises the cost benefit of supporting staff in this way.

By the year 2004, the personnel and HRM function could be radically different to the one we can observe presently and personnel specialists will have an increasingly important role in assisting such changes.

─────────────── **KEY POINTS** ───────────────

- Understanding and practice in managing people is developing and altering rapidly
- Demographic trends, which hospitality operators have no influence on directly and indirectly, affect how organisations and businesses operate
- A key skill required of personnel specialists in the future will be to analyse market changes and demands in respect of manpower strategies and policies
- The decrease in school leavers combined with other social and economic trends will cause hospitality operators to alter their personnel and staffing profile radically
- The functional side of personnel management will decrease, with operators increasingly making use of technology and external assistance
- Legislation will place ever-increasing demands on hospitality operators in respect of training and development

- Increasing numbers of operators will move towards quality management initiatives including 'Investors in People'
- Line managers will increasingly take on personnel responsibilities and the emphasis will be on a team approach to person management and development
- There will be a growth in more flexible wages and benefit packages with employees negotiating varied packages to suit personal circumstances, which will prove beneficial to both employer and the employee
- Training and development will increasingly occur between teams and be facilitated by line managers

QUESTIONS

1 List and explain the effects of demographic trends on the recruitment and selection of personnel for a national catering organisation.
2 Describe the possible structure and responsibilities of a personnel department of a contract catering company in the year 2000.
3 Explain the impact quality assurance and management systems will have on the personnel function in the future.
4 List and explain the advantages to an independent operator of using external personnel specialists.
5 Describe the possible differences in approach to HRM in the next decade between an independent hotel operator and a national company operating budget style travel accommodation.

HUMAN RESOURCE MANAGEMENT ASSIGNMENTS AND EXERCISES

—

INTRODUCTION AND GUIDE TO USE

The assignments and exercises detailed in this section could be used in a variety of ways:

- to provide underpinning knowledge for students studying for NVQ/GNVQ units and elements and other programmes
- to provide written evidence for specific NVQ/GNVQ units and elements
- as individual or group exercises alongside related questions (provided at the end of each chapter)
- as practical development exercises related to the unit in which an individual works
- completed assignments could be used to further enhance an individual's portfolio, CV or record of achievement folder. *Note:* There exists no one correct solution to the assignments.

Other points on the use of assignments and exercises:

1 The exercises and assignments relate to particular chapters and sections within the text. As this is an introductory text, you should turn to other reference material where appropriate.
2 The assignments are designed to act as individual pieces of work related to specific areas and competencies. If all the assignments are undertaken, it is recommended that the student identifies one particular establishment or company that will agree to a more in depth study (obviously there exists some benefit to an organisation of such a project).
3 There are obvious advantages and disadvantages in using a single organisation. By concentrating on one particular unit the student will reduce the overall workload and have the experience of analysing a unit's performance in depth. By using different units for each assignment, the student will gain wider experience of the varying approaches to HRM. Not all the assignments have to be completed to make up the package: only choose those relevant to your studies or work situation.

4   If the assignments are to be used for course assessment, certification, written evidence or as part of a personal portfolio, then consideration should be given to the professional presentation of the work; there are text books and guides on this subject in most public and college libraries.

5   I have not indicated an approximate time for the completion of assignments, as this will depend on the way the work is undertaken. However, setting targets and managing time is a skill required of all managers, so apply this rule to the work.

6   For trainers, managers, lecturers or tutors using this text I would advise discussion with the student at the outset to clarify objectives, overall context and presentation.

Final points

I have used many of these assignments in both training and tutoring situations with young students and adults. A number are based upon my direct experience within the industry as a consultant and trainer. It is my experience that the careful use of practically based assignments provides students with a variety of learning opportunities not available in more traditional training and teaching situations. Additionally, because the assignments are also designed for use within the workplace, creating real solutions to business needs, they hold particular relevance. The exercises can also be used in group work or brainstorming exercises.

Below is an outline plan which places the assignments in relevant order and identifies the area and unit they cover.

ASSIGNMENT PLAN

If you decide to complete all or a number of the assignments based upon one particular unit, it is recommended you follow the sequence outlined below. For a hospitality employee this would allow for the comprehensive analysis of the company and promote possible ideas for improvement in the HRM function. For a student this would allow for the integration of the various disciplines introduced throughout the text.

It should be noted that each assignment is designed to be 'free standing' and each can be expanded to encompass other considerations.

As stated you, the reader, can complete a number of assignments to satisfy course or competence requirements. As such they are particularly suitable for providing written evidence. The plan below sets out a group of assignments and exercises that make up a complete package and is an obvious sequence.

Good luck with the assignments and exercises, take enjoyment in the challenge and satisfaction from their completion.

REFERENCE TITLE			CHAPTER REFERENCE	
Assignment 3	Manpower audit		Chapter 2	Manpower planning and strategy
		↓		
Assignment 4	Personnel manual		Chapter 3	Personnel policies and procedures
		↓		
Exercise No.7	Job description / specification		Chapter 3	Personnel policies and procedures
		↓		
Assignment 5	Induction of personnel		Chapter 4	Recruitment and selection
		↓		
Assignment 6	Personnel and training audit		Chapter 5	Training and development
		↓		
Exercise No.11	Departmental training plan		Chapter 5	Training and development
		↓		
Exercise No.12	Skills training		Chapter 5	Training and development

Special note

Certain of the assignments and exercises will need to be altered slightly to suit completion for a specific hospitality business or unit. This would result in the student undertaking a considerable amount of work which, if appropriate, would be of benefit to the operator.

ASSIGNMENT 1
Human Resource Management

IDENTIFY THE HUMAN RESOURCE FUNCTION

The aim of this assignment is to introduce you to the key roles of people management within the hospitality industry.

TASK

With reference to this text and other sources of information, complete a written report identifying the key roles and functions of HRM. Provide for at least two of the functions a detailed explanation of how effective implementation of these functions assist the success of a hospitality business.

EXERCISE 1
Human Resource Management

KEY PERSONNEL AND HUMAN RESOURCE FUNCTIONS
(GROUP EXERCISE)

The aim of this activity is designed as a group exercise which will allow students to study and report on key functions of Personnel and Human Resource Management.

TASK

In pairs, identify a key function and prepare a five to ten minute presentation for the rest of the group, covering the following aspects:
- description and outline of the function
- list of benefits to a hospitality business of undertaking such a function effectively
- identification of any specific legislation which affects the particular function
- reference to sources of information

Use should be made of audio visual aids, such as an overhead projector or flip chart. Accompanying the presentation should be a summary report to be distributed to other students, covering the points identified above.

EXERCISE 2
Human Resource Management

IDENTIFYING THE BENEFITS OF HRM TO THE BUSINESS

The aim of this exercise is to allow you to develop a greater understanding of the role personnel and human resource management plays in the success of a company or business.

TASK

1 Working with a hospitality unit of your choice, interview the senior manager, owner or personnel manager, identifying the following:
- the overall approach to personnel management
- key personnel systems
- the benefits the individual sees in both approach and systems in respect of maintaining and improving the business
2 Complete a brief written report on your interview.

ASSIGNMENT 2
The Practice of HRM

IDENTIFYING LEADERSHIP AND MANAGEMENT STYLES

The aims of this assignment are to allow you to explore and identify leadership and management styles related to specific positions within a given catering organisation.

TASK

Working with a hospitality unit of your own choice, prepare and conduct interviews with three individuals who have responsibility for sections of staff within their unit.

Identify and report on how the supervisors and managers approach the following elements:

* staff scheduling
* training and development
* standards of performance
* conduct and discipline
* team building

Obtain from the individuals their perception of their leadership style.

Complete a written report on your investigation, detailing your findings, with comments on the various styles and approaches.

EXERCISE 3
The Practice of HRM

THE ROLE AND FUNCTION OF PERSONNEL AND TRAINING DEPARTMENTS

The aim of this exercise is to allow you to research and report on the role and function of personnel departments across a range of operators.

If this task if given to a group of students, then it may be advantageous for individual participants to select from a range of hospitality companies provided by the tutor. The subsequent reporting will then assist the coverage of a full cross-section of the industry.

TASK

I   Contact two hospitality personnel departments from different sections of the industry and, by research, interview, questionnaire and analysis of information, compile a report to include the following:

  · brief description of company (number of units/employees)
  · organisational structure of their personnel and training department

- the roles and responsibilities of the training and personnel staff
- any form of evaluation conducted by the organisation on the effectiveness of the department and its activities

2 Compare the way in which the two organisations undertake the Personnel and Training function, identifying particular strengths.

3 Include within your report any policy statements or information provided by the companies.

Suggested sources of information for addresses of companies and names of personnel managers:

- HCIMA Year Book
- *Caterer & Hotelkeeper*

EXERCISE 4
The Practice of HRM

THE ANALYSIS OF HRM THEORIES AND APPROACHES
The aim of this exercise is to allow you to research and analyse relevant theories and approaches related to human resource management.

TASK

1 From the list provided below, select one topic for research and analysis:

- employee motivation
- leadership styles
- management by objectives
- organisational theory
- quality circles
- team working
- empowerment
- quality of working life

2 Prepare a written paper which outlines past and current theories on the topic and explain the importance of such theories to the development of effective human resource management.

Note: This exercise will require you to research various texts and articles, some of which may be concerned with other industrial sectors or be general texts on personnel, HRM and management theory. This is a deliberate ploy to encourage reading from sources other than hospitality management texts!

ASSIGNMENT 3
Manpower Planning, Strategy and Practice

MANPOWER PLANNING

The aim of this assignment is to allow you to prepare for, conduct and report on manpower requirements for a hospitality operation.

Note: The assignment can be extended to include a cross-section of hospitality units, representing an appropriate range from the industry.

TASK

With the help of a hospitality operation within your area, complete the following tasks:

1　Research and obtain information on existing staffing levels within the unit.
2　Compile a statistical report, using graphs and charts where appropriate, identifying characteristics of existing staffing levels (e.g. length of service, status, gender).
3　Conduct an interview with the management of the unit to identify any projected alterations to staffing levels.

Analyse the outcome of statistical report and interviews and compile a report to the management, identifying recommendations for a manpower plan for the forthcoming year. The report should include reference to any identified weakness in current staffing level/manpower plan, and may require you to identify specific recommendations for particular departments within the operation.

EXERCISE 5
Manpower Planning, Strategy and Practice

MANPOWER PLANNING I

The aim of this exercise is to allow you to identify and plan the staffing requirements for a food production and service event.

TASK

1　For an identified food production and service event, prepare the following:

- list of overall staffing requirements
- duty of work rota identifying individual responsibilities and duties
- a briefing document for all staff involved covering the event
- a list of key tasks for individuals

2　Following the event, produce a report identifying the procedures you undertook and an evaluation of your planning and delivery.

EXERCISE 6

Manpower Planning, Strategy and Practice

MANPOWER PLANNING II

The aim of this exercise is to allow you to analyse the manpower requirements for a large outside catering event.

Background

Executive Catering is a small event catering company, specialising in quality catering for up to 500 people. They have a production unit, staffed by four full time chefs and three assistants, where the majority of foodstuffs for events is prepared. Other full time staff (excluding senior managers) include the following:

- Operations Manager, responsible for overseeing events
- Food Services Manager, responsible for all food and beverage service
- Transport Manager + 3 Drivers, responsible for transport and delivery of all foodstuffs
- Site Manager + 1 Assistant, responsible for provision, setting up and maintenance of marquees and equipment
- Steward, responsible for cleaning and hygiene

All other staff are hired for specific events from a pool of trained casual staff.

Executive Caterers have been approached to undertake a reception and buffet for the official opening of a new factory for a multinational manufacturing company. The event will cater for 400 invited guests in two marquees, provided by Executive Caterers, and will include:

- reception
- formal sit down meal
- speeches by manufacturing company's Managing Director and Chairman

The menu will comprise a cold starter, soup, main course, sweet and coffee. Wines will be a choice of red or white served throughout the meal. Sherry and champagne will be served at the reception. The Managing Director has requested champagne for a formal toast at the end of the meal.

Staff (casual rates) are as follows:

- chefs – £5/hour
- food service personnel – £3.50/hour
- kitchen assistants – £3.00/hour
- general assistants – £3.00/hour

TASK

As Operations Manager (with responsibility for staffing), you have to compile a detailed report and outline costed manpower plan for the event.

1 Identify staffing requirements for the event, broken down into areas of:
   - Food production
   - Food and beverage service
   - Set up of event site and maintenance
   - Transportation
   - Management
   - Stewarding

2 Provide an estimate of staffing costs for all non-full-time personnel

---

ASSIGNMENT 4
Personnel Policies and Procedures

PERSONNEL PROCEDURES MANUAL
The aim of the assignment is to allow you to research and report on the contents and use of an operator's personnel procedures manual.

TASK

The owners of a large independent 3-star hotel have asked you to compile a comprehensive personnel procedures manual.

Whilst the hotel has been operating successfully for a number of years, it has never used standardised procedures. With an expansion of business, coupled with a need to adhere to the increase in legislation, the owners have decided that such a manual is required.

At this stage all they require is a list of all the areas to be included, with two examples of detailed procedures – one on disciplinary and grievance procedures and one on staff action on discovering a fire.

Prepare the list of contents, accompanied by a brief explanation of why each item needs to be included. Accompany this list with the two detailed procedures.

EXERCISE 7
Personnel, Policies and Procedures

JOB SPECIFICATION AND DESCRIPTIONS
The aim of this exercise is to enable you to research and prepare job specifications and job descriptions for a variety of positions across a range of sectors.

TASK

1 Research the requirements for job specifications and job descriptions.
2 Compile a job specification and job description for the following positions:
    - room attendant/chambermaid full time in a small to medium hotel
    - deputy manager in a 3-star business hotel
    - chef for a large unit of a contract catering company
    - bars manager in a town centre leisure and conference facility
3 Present information in standardised format.
4 Provide written explanation of the benefits of using such documents in respect of effective recruitment and selection.

EXERCISE 8
Personnel, Policies and Procedures

THE DISCIPLINARY INTERVIEW
(GROUP EXERCISE)
The aim of this exercise is to allow a group of students to prepare for, conduct and evaluate a disciplinary interview. As there exist a considerable amount of learning and development opportunities within such an exercise, appropriate briefing and preparation is of great importance.

Outline

Participants should have received or be required to research the necessary guidelines to the effective conducting of disciplinary interviews.

As with all role play exercises, the outcome is not so important as the manner in which learning opportunities are used.

THE BACKGROUND

The Brooks Hotel is a privately owned 3-star 70-bedroom city centre hotel with extensive banqueting, function and leisure facilities.

THE CHARACTERS

- J. Welcome, General Manager
- P. Smythe, Personnel & Training Manager
- G. Attercliffe, Food Service Assistant

THE SITUATION

G. Attercliffe has been reported for being late and untidily dressed. This individual has worked for the hotel for over two years full time, following part-time employment of approximately six weeks. This has been the second time this employee has been reported for such a discrepancy.

The task is to conduct an interview following the appropriate guidelines and identify an appropriate outcome.

It is suggested that individuals choose or are chosen for the specific roles, along with an observer whose role it is to report on the process and outcome of the interview.

CHARACTER BRIEFS

J. WELCOME, GENERAL MANAGER

You have been in post just over one month. An experienced individual this is your first job as General Manager and you are keen to succeed and make your mark. One of the targets you have set yourself is to improve standards all round and this includes the motivation and standard of staff. This is your first disciplinary interview and you have asked for details from the Personnel & Training Manager, who has been in the hotel for just over six months. The report given to you was as follows:

This employee is not performing well and colleagues have commented to me on lateness on a number of occasions recently. When I delivered a reprimand in front of her colleagues, I received no explanation and, knowing how keen you are to stamp out or get rid of poor employees, I think this employee should leave.

You now have to conduct the interview and have asked the Personnel Manager to report to your office immediately along with G. Attercliffe.

P. SMYTHE, PERSONNEL & TRAINING MANAGER

You have a very pressurised job, which involves duty management and banqueting alongside tackling the personnel and training function. This aspect you inherited and it is a job you would really like to do well, if you had more time and training. The General Manager asked you to prepare an employee handbook covering all the aspects related to working in the hotel, but as yet it is unfinished. You have some sympathy with G. Attercliffe as overall, in your opinion, this employee works well.

G. ATTERCLIFFE, FOOD SERVICE ASSISTANT

You have enjoyed working at this hotel in the past, although you do not get on with some of your colleagues. The restaurant is a good place to work as there are lots of perks, including the opportunity to take home items of food. All the other food service staff take similar opportunities and nobody seems to mind.

Lately work has increased and you have put in a lot of extra hours with a vague promise of time off when it's quieter. When P. Smythe reprimanded you it was in front of your colleagues and you felt rather humiliated. In addition to your work you have recently started a management course in your spare time which the Personnel Manager would not fund. You really want to improve and develop your career, but think this hotel and the new manager does not care for its staff.

Added notes: tutor guidance

As with all case studies/role play exercises, there can exist a variety of outcomes. Within the field of HRM it is important to concentrate on the key aspects. Consider the following factors:

- legal factors
- standard codes of practice on disciplinary procedures
- personalities and experience
- and, most importantly, developing a positive outcome.

Standardised, well-documented employment procedures and conditions may identify bench marks on which to base disciplinary decisions, but HRM is concerned or should be concerned with a positive outcome wherever possible.

ASSIGNMENT 5
Hospitality Recruitment and Selection

INDUCTION OF PERSONNEL

The aim of this assignment is to enable you to research, report on and compile an induction programme for newly appointed personnel.

TASK

1 Contact a minimum of three hospitality operators to obtain copies or details of their induction programmes. The three operators should represent a cross-section of the industry.
2 Prepare and compile an induction programme for a hospitality operator not represented in sectors from which information has been obtained.
3 Present your information in written format accompanied by a detailed explanation on:
   - the benefits of using a standardised induction package
   - legal considerations required

Include within this report the prepared induction programme presented in an appropriate format for use by an organisation.

EXERCISE 9
Hospitality Recruitment and Selection

BASIC INTERVIEWING SKILLS
(GROUP EXERCISE)

The aim of this exercise is to allow students to experience the basic interview process and to assist the development of listening skills. The exercise can be used successfully with participants prior to the Group Exercise No.10 on interviewing and selection.

Notes

There are a variety of methods for undertaking such an exercise and the method chosen is dependent upon the number of participants, knowledge, time and facilities available. Whilst a tutor could provide the schedule and timings, this aspect could also be given to the group to undertake.

THE KEY TASKS:

Every member of the group acts as an
- interviewer
- interviewee
- observer

Note: The minimum number for each group is three.

The interview can be on any subject, but designed to solicit information from the interviewee. As a guide the interview should last 10 minutes. With a three-number group the sequence could be as follows:

- A interviews B taking no notes (10 minutes)
- A provides verbal feedback on interview to B (2 minutes)
- B interviews A taking no notes (10 minutes)
- B provides verbal feedback on interview to A (2 minutes)
- C provides verbal feedback on observations of style, body language and feedback to A and B (5 minutes total)

The roles can then be changed as desired, for instance with C becoming the interviewee and so on.

Alternatively, the interviews could be conducted in a straightforward manner and, upon completion, three member groups could join with others to conduct the feedback sessions.

The basic skills learnt in this exercise are listening, communicating and providing feedback, all key aspects of interviewing skills.

EXERCISE 10

Hospitality Recruitment and Selection

INTERVIEW AND SELECTION
(GROUP EXERCISE)

The aim of this exercise is to allow students to prepare, conduct and evaluate an interview and selection situation and it is linked with exercises and assignments related to job specifications and descriptions.

TASKS

The following tasks should be undertaken:

- preparation of job specification and job description
- identification of individual roles, e.g. interviewers, applicants and observers
- preparation of job application form (unless group uses existing one)
- preparation of job advertisement
- finalisation of application/shortlisting, interview/evaluation schedule

Suggested schedule:

- job details issued
- applicants apply
- initial shortlisting
- interview
- selection
- evaluation

Guidance notes

1 The group may wish to invite an experienced personnel and training manager from a local hospitality unit to provide assistance.
2 All the group should be involved and 'unsuccessful' applicants should act as observers during the process of interview and selection.
3 Consideration should be given to all the relevant legislation governing recruitment and selection.
4 The evaluation of the exercise is an important component and time should be scheduled to allow for feedback on all aspects.

Guidance to tutors/trainers

This standard exercise is a useful way for students to experience the process of recruitment and selection. Considerable teaching and learning opportunities exist, both on an individual and group basis in respect of procedures, systems, legal aspects, interview skills and techniques.

Careful briefing is required; however, the exercise can be adapted for various levels of courses and can provide participants with evidence for unit/element accreditation. Prior skills training should be provided in respect of interviewing skills (see Exercise No.9).

ASSIGNMENT 6
Hospitality Training and Development

PERSONNEL AND TRAINING AUDIT

The aims of this assignment are to allow you to prepare, complete and report on the training and development needs of a single hospitality operator. This assignment covers a variety of tasks and skills including the interviewing of staff, compilation of questionnaires, analysis of data and report writing.

TASKS

1   Using a catering operation within your vicinity, conduct a personnel and training audit with the aim of identifying training requirements for the operation at unit, department and individual level.
2   Prepare for and conduct a preliminary interview with the unit's general manager and personnel and training manager.
3   Obtain appropriate and relevant manpower statistics representing staffing levels, age and gender breakdown and years of service.
4   Conduct an analysis on these statistics.
5   Prepare for and conduct interviews with a cross-section of identified personnel, e.g. management, supervisory, heads of department, operatives and part-time employees, using a standardised interview form of your own design.
6   Obtain details of any existing or planned training.
7   Prepare a detailed report on your findings presented as follows:
    · Introduction
    · Report of activities undertaken
    · Analysis of manpower investigation
    · Findings and outcome of interviews
    · Identification of training and development priorities
    · Recommendations
    · Conclusions

Careful consideration should be given to the presentation of the report and appropriate graphs and charts should be included.

Notes and guidance

This is a fairly complex undertaking and consideration should be given to the sensitive nature of the investigation. For a larger hospitality unit it may be appropriate to concentrate on one particular department. Advice should be sought on the preparation of the audit and schedules discussed with tutors. Whilst examples are provided within the text on conducting such an exercise and the use of questionnaires, students are recommended to test the validity of the questionnaire prior to use in the field.

EXERCISE 11
Hospitality Training and Development

DEPARTMENTAL TRAINING PLAN

The aim of this assignment is to allow you to research and analyse the training needs of a specific department within a hospitality unit, and to prepare a detailed training plan for a given period.

TASKS

1 In consultation with a hospitality operator identify a specific department possessing a range of personnel.
2 Conduct research by interview or questionnaire on current skill levels, qualifications and training requirements.
3 Compile a training plan for the department in priority order, identifying training activity, target audience, reason for training need and, if possible, costings and responsibility.
4 Identify an appropriate method for evaluating the effectiveness of the training.
5 Present your findings in a written form with an explanation of how research was carried out and a brief summary identifying your main recommendations.

Notes

1 This assignment could be linked to Assignment 6.
2 Use should be made of information within this text.
3 Consideration should be given to the confidential nature of the work being undertaken.
4 The assessment of this assignment could be further enhanced by involving the Management and/or Head of Department used.

EXERCISE 12
Hospitality Training and Development

SKILLS TRAINING – DESIGN, DELIVERY AND EVALUATION

The aim of this two-part exercise is to allow you to research, design, prepare, deliver and evaluate a skills training exercise. The exercise is separated into two parts. The first concerns the identification of levels of competence or skills required. The second is concerned with designing, delivering and evaluating a training session against the previously identified standards.

TASKS

PART A: Identification of performance standards

1   For one specific task, job or process compile a list of measurable performance standards. These performance standards should identify precisely what level an employee would need to reach if performing the task unaided and competently.

PART B: Design, delivery and evaluation of training

2   Research, prepare and compile a training session for the skill, process or task to deliver to a suitable candidate.

3   Identify a suitable candidate and brief them on the schedule for the training.

4   Deliver the training session using prepared training notes and required resources.

5   Conduct an evaluation with the trainee on the outcome of the training, identifying whether the trainee is now competent in the task.

6   Compile a written report on the exercise, including the outcome of the evaluation and assessment of competence, and present with copies of performance standards and training notes.

ASSIGNMENT 7
Future Role of Human Resource Management

The aim of this assignment is to enable you to research, analyse and report on potential changes to HRM.

TASK

1   Contact a hospitality operator from three different sectors and identify by interview, questionnaire and research, potential developments in their approach to personnel and human resource management

2   Analyse your findings and compile a report describing briefly each sector, specific operator and identifying the key developments in relation to HRM and personnel approaches

3   Provide explanations of external and internal influences on the identified developments, using, where appropriate, reference to research conducted

4   Include within the report, graphs, results from questionnaires and other sources of information which support the need for such developments

Guidance notes

1   Ensure that any contact or request to personnel managers or specialists is completed professionally.

2   Use reference sources contained within Appendix B.

3   When compiling a questionnaire, ensure that it is laid out clearly and it can be understood and completed easily.

4   Plan and schedule your work: this assignment will take a number of weeks.

EXERCISE 13
Future of Human Resource Management

QUALITY DEVELOPMENTS IN HUMAN RESOURCE MANAGEMENT

The aims of this exercise are to allow students to research and understand quality approaches related to HRM and personnel practice.

TASKS

Allocate tasks to the group to investigate and report on the following:

· BS5750 – IS9000
· Investors in People
· Total Quality Management
· Team working

Each group should present a brief verbal report to the whole group, providing a description of the particular development or initiative; examples of use within the hospitality industry and explanations of the benefits to operators in relation to HRM and personnel practice. The verbal report should be backed up by a written brief outlining the main findings, source information and suggestions for future reading and research.

EXERCISE 14
Future of Human Resource Management

EFFECTS OF TECHNOLOGY ON HUMAN RESOURCE MANAGEMENT IN THE FUTURE

The aim of this exercise is to allow you to research, analyse and report on the effect of technology on human resource and personnel management issues.

TASK

Prepare an outline of the possible effects of technology on HRM and personnel issues, exploring the disadvantages and advantages of such elements as computerisation and centralised personnel systems.

SUMMARY

Completing the assignments and exercises in the manner identified should have resulted in the reader proving real learning has taken place. You will have learnt the relevance of undertaking the practice of HRM in realistic situations.

Nothing, of course, can replace the learning that occurs when performing such tasks routinely as part of an individual's specific job role. Competent managers are ones who can perform duties to the standard required in a variety of situations.

However, the completion of these assignments and exercises will have started this competence curve.

ADDITIONAL SOURCES OF INFORMATION

—

For the trainee or acting personnel specialist, there are a variety of organisations which can provide information, guidance and assistance with regard to personnel, employment and human resource management issues.

The following pages provide details of such organisations (addresses correct at time of compilation). Whilst I have listed certain organisations under specific headings, many offer a variety of assistance to both employers, employees and personnel specialists.

MAGAZINES AND JOURNALS

- HCIMA Journal *Hospitality*, issued to members
- *Caterer and Hotelkeeper*, weekly magazine
- *Personnel Management*, monthly magazine of the Institute of Personnel Management
- *International Journal of Contemporary Hospitality Management*, available from: MCB University Press/HCIMA, 60/62 Tuller Lane, Bradford, West Yorkshire BD8 7BY
- *Restauranteur* magazine

HEALTH, SAFETY AND WELFARE

Health Education Authority
Hamilton Place
Mabledon Place
LONDON WC1H 9TX

Health & Safety Executive
Information Centre
Broad Lane
SHEFFIELD S3 7HQ

Local health authorities will have a health education department and the address can be found in local telephone directories.

British Association for Counselling
37a Sheep Street
RUGBY CV21 3BX

Action on Smoking and Health (ASH)
5–11 Mortimer Street
LONDON W1N 7RH

The National Aids Helpline
Telephone: 01800 555777

National Aids Trust
286 Euston Road
LONDON NW1 3DN

Royal Society for the Prevention of Accidents (ROSPA)
Canon House
Priory Queensway
BIRMINGHAM B4 6BS

Alcohol Concern
Workplan Advisory Service
305 Grays Inn Road
LONDON WC1X 8QF

The Terrance Higgins Trust
BM/AIDS
LONDON WC1 3XX

Drugs Training Project
Department of Sociology
University of Stirling
STIRLING FK9 4LA

Additionally, such bodies as the HCIMA, Confederation of British Industry, Trades Union Congress, Institute of Personnel Management and the Employment Department have produced studies and reports on health issues. The contact addresses for these are provided below.

EQUAL OPPORTUNITIES

The following organisations all offer advice and information relating to equal opportunities:

The Equal Opportunities Commission
Overseas House
Quay Street
MANCHESTER M3 3HN

The Commission for Racial Equality
Yorkshire Bank Chambers
1st Floor
Infirmary Street
LEEDS LS1 2JP

The Race Relations Advisory Service
(Department of Employment)
City House
New Station Street
LEEDS LS1 4JH

GOVERNMENT AGENCIES

British Standards Institute
Lynford Wood
MILTON KEYNES
MK14 6LE
Tel: 01908 22166

BTEC
Central House
Upper Woburn Place
LONDON WC1H 0HH
Tel: 0171 413 8400

Department of Employment
Advisory, Conciliation and Arbitration Service
27 Wilton Street
LONDON SW1X 7AZ

Investors in People (UK)
Room N805
Employment Department
Moorfoot
SHEFFIELD S1 4PQ
Tel: 0114 25 93427

National Council for Vocational Qualifications
222 Euston Road
LONDON NW1 2BZ
Tel: 0171 387 9898

MANAGEMENT BODIES AND ASSOCIATIONS

The following organisations all offer training, consultancy, research, advice and information related to management issues.

Institute of Personnel Management
IPM House
Camp Road
Wimbledon
LONDON SW19 4UX

The Industrial Society
Robert Hyde House
49 Bryanston Square
LONDON W1H 7LN

Management Charter Initiative
Russell Square House
10-12 Russell Square
LONDON WC1B 5BZ

The Tavistock Institute
Tavistock Centre
Belsize Lane
LONDON NW3

The Institute of Management
Management House
Cottingham Road
CORBY NN17 1TT

Confederation of British Industry
Centre Point
103 New Oxford Street
LONDON WC1A 1DU

Institute of Manpower Studies
University of Sussex
Mantell Building
Falmer
BRIGHTON BN1 9RF

HOSPITALITY ASSOCIATIONS AND PROFESSIONAL BODIES

Hotel, Catering and Institutional Management Association
191 Trinity Road
LONDON SW17 7HN

British Hospitality Association
40 Duke Street
LONDON W1M 6MR

Hotel Industry Marketing Group
Wood Farm
Norwich Road
Denton
Nr. HARLESTON IP20 0BA

Confederation of Tourism
Hotel & Catering Management
204 Barnett Wood Lane
ASHTEAD KT21 2DB

Craft Guild of Chefs
Cooking & Food Association
1 Victoria Parade
331 Sandycombe Road
RICHMOND TW9 3NB

EMPLOYMENT DEPARTMENT PUBLICATIONS

The following booklets can be obtained, free of charge, from the offices of the Employment Service:

- Trade Union Political Funds (PL868 (Rev1))
- Union Membership and Non-Membership Rights (PL871 (Rev1))
- Trade Union Executive Elections (PL866 (Rev1))
- Union Secret Ballots (PL701)
- Industrial Action and The Law: A Guide for Employees, Trade Union Members and Others (PL869 (Rev1))
- Industrial Action and The Law: A Guide for Employers, Their Customers, Suppliers and Others (PL870 (Rev1))
- Statutory Code of Practice: 'Picketing'
- Written Statement of the Main Terms and Conditions of Employment (PL700)
- Itemised Pay Statements (PL704)
- Guarantee Payments (PL724)
- Time Off for Public Duties (PL702)
- Employment Rights for the Expectant Mother (PL710)
- Suspension on Medical Grounds under Health & Safety Regulations (PL705)
- Employment Rights on the Transfer of an Undertaking (PL699)
- Redundancy Consultation and Notification (PL833)
- Facing Redundancy? Time Off for Job Hunting or to Arrange Training (PL703)
- Redundancy Payments (PL808)
- Employees' Rights on Insolvency of Employer (PL718)
- The Law on the Payment of Wages and Deductions (PL810)
- Unfairly Dismissed? (PL712)
- Fair and Unfair Dismissal – A Guide for Employers (PL714)
- Rights to Notice and Reasons for Dismissal (PL707)
- Rules Governing Continuous Employment and a Week's Pay (PL711)
- Limits on Payments (PL827)
- Recoupment of Benefit from Industrial Tribunal Awards: A Guide for Employers (PL720)
- Individual Rights of Employees: A Guide for Employers (PL716)
- Industrial Tribunal Procedure (IT1)

ACAS publications

ADVISORY HANDBOOKS

- Employing People: A Handbook for Small Firms
- Discipline at Work
- Employment Handbook

ADVISORY BOOKLETS

1 Job Evaluation: An Introduction
2 Introduction to Payment Systems
3 Personnel Records
4 Labour Turnover
5 Absence
6 Recruitment and Selection
7 Induction of New Employees
8 Workplace Communications
9 The Company Handbook
10 Employment Policies
11 Employee Appraisal
12 Redundancy Handling
13 Hours at Work
14 Appraisal and Related Pay
15 Health and Employment
16 Effective Organisations: The People Factor
17 Supervision
18 Recruitment Policies for the 1990s

Additionally, ACAS publish occasional papers, QWL reading, codes of practice and annual reports.

BOOK SUMMARY

———

This text has provided you with an introduction to both the theory and practice of HRM. There is an initial outline of the importance of this function, further sections identified and explained the various strategies, policies, procedures, methods and actions operators undertake to maintain and develop this key function.

Throughout the text, I have attempted to outline the need for a clear understanding and a positive approach to the management of people. In using the term 'Human Resource Management' critics would argue that you are defining individuals and teams as units of resource which, if moulded and trained, will perform to the required standard. In reality, as the majority of professional human resource managers would agree, the most effective systems are ones which treat people as individuals.

The development of the personnel role away from a function-based approach can be clearly identified over the past decade. Whilst there is an obvious need for systems and procedures, effective organisations are looking increasingly towards strategies and practices which reflect the movement towards a quality team approach.

Positive personnel practices based on sound systems provide both the employer and employee with a base for effective working partnerships which, in turn, maintain, develop and improve the sound management and service to the customer.

The interest shown over the last few years in such approaches as Total Quality Management and schemes such as National Training Awards and Investors in People reflect many organisations' acceptance that investment in staff is not just limited to finance. Yet increasing Government and EEC legislation related to employment law, coupled with the increase in employers' responsibility under such legislation as the Health and Safety at Work Act, have also pressurised operators to create some fairly rigid personnel practices.

Personnel managers and operators within the industry have also had to take the pressure of economic recession which has and will have in the future an increasing effect on personnel policies and practices.

No business can afford to ignore the positive contribution effectively managed staff can provide and all, regardless of size, will require a strategy for the focusing of this aspect of management. The importance of manpower planning, which for larger organisations is a never-ending cycle, has been stressed. Contained within this cycle is the process of recruitment and selection, which for many personnel managers forms the focus of activity. Key stages and elements of this process should now be recognised. If strategic planning forms the first part of the HRM function, then recruitment and selection is the obvious second part. However, as identified, all aspects of the process are interrelated and need to be based on sound procedures and systems.

Upon employment, personnel require ongoing training and development if an organisation is to survive in today's highly competitive market. The investment in ongoing training by hospitality operators has increased rapidly over the past decade, with a trend towards multi-skilling, job flexibility and empowerment.

The need for more flexibility by employees is a natural occurrence from the decrease in demand, advances in technology and increasing pressure to reduce staffing costs. Whilst predictions for the future are always difficult, I have attempted in the final chapter to provide some indication of the role of HRM in the next decade.

However, it should be realised that hospitality operators cannot rely solely on developing effective HRM practices. There exists the need for sound financial management, targeted marketing and sales activities and solid operational management. The understanding of complex management theories on leadership and motivation and task analysis, whilst important, should not outweigh the need for practical and effective person management skills.

Those of you who have worked through this text and used the assignments in Appendix A should now have a much clearer understanding and knowledge of the HRM function. I hope you have enjoyed both reading and working through the text. It has been successful if it has provided you with a sound base on which to build further skills and expertise.